D1195529

PEOPLE'S BANKER

THE STORY OF ARTHUR T. ROTH AND THE FRANKLIN NATIONAL BANK

PEOPLE'S BANKER

THE STORY OF ARTHUR T. ROTH AND THE FRANKLIN NATIONAL BANK

by Walter S. Ross

Author of *The Last Hero: Charles A. Lindbergh*
Former Roving Editor, *Reader's Digest magazine*

KEATS PUBLISHING, INC. New Canaan, Connecticut

PEOPLE'S BANKER
The Story of Arthur T. Roth and the Franklin National Bank

Copyright © 1987 by Arthur T. Roth and Walter S. Ross

Library of Congress Cataloging-in-Publication Data

Ross, Walter Sanford, 1916-
   People's Banker.

   Bibliography: p.
   Includes index.
   1. Roth, Arthur T. 2. Bankers—United States—Biography.
   3. Franklin National Bank. 4. Bank failures—
   United /States. I. Title.
HG2463.R68A3   1987   332.1′223′0924 [B]   87-4066
ISBN 0-87983-429-3

Printed in the United States of America

Published by Keats Publishing, Inc.
27 Pine Street (P.O. Box 876)
New Canaan, Connecticut 06840

CONTENTS

ACKNOWLEDGMENTS

The following people were kind enough to grant taped interviews. Tapes and transcriptions are in the possession of Mr. Arthur T. Roth and are open to responsible researchers.

Hon. Charles B. Brownson, Mr. Patrick J. Clifford, Dr. Edward J. Coyle, Mr. George Fernandez, Mr. Luiz Gastal, Mr. Herman Goodman, Hon. Leonard W. Hall, Dr. R. Gordon Hoxie, Hon. Eugene Keogh, Hon. John Martin, Mr. Charles McNeill, Mr. Frederick Mortensen, Professor Paul S. Nadler, Mr. Willard C. Rappleye, Jr., Gov. L. J. Robertson, Mrs. Arthur T. Roth, Hon. James Saxon, Mr. H. Vernon Scott, Hon. Cyrus Upham.

The facts in the Postscript come primarily from pages 130–214 of Luigi DiFonzo's meticulously researched book *St. Peter's Banker: Michele Sindona* (New York: Franklin Watts, 1983), 308 pages.

\

FOREWORD

Arthur Roth is a legend in his own time.

He took a tiny bank on the verge of bankruptcy in 1934, with total deposits of $464,000, and built it into the 18th largest bank in the nation. A single share of Franklin National Bank stock, sold for $10 when Arthur Roth started, was valued at $25,000 when he resigned his executive responsibility in 1968.

He revolutionized banking nationwide by innovative marketing of services that included parking areas, drive-up windows, garden banking, Christmas shows and lollipops for children, and dramatic speeding-up of mortgage and loan procedures. Banking owes its entry into credit cards to his innovations.

Over thirty years ago he pioneered in employing the handicapped and students who were attending high school, provided community rooms, and introduced life and medical insurance as well as purchase clubs and appliance displays. He issued annual reports, operated like a department store, and offered certificates of deposit for savings.

In other areas, he led the nation's commercial bankers in winning a United States Supreme Court decision to permit use of the word "savings" and in opposing ex-President Hoover's plan for weakening the Comptroller's office, which regulates U.S. national banks. Additionally, he won the fight to remove savings banks from the American Bankers Association because of their avoidance of federal income taxes, and spearheaded the campaign to save the U.S. from possible financial chaos in 1968.

Through creative banking and businesslike services, he led in financing the building of Long Island from only 604,000 residents in

1940 into the bustling commuting, office, and industrial region of 2,600,000 it is today, boasting the lowest unemployment rate in the country, the highest per family expendable income and, according to national surveys, the finest quality of life.

He became widely known, the subject of articles appearing in over 50 national publications. *Reader's Digest* in 1945 headlined a story on him with "Here is a Banker with Imagination," and *Fortune* in 1946 wrote, "Roth has emerged as a disquieting phenomenon in U.S. banking. In a white-cottage, white-collar suburb with no industry, no railroad station, and very little money, he has developed a way to triple normal banking profits."

Arthur Roth also gave social and cultural leadership to Long Island, serving in key positions on the boards of the Long Island Rail Road, Long Island University—as well as Georgetown University in Washington, D.C.—Mercy Hospital in Rockville Centre, the Long Island Association of Commerce and Industry, and Abilities, Inc.—a firm employing handicapped people—and pioneering area beautification, smoking bans and historical preservation. His interest and expertise in history was demonstrated when he originated two colonial balls in authentic costume and with food, dancing and table settings of the period.

Arthur Roth, at eighty-one, is still an active leader as a Director of Extebank; Director and Past Chairman of the Watchdogs of the United States Treasury and the Bankers' Committee of Tax Equality in Washington; Founding Director Emeritus of the Library of Presidential Papers; Director Emeritus of Textron Inc.; and Trustee Emeritus of the Museums at Stony Brook.

There is one Shakespearean irony in this tremendous career. Four years after he retired from Franklin, the monument to the success of his innovative approach, and despite his pleas to the bank directors and stockholders and repeated warnings to federal banking authorities, the bank became insolvent through criminal looting, resulting in the biggest bank failure in the nation's history.

Over these many years, as editor of the region's business newsweekly, and an associate of Arthur Roth in many regional betterment projects, it has been a source of pride to be a friend of this great man.

Reading his story, you too will come to know a uniquely innovative banker, an entrepreneurial businessman, and a tireless worker for a better community and nation.

Paul S. Townsend
Editor, *Long Island Business*

PEOPLE'S BANKER

THE STORY OF ARTHUR T. ROTH AND THE FRANKLIN NATIONAL BANK

Introduction:
250,000 Percent Profit

Most of us share in the jackpot fantasy; picking up a few million in the lottery, rolling a string of sevens at a casino. Part of the folklore of our time are the fortunes made from prescient investments in high-flying stocks if you got in on the ground floor. Risking a small investment in the initial offering of IBM at $125 a share, or Minnesota Mining & Manufacturing at $60, would have reaped enormous rewards. Same for Syntex, Polaroid, Genentech, and others.

These explosive growth stocks are held in awe by investors because they multiplied a dollar by 100 or 200. Yet there was a much higher flier, unknown to many, that paid off at twenty times the rate of these fabled stratospheric shares. A $1 investment in an obscure local bank would have brought you more than $2,500 in dividends and stock bonuses thirty years later. Gambling a mere $100 in the stock of the tiny Franklin Square National Bank—later the Franklin National Bank and now the European-American Bank—back in the mid-1930s would have returned a quarter of a million dollars in 1968; $1,000 left to grow in the stock of that obscure crossroads bank would have made you a millionaire twice over.

The bank itself had total assets of less than a half-million dollars in 1934. By 1971 it had grown into a financial colossus worth more than $3 billion. And while it was growing, it earned more per invested dollar than any bank in the country, large or small.

Financial growth as explosive as this is fascinating. But the economic framework alone is too narrow to contain the whole story. Franklin is interesting not only because it grew geometrically but be-

1

cause behind the growth is a story with many dimensions, only one of which is measurable in money.

In order to grow as fast and as big as it did, the bank had to become a major force in changing American banking from a rather distant and disdainful profession into one responsive to the needs of local people, communities, small businesses. During the past forty-five years, this has caused a fundamental shift of economic power with powerful effects on the kinds of lives Americans live, and on the U.S. economy.

Another dimension of the Franklin phenomenon is that it was largely the result of the ideas and energies of one man. Yet, near retirement, he was stripped of his authority and eventually forced out of the bank he had done so much to build and saw it taken over by people several of whom were incompetent or dishonest. In a couple of years they destroyed the institution, aiding the process in no small part by abetting an international criminal who bought control of Franklin.

If anything, the destruction of the bank only added luster to its fabulous growth under Arthur Roth. In 1971 the First California Company, securities brokers, sought to gain a bit of reflected glory for a client bank by publishing brief sketches of four "master builders" of banking who had created "a great economic corporate and investor wealth in America." The four:

J. P. Morgan (1837–1913)
Andrew W. Mellon (1885–1937)
A. P. Giannini (1870–1949)
A. T. Roth (1905–   )

The first three names are familiar to most Americans, but who was, or is—since he is the only one on the list still living—A. T. Roth?

Morgan, founder of Morgan Guaranty Trust Company, the country's fifth-largest bank, once lent the United States government enough of his gold so that it could remain solvent during the panic of 1895.

Mellon built the Mellon National Bank & Trust Company, fifteenth-largest in the country. His brilliant nine-year career as Secretary of the Treasury is well known; his art collection (and endowment) are the core of the National Gallery of Art in Washington, D.C.

A. P. Giannini started the Bank of America, once the world's largest publicly owned bank.

And Roth? According to the First California prospectus, Arthur Roth of the Franklin Bank was the spark plug behind the bank's growth through brilliant mergers, acquisitions and new branches on Long Island. . . . In the 20-year span [1949–69] Franklin grew from $44 million in resources to $3.2 billion until it is now the 21st largest in the United States. A. T. Roth was aggressive and brilliant.''

Intrigued but unsatisfied by this thumbnail information, I asked the California brokers why they had placed Roth alongside three undoubted financial titans. Mr. George Fernandez, who prepared the report, replied:

> We feel very strongly that a very well-run company is guided by an individual at the top who has thought out the parameters to make the company successful in its industry. This has been true in the early stages for IBM (Watson), Ford Motor Co. (Ford), E. I. DuPont (DuPont), Bank of America (Giannini), and Franklin National Bank (A. T. Roth).
>
> We became interested in Franklin National Bank in 1950, at which time Mr. Roth was president. The growth record since that time . . . has been spectacular. . . .
>
> Mr. Roth was no ordinary, self-satisfied banker. We note that the man had

A. VISION	by capitalizing on Long Island's future growth prospects through the concept of a multioffice banking system. (This was uncommon in the Empire State in those years).
B. COURAGE	to struggle with the regulatory bodies and the banking fraternity as he strove to accomplish (A) above. He took firm positions on his beliefs and carried them through.
C. DEDICATION	to the creation of his dream in (A) above. Franklin National and he became identified as one.

> . . . Shareholders in California, at one time, owned about 10% of the outstanding shares of the bank in the late Fifties [N.B.: This, too, was unusual; most small banks are owned locally.] Californians like growth and aggressiveness in their investments; Franklin National Bank was their meat. A. T. Roth made it possible and they bought him.

This is, of course, largely a financial assessment of the accomplishments of Arthur T. Roth, but there are references to those other dimensions.

Banking is one of the most basic of human activities. This is so in many primitive societies, as well as in all types of modern industrial economies—communist Russia and China; all the communist countries, in fact—as well as capitalist Europe and the Third World. The kind of banks a country has, their number, their size and disposition tell you what sort of country it is. There are more branch banks and local banks in this country than in much of the rest of the world.

Banking—the word derives from *bench*, on which cash was counted—is a business whose stock is money. In the United States it is a controlled business—bankers are regulated toward prudence by federal and state laws and authorities. Most are ultraconservative, even retrogressive. Their buildings are generally large and somber, designed to cow the customer. Your typical American commercial bank leader is a graduate of Exeter, Andover, or Groton; of Harvard, Yale, or Princeton. He belongs to an exclusive club, worships at an acceptable church, is almost always a WASP. There are few Jews or blacks in the upper reaches of commercial banking in this country, and not many Catholics.

Banking in most of the United States sixty years ago when Arthur Roth began his career was hidebound and uncreative; unheeding of most people's needs and wants, ignorant of or opposed to social trends in government and industry, unaware or unbelieving in new currents in economic thinking. Bankers took in money from individuals but lent it capriciously, often unwisely or selfishly, rarely to average people or small businessmen. Their ideal was liquidity. They invested heavily in corporate and foreign bonds, which were supposed to be safe, and waited inside their citadels for the next depression.

Until 1933 the majority of U.S. banks were small and run by people who knew little or nothing about banking. They failed regularly by the hundreds, and in these cases depositors rarely collected 100 cents on the dollar. Not only did banks not protect their depositors, they simply did not do their basic job, which is to help the economy grow. As a result, new business and industry were starved for capital; it was difficult, often impossible, for most people to own their own homes.

The New Deal changed the rules of banking, at first keeping banks alive with infusions of capital, later offering a number of programs by which banks could help finance the country out of the depression.

But the vast majority of bankers were suspicious of these changes and were uncooperative. Not so Roth; he was often the first to see the value in federally backed finance. But he went far beyond this to provide new kinds of banking. He was skeptical of the practices of the past and was willing to ask daring questions and accept challenges. Nor was he averse to shattering myths or breaking idols. And he was not afraid to be creative, innovative—attitudes that are still anathema to many bankers.

He never conformed to the image of the banker. He didn't go to the right school or college; Townsend Harris Hall High School in Manhattan was the end of the line for him. He has a big nose and a name borne by many Jews. He has often been contentious and hence to other bankers he was—and is—an upstart Jew. Actually, Roth is a devout Roman Catholic, a pillar of his church, descended from a long line of Bavarian Catholics, if that matters. It certainly mattered to many bankers and to banking authorities.

But more important, Roth's philosophy of banking is pragmatic: He believes banking is a business that should run on business lines, use business techniques, serve the largest number of people, and make an honest profit.

It was the application of his philosophy of "retail banking" (his term) to Long Island, New York, that created what can only be described as a revolution. What we accept as commonplace today in our banks—the full-service bank with its installment credit, easy financing, quick business loans, long-term mortgages to build or renovate houses, checking and savings accounts under the same roof, credit cards, giveaways, gimmicks, hard-sell bank advertising—are to a significant degree the result of Roth.

The proliferation of bank branches was started in California by the Bank of America. In the rest of the country, there were few branch banks until Franklin began to sprout in the 1940s. In good part, today's ubiquitous banks and banking services, as accessible as supermarkets (and sometimes *in* supermarkets), are a by-product of Franklin's method of growth.

While tending his bank, Roth did not just mind his own business. When he found the regulatory environment hostile, he tried to change it, and frequently succeeded. This often meant espousing lonely, unpopular causes and fighting with governors, senators, congressmen, the banking establishment, and the comptroller of the currency, who controls all national banks. Roth's motives were often self-protective or self-advancing for his bank, but not invariably and never solely. His basic motivation was usually one of principle; more than once, Roth went against self-interest and even the interests of his shareholders.

As an example, he was one of only three bankers in this country (the others were Shirley Tark of Chicago and Howard Stoddard of Michigan) who had the courage to testify before a U.S. Senate Committee that the government ought to withhold income tax on the interest earned by depositors' savings accounts, the way it did on salaries, since much bank interest was not reported. Other bankers dared not grasp this nettle. Roth was able to get away with it simply because his bank was so successful. The outcome was tax form 1099, on which tax authorities now require banks to report all individual interest payments.

Millions of Americans have their first experience of banking with the savings accounts they start in mutual savings banks while in school. Hence, in the seventeen populous eastern states where they mainly exist, mutual savings banks have been nearly as sacred as motherhood. To Roth, the commercial banker, savings banks were unfair competition. He horrified his colleagues when he fought savings banks for the use of the word *savings* to which they held exclusive title in New York State banking. When he won in the U.S. Supreme Court, other commercial banks quickly began using the word.

Commercial banks pay about the same income taxes as other businesses. By special dispensation of the Internal Revenue Act, savings banks were practically exempt from income tax. Roth found this inequitable and unacceptable. He forced commercial bankers to take a consistent position on this by getting the savings banks out of the American Bankers Association. Then he persuaded President Kennedy to include an increased tax on savings banks as part of his special message to Congress in April 1961. As a result, mutual savings banks do pay some income tax today—not as much as commercial banks, but a more equitable proportion.

Roth was the first banker in the country to systematically employ handicapped people in his bank. It was a move dictated by sentiment, not sentimentality; he believes that people respect themselves more when they can help themselves. He financed personally, and through the Franklin Bank, the now famous Abilities, Inc., of Henry Viscardi, a successful Long Island subcontractor that employs only handicapped men and women.

I came across Roth's trail when researching an article for *Reader's Digest* on the economic costs of smoking cigarettes. An old news story, dated 1963, stated that he had forbidden employees to smoke in all of Franklin's branches during working hours. His motivation, he told me, was partly personal: Never a smoker himself, he found that the smokescreen at directors' meetings usually brought on one of his sinus headaches. But he was also convinced that smoking was dangerous and certainly costly. Proving the latter to his directors was the basis for his interdiction.

He made a study of what smoking employees cost the bank, in lost time on the job, in extra absenteeism (smokers get sick more often and more seriously than nonsmokers), in burned furniture and rugs. The cost came to $7 per smoker per week. Since the bank had 2,400 employees at the time, half of whom smoked, the loss amounted to $8,400 per week, or more than $400,000 per year. Roth translated this at about 1.5 percent of the bank's profits.

Even the most confirmed smokers on the board of directors were convinced that this was costing shareholders a lot of money, so they offered little resistance when Roth suggested that they no longer smoke at directors' meetings, setting an example for officers and employees.

The prohibition lost the bank some business from vending-machine companies and some potential deposits from a couple of tobacco manufacturers. But it won compliments from many customers. And the no-smoking edict made news, like a good many of Roth's moves.

He has a talent for combining private profit with public weal. In building his bank, he also arranged to build houses for his neighbors, at least 25,000 in Nassau County alone. Probably more than any other individual, Roth is responsible for helping to change Long Island's Nassau and Suffolk counties with their more than 2.5 million people, from a bedroom of New York City into a self-sustaining economy. Franklin financed hundreds of small factories and other light enterprises that provided jobs in business and industries that did not create large amounts of pollution, and whose architecture was not a blot on the landscape. From the beginning Roth has been a believer in the kind of planned growth that enhances not only the economy but the quality of life.

A tall, stately man—many have remarked on his resemblance to the late General Charles DeGaulle—Roth is known as unruffled and unflappable. During his many controversial clashes, few heard him raise his voice. His wife used to think there was something wrong with him because he never lost his temper at home.

He has few hobbies; mainly, he enjoyed his work. He was never interested in being very rich; he is certainly well-to-do, but even at the height of his success, his main residence was the house—in which he still lives—that he bought when he was cashier of the Franklin Square Bank in 1937. He could have greatly expanded his wealth if he'd sold the stock he owned in his bank, but he gave much of it away when it was valuable, or sold it at cost to employees. Not wanting to jeopardize the bank's future when he left, he and his family held the stock they still owned. This decision cost them several million dollars.

Arthur Roth is an unusually open man, speaking his mind without regard to consequences to himself. Hence, it seemed best to let him tell his own story largely in his own words, except mainly in this introduction and the final chapter, plus several introductory sections to chapters 2, 4, 9 and 10 and the postscript. The rest of the words in this book were taken from numerous lengthy interviews, which were taped and transcribed by me; his written words come from his private papers. The author has had a free hand in the selection of topics and what he wished to say about them. Mr. Roth did not ask for substantive changes in the manuscript. Factual material was taken from and checked with responsible sources.

W.S.R.

1 • Beginnings of a Banker

I got into banking simply because I could get a job in a bank. It started when I was seventeen, after graduating from Towsend Harris Hall High School. My father was a builder—a German immigrant bricklayer who had become a housing contractor—and my brother and uncle worked with him: Roth, Fecher & Roth. I did have a good head for figures; even while going to school, I used to keep their books. I would certainly have been welcomed into the family business, but my mother couldn't see it. She wanted me to have a more professional career. She was the strong person in the family. She made the policy decisions. It was she, for example, who decided that the family needed to own its own house. She took money she'd saved out of household expenses and signed the papers for a three-family house at 1120 Intervale Avenue in the Bronx. Then she took my father to see it and said, "Look what I decided to buy." It gave my father an incentive to work harder, to pay off the mortgage.

Both my parents came from the same village, Meinaschoff, on the River Main near Aschaffenburg in Bavaria. Philip Roth and Therese Fecher belonged to the same Catholic church as their parents, grandparents, and theirs before them for as far back as the church records go. They both came to America in the same year, 1888, with their respective families. They had known each other in Germany. Both settled in the German section of the Bronx, on Third Avenue near 156th Street, where they met again and were married.

I was the last of their four children, three boys and one girl, born on December 22, 1905, at home. The Bronx was almost rural in those days. There was a real feeling of neighborhood; you and your friends went to the same local public school and then to the same high school. You played ball in the streets; we had a backyard, too, with some grass, shrubs, trees and a vegetable garden.

My mother was the most courageous and energetic person I've ever known. I had a sister who was, mentally, extremely retarded. She had the mind of an infant, although she grew large and heavy, and lived until the age of twenty-eight. My mother would never think of putting her in an institution; our sister stayed with us all the time, in her own room. She really needed a nurse, a full-time attendant, to take care of her; but of course that was beyond our means. My mother did everything that was needed. That was her burden, her responsibility, and it was an enormous responsibility. She insisted bearing on it.

We used to wonder why all the cracks in the window and door in my sister's room were always stuffed with paper. Only many years later, after my sister died, did my mother tell me: If she felt that she herself was going to die, she intended to turn on the gas and take my sister with her. She wasn't going to leave her to be cruelly treated by some institution; we boys would not have been able to care for her, or to pay for the kind of private nursing she would need.

Yet with that tremendous, unrelenting responsibility for her retarded child, she never stopped doing all that was needed and much more, for her three sons, and for many neighbors. She had a vegetable garden in back of the house and grew enough to feed us fresh vegetables and to give plenty to neighbors. She canned the rest. We lived on that garden a good deal. She was a great cook, too. And was always putting up jams and jellies and preserves, and she'd give them away to people in the neighborhood who weren't maybe quite as well off as we. And she did a lot of needlework. Of course, she kept house without any help.

Then, later in her life, which Lord knows was a hard life, she had other burdens. When my father had a stroke, she nursed him at home for at least a year, or two, until her physical strength gave out. We never thought that would happen; she'd seemed indestructible.

She was an old woman by the time she was fifty; wore herself out in the service of others. But she kept on going for more than thirty more years; she died at eighty-three. Her late years were a daily physical struggle with poor digestion, yet she got up every morning at 5:00 A.M. and began baking. Cakes, breads, pies—things she could not eat herself. She just enjoyed doing for others.

If mother had had her way, if the money had been available, I would have gone on to college. But it simply wasn't in the cards. From the time I was nine, I'd had to work in my spare time—after school, weekends, and holidays. I used to deliver bread and rolls for a local baker. But there was never any feeling of being deprived; everybody in the family worked hard, and I was just doing my share. It seemed just as natural to live like that, then, as it is for today's youngsters to have cars and European vacations.

I went to the local grammar school, P.S. 20, which was only two blocks from where we lived. My friends and I did the usual things that boys do—explored the neighborhood, played around construction sites. I remember one incident very clearly. We lived not far from the elevated line of the subway. The structure was quite high, perhaps fifty or sixty feet above the street, and we used to climb its columns on the rivets.

Then there was the bridge over the railroad tracks, where we often played at dangerous things. The bridge was suspended by hollow girders that were solid steel on two sides, the other two sides were a latticework of steel strips in the form of XXXXX. On a dare, I got inside one girder through a small opening and climbed up at a forty-five-degree angle, and then down again. When I reached the bottom, which must have been about fifty or sixty feet from the entrance, I was wedged headfirst into a tiny space, with no way to turn around.

The angle was too steep to crawl up backward. I had visions of suffocating in that dark, cramped space. I was really scared. Fortunately, two men came to my rescue. They discussed sawing through the steel strips, but this might weaken the bridge. In the end they decided to turn me around. It took I don't know how long. Then they pulled me through a space in the X's. I suppose if I'd been an inch taller or a few pounds heavier, I wouldn't have been able to manage.

For years after, I had nightmares about that experience, the one truly frightening memory of my childhood, which was really quite a happy one. Although poor, we were brought up with the feeling that we could always manage somehow. And we always did. As a matter of fact, aside from that constant trauma of my sister, our life improved over the years. There is great satisfaction in knowing that this has happened through your own efforts—as an individual, as a family. That is the strongest sense of security that anyone can have, and one I hope I've been able to instill some of in our own two children. It has also governed my relationships with people in business—I've tried to give my colleagues the opportunity to better themselves. It seems to me that true charity is not a handout but an opportunity to fulfill your ambitions and exercise your talents. This has governed my dealings with people who are physically handicapped, too, both in and outside the bank, and I've seen it work.

There was no opportunity to go to college—and in fact I was able to complete high school only because Townsend Harris Hall had a three-year cram course that gave you the same diploma as a normal four-year course. Then, at age seventeen, I had to look for a job.

This was in 1923, when the country had come out of the war and postwar depression and was entering an era of inflation. Of course, I didn't know that, but it did create an economic climate in which one could get a job.

There was no special reason to pick banking as a career, except that I'd had some experience keeping books for the family building business. And, incidentally, had learned the details of that business, which gave me understanding of the field that was later to be extremely useful when it came to making loans to builders.

The only contact I'd ever had with a bank was with the German Savings Bank on Third Avenue in the Bronx, where my mother kept her savings as many German families did in those days. It was an imposing building, like most bank buildings, and I suppose I was properly awed as a youngster by the marble and stone. One looked up to bankers, as one did to other successful people, but there was no special contact that made me want to follow in anyone's footsteps.

When I was seventeen and needed a job, I read the want ads like anyone else, and saw that a messenger was needed at the Columbia Bank at 415 Broadway, corner of Canal. I applied and got the job at $10 per week. A year later the Columbia bank merged with the much larger Manufacturers Trust Company, and I continued on with the new employer.

Manufacturers was, incidentally, a Jewish-owned bank; Nathan and Ralph Jonas were the chief executives. This was, and is, rare in American commercial banking. At that time there was one other important Jewish commercial bank, the Bank of the United States—which later failed rather disastrously although all depositors were substantially paid off.

The world of commercial banking has always looked down on Jewish bankers although this topic is never, of course, discussed openly. And because I have a family name that is borne by many Jewish people, because of that early connection with the Jonases, and perhaps because of my appearance, many of my colleagues and competitors assumed that I was Jewish. In some ways this was an advantage, especially in dealing with Jewish customers, who are no different from others in feeling more comfortable with their own people—this is just as true of Irish Catholics and Scotch Presbyterians. And in some ways it was disadvantageous—in getting ahead in banking and in dealing with banking authorities, there was always that unspoken barrier of anti-Semitism. Obviously it hasn't hindered my career, but perhaps it did add some difficulties. The one problem that I have found personally annoying, created as a result of this misconception, is that all my life I've had a great deal of mail from Jewish cemeteries.

With my upbringing there was never any question about working hard. I'd do as much work as the bank gave me, and more; I was young, ambitious, energetic. Pretty soon they advanced me to "rack" clerk, which meant sorting out checks by hand into racks, and running an adding machine. The next step up the ladder was to statement clerk, preparing monthly statements for checking accounts. And then to Boston ledger bookkeeper. The Boston ledger was a three-foot-square ledger in which all of the bank's transactions were posted daily, by hand, in pen and ink. Having a neat, small script helped in that work.

The Boston ledger was the bank's permanent record; there were also daily ledgers from which the bank struck trial balances at the close of every business day. I was moved into that work, then to collection clerk, and note teller. This put me at a window on the first floor.

I go into these details because they were important in my training; I worked in just about every department of the bank in a day when all these things were done by hand. It was invaluable in learning the banking business, especially the detailed administrative side of it, which is really the heart of any bank—in fact of any business. Many times in later years I went back to the fundamental operations whenever there were major problems, and it was here that solutions often became apparent.

After four years of this kind of training, I was taken into the controller's office at the bank's headquarters at 139 Broadway. Here one could get a picture of the total operation, which, while not as large as Chase, National City, or Guaranty Trust, was one of the largest in the country. And it was expanding, merging with many smaller banks, which became branches all over the city. We got to know and deal with all the different ethnic groups.

When the Bank of the United States went under in 1928, taking with it the assets of thousands of poor immigrants, Manufacturers had recently merged with the State Bank on the Lower East Side, which had many similar accounts. The sudden closing of what had been regarded as a solid financial institution spread fear and panic among the immigrant colony, many of whom were illiterate. Their banking was done not by signature but by fingerprint.

Just about every depositor in Manufacturers' State branch at the corner of Grand and Ludlow Streets came to the bank to take out his money. I was sent over to supervise. At first we paid out as fast as we could, but as the lines outside grew longer, we deliberately slowed down to conserve cash. When closing time came, there were still hundreds of people on the streets. We told them to come back the next day, that we would reopen in the morning. But they were so panicked by the closing of the Bank of the United States that even though it was nearly freezing, most of them sat on orange crates in the streets all night long. Peddlers sold them hot knishes and other food.

Since the numbers of withdrawals continued into the next day, we decided to pay out as slowly as possible—in dollar bills. This took many minutes for each customer, and those waiting outside became very angry. Many took their passbooks over to the nearby Bowery Savings Bank, which accepted them and told the people that the money would be collected for them.

When the Bowery sent over hundreds of fingerprint passbooks for collection, I refused to accept them. Our president, Nathan Jonas, was told about it and called up our branch manager, who asked me if the story was true. "Yes, I sent them back," I told him. "We couldn't afford to pay all those accounts—we might as well have closed the bank. Besides, I had good reason to refuse: Those were fingerprint passbooks, and a lot of the withdrawal slips didn't compare with the signature cards."

"President Jonas told me to tell you it was a terrible thing to do," the manager said, "and that he was glad you did it!"

It was, of course, a tremendous decision for a youngster of twenty-two to make, and one I didn't like having to make. I knew our bank was sound and that when the panic blew over, these people would redeposit their money. But meanwhile they could have wrecked the bank, since no bank is prepared for so large a payout on such short notice. Later, during the banking crisis of 1932–33, many large banks made it a policy to restrict withdrawals to a tiny percentage of each account in order to conserve their liquidity.

While still at the former Columbia bank, I worked with a pretty brown-eyed brunette in the bookeeping department, named Genevieve

Kolczynski. When I was moved downtown, we continued to see each other. We were engaged and later married on January 26, 1930, and set up housekeeping at 615 Pelham Parkway North in the Bronx in a $60-a-month apartment.

My wife encouraged me to try to make up for the lack of college training by studying accounting and economics at the Walton School of Commerce; also, I attended a course given by the W. H. Leffingwell Company on "the art of supervision."

From 1930 onward, things got progressively more stringent in banking. My salary was cut back to $130 a month, which forced us to give up our flat and find less expensive quarters. My wife, who'd left her job when we got married, found another with a jeweler.

But things were much worse for other employees. I became a kind of troubleshooter, "efficiency expert" because of my knowledge of operations. I was given the responsibility of reducing overhead, which meant not only cutting salaries but eliminating jobs. Some of this happens by attrition in any large organization: When people leave or retire, you just don't replace them. But more rapid retrenchment was forced on us by the depression; we had to fire many people.

As an example, my boss, Controller Charles Clough, told me one day that our new president, a Mr. Harvey Dow Gibson, had pointed out to him that a branch of the New York Trust Company on Fifth Avenue ran quite efficiently with only twenty-three employees; while our branch on Southern Boulevard in the Bronx, which had about the same amount of deposits, was staffed with forty-three people. Mr. Gibson wanted us to cut back to twenty-three people on Southern Boulevard.

I said, "That's impossible. The New York Trust has only a handful of large accounts. Our Bronx branch has hundreds of small ones. They require much more service."

Still, it was an order. So I went to the Bronx and began analyzing operations, simplifying procedures, drawing up new forms, the sort of thing I'd been trained to do. And within a couple of months, we were able to eliminate those twenty jobs.

In a way this was a triumph. But for me it left a bitter taste. It had meant firing twenty good, honest, hardworking people. And since the object was payroll reduction, one got rid of the highest-paid people. This meant older folk with families, responsibilities. And older people just couldn't find jobs readily. Besides, at that time there was little severance pay, no unemployment insurance, no Social Security retirement, no private pension plan in the bank. These people were being thrown out of work through no fault of their own at the worst time in their lives, and at the most desperate economic period in our history.

Frankly, I hated having to be responsible for that, and I wanted very much to get out of that kind of work. I needed a job myself, of course. My wife was pregnant with our first child, so I couldn't afford to just walk out. But I was wide open for any opportunity where I could make a positive, rather than a negative, contribution.

2 • Surviving the Crisis

Background

Even during the prosperous 1920s, when the economy grew almost as fast as the Dow-Jones index, banking in the United States was in deep trouble. Wrote Jesse Jones, head of the government's Reconstruction Finance Corporation. "Between January, 1921, and September 30, 1932, more than ten thousand banks in the United States went out of existence—a truly shameful record for the richest country on earth."

It was no wonder that banking had a bad name, and it got worse after the 1929 stock-market crash. Bank failures mounted: more than 1,000 in 1930; over 2,000 in 1931.

The private banking system on which the American economy rested continued to degenerate. Hundreds of isolated small country banks closed. Then in October 1932 the governor of Nevada declared a statewide moratorium on banks. Not all closed, but some stayed shuttered for months while people scraped along on barter, cash, and personal IOUs.

The Nevada closing did not have immediate national repercussions; the state was isolated (distances were greater in those days), thinly populated, and sparsely banked—there were only twenty in the entire state. But confidence in banks was evaporating fast; people withdrew more and more cash and gold; hoarding replaced depositing.

As mistrust spread, the banks of whole cities were bled white by withdrawals. It started in smaller towns before Christmas 1932; cash hemorrhages spread to bigger cities: Memphis, Cleveland, San Francisco, New Orleans. In February 1933, with General Motors common stock selling at 10, the leakage reached Detroit; Michigan's governor was forced to close not only the banks of that city but every one in the state, since all were linked in some way with the automobile industry. Next Maryland had a three-day bank holiday.

Trust—without which banking cannot exist—disappeared. Bank holidays were declared in Alabama, Louisiana, Oklahoma; then in seven more states; then four more. "After midnight of March 4," Jones wrote, "a few hours before the sunrise of [Franklin D. Roosevelt's] Inauguration Day, state moratoriums were declared in New York and Illinois. That was the knockout blow. By breakfast time every state that still had any banks in operation ordered them closed."

When President Franklin D. Roosevelt entered the White House in March 1933, he had with him two rough-drafted presidential proclamations. One announced an immediate national banking holiday, taking the onus of bank moratoriums off both bankers and state governors. The second convoked a special session of Congress. Roosevelt ordered his newly appointed secretary of the Treasury, William Woodin, to have a banking bill ready for that session on March 9, five days after the Inauguration.

The mood of the country was so desperate that the president could have done as he pleased. Many thought he should nationalize the banks which had compiled such a sorry record. But Roosevelt preferred to rescue the system of private banking which bankers could not, or would not, do for themselves.

Woodin ordered the Federal Reserve to print bank notes, backed by bank assets. He wrote into the new banking bill provisions for the review and reopening of closed banks, and a system of "conservators"—"a title akin to receiver, but less harsh on the public ear"—to take over and operate banks too shaky to stand alone.

The bank holiday lasted for ten days. Roosevelt announced that banks in Federal Reserve cities and in 250 cities with recognized clearinghouses would open on March 13, and in the rest of the country on the 15th. Thousands never did open—more than 4,000, in fact, went under in that year of 1933. And Jesse Jones estimates that of those allowed to open, about 4,000 were really unsound, while hundreds—including many savings banks, which had boasted that none of their number failed—were put under "conservators."

The main thing Jones did to save banking was brilliantly simple. Instead of forcing loans on banks as the Reconstruction Finance Corporation (RFC) had been restricted to doing under Hoover, he got the law rewritten so the RFC could inject capital into banks. Then he cajoled, persuaded, urged, and forced bankers to issue preferred stock, or capital notes, which the RFC bought. The resistance was glacial; the banking world believed that the government was using its stock-buying powers to take over banking.

It took Jesse Jones seven months to persuade the biggest New York banks to issue and sell preferred stock to the RFC—National City,

$50 million; Chase National, $46 million. When the big banks who weren't in deep trouble took this step, the smaller banks, which were in serious difficulty, felt able to follow without being shamed.

The 1933 banking crisis was, of course, in good part a result of the economic debacle of the country. But the causes often lay in poor management. And the greatest reason for bank failures in good times had been undercapitalization. Eighty-eight percent of American banks had only $100,000 or less in capital and reserves. Forty percent began with less than $25,000. The bars were obviously much too low. Anyone could start a bank, and just about everyone did. Thousands were in communities with fewer than 5,000 inhabitants. These institutions weren't necessary, or even useful; they were status symbols, like flag-carrying airlines of underdeveloped countries.

In 1930, with only $41 billion total deposits, there were more than 29,000 banks in the United States; in 1972, with nearly $600 billion on deposit, there were fewer than half as many banks, only 14,000.

Under the standards forced on bankers by the New Deal, bank failures were rare for many years after 1934. From 1940 until 1981 there was no year in which ten U.S banks failed. However, since then bank closings have been on the rise: forty-two in 1982, forty eight in 1983 and they have continued to increase; in 1986 one hundred and thirty-eight banks failed in the United States: depositors are insured for up to $100,000.00 by the Federal Deposit Insurance Corporation.

Most bankers couldn't see, nor would they ever admit, that not only the private banking system but the entire capitalistic system in the United States had been saved by Roosevelt's New Deal. Few cooperated, and then only under pressure, with the various government financial programs designed to cool the panic, save the nation's homes and businesses and get the economy moving again.

The Franklin Square National Bank was an almost perfect example of what was wrong with American banking in the 1920s. It was started in a tiny village of less than 5,000, which had no industry, little commerce, and not even a railroad to serve it. Its founders were almost totally ignorant of professional banking. With a total capital and surplus of $62,500, the bank was underfinanced. Chartered on October 13, 1926, it began operations on November 1 in a rented store only 16 by 60 feet—but even that was much too large for its needs.

The goal was to make money and to "put Franklin Square on the map," as its first president, Arthur C. Phillips, the lone board member with banking experience, said. Also being on the board of directors of a bank elevated one's standing in the community. And, of course, the directors regarded one another as prime lending risks.

Although Phillips was innovative—he added evening banking hours, for example, to attract shoppers; made arrangements with the utility companies for people to pay their bills at the bank—Franklin Square National was so small that it took nearly three years to reach $1 million in total assets. That was in October 1929, a few days after the stock-market crash, and from there on it was all downhill for the next five years.

In 1930 deposits had dropped to $830,000; in 1931 to $730,000; and in 1932 to less than $600,000.

In Franklin's early days—as today—every national bank kept its primary reserves in United States government bonds. But their secondary reserves, which were the major portion of the bank's security, were invested in foreign-government, and so-called high-grade corporate bonds.

Franklin was no exception. Its first president considered himself an expert in bonds, and ten days after the bank opened he invested $65,000 of the $67,500 in capital and reserves in Argentine government 6-percent golds and Chicago Rock Island & Pacific Railway 4 percent. Both securities died before maturity.

President Phillips realized that things weren't going well in 1930 when he told his board that the bond account showed an average drop of nine points (i.e., $90 per bond, 9 percent of the par value). He was working closely with "bond experts" E. H. Rollins & Sons, and the Hanover National Bank. (One reason for Phillips's imprudent investments was that small banks, like Franklin, were dumping grounds for the big banks who underwrote the sale of foreign bonds.) Phillips asked the board for future guidance. Being even more ignorant about bonds than he, the board gave him a vote of confidence and asked him to "continue to handle the account in the same manner as heretofore."

That manner cost them another $44,578.03 the next month, when the chief bank examiner for the comptroller of the currency told them they had to cover the shrinkage in their reserves resulting from the depreciation of their bonds. They had to put this money up out of their own personal resources.

In November 1931, the bank held $480,000 in bonds, which had depreciated by $123,609. That was only part of its problem. The bank's directors had been lending themselves money for their various enterprises. Nearly a quarter of their outstanding loans were to each other. As they were no better risks than their neighbors, most of those loans were in default.

The directors also failed in two other areas. They had been unable to hire a competent cashier—the chief operating executive in a bank of that size. Their first cashier had got them mired in a failing duck farm, which cost the board, collectively, $29,791.09 out of their own pockets.

Their second cashier wasn't much better. And with deposits shrinking, the bond account leaking capital, and loans overdue, it was a wonder that the bank survived until the state bank moratorium.

The economy was at its low point in 1932, with the national income down by 50 percent (to $41 billion) and 13 million people—a quarter of the labor force—out of work. Franklin was as sick as the economy around it, but it managed to keep afloat while several other Long Island banks went under. Still, its bond account had shrunk to nearly half its face value before the bond market rallied and raised the value of Franklin's securities by more than $70,000.

In February 1933, the bank was so poor that it had to borrow $15,000, this time from the Bank of New Hyde Park (secured by mortgages), in order to pay cashed checks.

Like many other banks, it was reprieved that year by the state bank moratorium and the ten-day national bank holiday.

After that, according to early director Herbert Mirschel, "We weren't too sure that we were going to open. . . . We didn't know how badly off the other banks were, but we imagined we were one of the worst. . . ."

They were badly enough off to be told by the Nassau County Clearinghouse that they could not reopen unless the board of directors put up another $50,000. It cut deep. Most of the directors were forced to put up all the property they had left. But they were a stubborn lot, and Franklin was the first bank on Long Island to open after the bank holiday.

It was far from solvent, however. Debts continued to pile up. The bank's cashier was responsible for a personal shortage of $6,500 from playing the stock market. Actually, several directors were involved. Three board members made good, but the bond account was deflating again, and this time not merely through depreciation but also through default.

Actually, part of their desperate condition was due to the fact that examiners of the time measured bank capital in terms of current bond-market values; today, the face value of the bonds is the criterion. By today's token, Franklin would not have been considered in quite such bad shape. But it wasn't a healthy bank by any standard.

The deputy comptroller of the currency in late 1933 warned the directors that they would have to replace any losses occasioned by "excessive or otherwise unlawful loans or investments authorized by them."

Two directors tried to take turns acting as a cashier, but one had to leave to tend to his lumberyard. On Sunday, April 15, 1934, Arthur T. Roth, then a rising administrative expert in the Manufacturers Trust Company, had the good or bad fortune to take a drive out to Wantagh on Long Island with his wife, Genevieve. As the Roths headed east, they passed a westbound car carrying Fred Schilling, a Franklin director, and his wife who was Roth's cousin.

Schilling blew his horn, both cars stopped, and the men got out. As Roth walked toward the other car, Schilling said, "I've been looking for you. We've got an opening at the Franklin Square Bank for a cashier." Arthur Roth recalls that day very clearly. . . .

When we met Fred Schilling that day, we were thinking about moving out to Long Island. My wife, who had been born in Bayshore, had very happy memories of her childhood in the country, and we wanted a house and grounds of our own to bring up our family the way she'd been raised.

And there was the other reason I was anxious to change jobs. I'd been working for Manufacturers Trust for nearly twelve years. Part of the work was something I liked and enjoyed, but there was the side to it that I didn't like at all: reducing the overhead by cutting the payroll. Frankly, I hated having to do that.

Because of this, and wanting to move out to the Island, the Franklin job was very appealing. But when I told my boss, he advised me not to take it. "You'll be on the wrong side of the tracks," he said, "in the area with the highest rate of unemployment. If you want to move out there, why not try a more prosperous place, like Garden City?"

I asked for a day off to visit Franklin. I found only four employees rattling around in an overlarge building. But I liked President Phillips, who seemed vigorous and dynamic.

Nobody told me during the interviews that the bank was in deep trouble; only that they needed a cashier. I asked some questions of a few people in the banking business, but nobody knew much about Franklin—it was such a small bank.

Probably I didn't ask enough people or enough questions, but it didn't seem necessary. Having lived through the bank holiday, I had seen thousands of banks close and stay closed. I assumed that Franklin was sound because it had opened so quickly. Else why would the comptroller let it open?

I took two days to think it over, and decided to accept the job. We moved out to Hempstead.

Only when I started working there, on April 30, 1934, did I find several severely critical letters in the files from the comptroller's office, warning Franklin to get its house in order or "serious results are likely to follow."

That was bad enough, but when I added up the bank's liabilities, I wondered why I'd ever gone there. Not only was it smaller than any of Manufacturers' thirty-five branches, but its deposits of $478,000 were shrinking in both time and demand categories.* There was a bond depreciation of close to $200,000 (against only $125,000 of capital), and about $50,000 in bad loans not yet charged off. Many were to directors, former directors, and directors' companies; and the comptroller said that the amount of money in this category was so far out of line it was illegal.

I wasn't about to move back to the city. The only solution was to try to put Franklin back into solvency.

One of the obvious places to start was on the loans to directors, and directors' companies. These had to be reduced, not only for the money involved but for the bank's reputation. This was put to them in no uncertain terms; at the end of the first week, these loans had been reduced by nearly 20 percent, from $60,000 down to $50,000. President Phillips said he was surprised at how vigorously I approached this problem.

One has to tell the story sequentially, but actually there was no time for priorities. The bank was in such bad shape, we had to try to handle all of the problems simultaneously. On top of this, I started work just on the day when statements had to be made up for depositors. We worked sixteen, eighteen hours a day, weekends and holidays.

Another thing we attacked was all the "bad loans." Many were too small to give to an attorney for collection. Some had dragged on for four and five years. But when we looked into them, we found not a group of willful delinquents but people who wanted to pay but just couldn't meet the terms of their loans.

They had to be interviewed and the notes renewed. It took a good deal of time; it was bad for their morale and for ours. And renewing the notes on the same terms did not speed up repayment.

Clearly, new tactics were needed. We decided to put the loans on an

*"Time" deposit is a savings account; a "demand" deposit is a checking account.

installment basis. This was during the beginning of installment lending in banks. (It all grew out of the Morris Plan, which had been invented by a Richmond, Virginia, lawyer named Arthur Morris. One of his clients needed money to pay his wife's hospital bills; Morris said he'd lend him the money, but the man would have to pay it back in monthly installments. And from that transaction had grown a system of Morris Plan banks.

State laws were passed to regulate the Morris Plan. Loans were limited to two years; beyond that, the law considered it usury. The Morris Plan also got into automobile financing.)

In those days there was a great deal of shame attached to any borrower who had to use the Morris Plan. But it was practical and it spread, and the big First National City Bank looked into it. They began installment lending; and at Manufacturers Trust before I left we had investigated and decided to do the same.

We adapted the idea to Franklin out of necessity, to pay off the delinquent loans. We gave the borrowers books of coupons made out in small sums that they could comfortably manage in monthly installments. On these loans, we would charge a 6-percent discount, which is an effective interest rate of 12 percent. And the borrowers were covered with life insurance to protect the bank.

Sometimes the installments were spread out over five and six years. Knowing the Morris Plan laws, I called up the national bank examiner to ask if we could start this installment-loan department. He referred me to Washington, to the comptroller's office; I believe the man I spoke to there was Cyrus Upham. I asked him whether it would be legal for us to start an installment-lending department.

He said, "It's not proper for a bank to get into that type of business. And especially a bank as small as yours."

I said, "All I asked was, is it legal?"

He said, "Yes, but I'm saying you ought not to do it."

I said, "Some of these notes may run as long as six or seven years. Is there anything illegal in that?"

He said, "No, but it's improper."

Perhaps it was, but we had no choice—we had to do it. But the comptroller's office was wrong about the law: There was no national law on the subject, but the state law stated clearly that loans over twenty-four months were usurious. Technically we were in violation on those stretched-out repayments, although nobody ever brought that up.

Giving borrowers coupon books made it possible for them to pay off—which they wanted to do—and it saved the bank's time and began recouping our assets.

One of them I remember was a plumber, Louis Anziano, who owed the bank $500. He was a slow payer, often delinquent. We put him on the installment plan and he began paying. Then he wanted to get married, and needed an additional $150. We lent him the money, and he got married and he was one happy fellow. Some of the directors regarded him as a poor risk—*anyone* who was behind on his payments was a poor risk, they thought—but you could tell that here was a man who was caught in the economic squeeze and was doing the best he could. Of course he repaid every penny. And later he became a millionaire.

We were forced to increase our capital. The directors couldn't add to it, and there was no market for Franklin stock. The Reconstruction Finance Corporation and the comptroller of the currency told us to issue $100,000 of two types of preferred stock. The RFC bought $50,000 of the Class A, and the other $50,000 was taken up by the conversion of the directors' guaranty into Class B preferred. We were also instructed to depreciate the value of our outstanding common stock from $100,000 to $50,000 to more nearly reflect its value; and we were told to wipe out our "surplus and undivided profits" as being illusory.

It was painful surgery, without anesthesia. Much of it was finished by July 26, 1934. Now that the bank was on a sound financial basis, we could begin to put our assets to good use, to build our financial strength, and perhaps even to turn a profit.

One of our first profitable deals was to buy Home Owners Loan Corporation bonds. The HOLC had been set up by Roosevelt to buy up mortgages from householders who couldn't carry them. It replaced the counterproductive 1932 Federal Home Loan Act, which had been supposed to encourage private banks to lend to mortgagees. In the first year of that earlier ill-conceived program, 250,000 American families lost their homes through foreclosures; the next year (1933) foreclosures were running 1,000 a day.

Roosevelt's HOLC immediately stopped this by providing government cash to finance taxes and repairs, and rewriting existing mortgages, stretching them out in time and making payments easier to meet.

At one time, the HOLC held mortgages on one out of every five urban houses in this country—about 16 percent of the total mortgage debt. Those homes would have otherwise been foreclosed. The HOLC kept millions from being literally forced out on the street. And it pumped new life into the real-estate market.

As Arthur Schlesinger says, "Probably no single measure consolidated so much middle-class support for the administration."

But bankers were suspicious of it. It was financed by bonds, for which the federal government guaranteed the interest payments. But they had not guaranteed the principal. As a result, the bonds were selling at only 80 to 90 cents on the dollar.

I was convinced that in for a penny, in for a pound; the government would be forced by the logic of circumstances to back not only the interest but the principal as well. So we bought up as many bonds as we could afford—about $150,000 at the discounted price. It wasn't very long afterward that the government did officially guarantee the principal, and the bonds shot up to par. The bank made a quick profit of $25,000.

Our posture was always to cooperate in the many government loan programs that were started by the RFC and other government agencies. Obviously the government had saved the banks—I couldn't see this as creeping socialism. They could have taken them over, had they wanted to. And they were saving homes and farms and businesses—the whole economy. Of course, there was risk; but there was more risk in sticking to the old ways that had so obviously failed. If the new ways didn't work, there was probably no hope for our system, anyway: What could we lose?

One of the things we did to build the bank was to go out and seek business. Now I have never cared for selling. It goes against my personality to go out and try to interest someone in a proposition. My interest lies in management. But at that time we all wore eight or nine different hats. So I put on my sales hat and went calling on local businessmen. And we were able to convince many to bank with us.

One was a very pleasant and friendly man named Philip Weisberg, who had a fuel-oil business, the Petro-Nassau Corporation, which included selling and installing oil burners. I offered him some ten shares of our bank stock, which was worth about $8 a share; and to sweeten the package, there were twenty shares of a local store called Franklin Shops. Mr. Weisberg said he'd be interested in the shops, but he'd think about the bank shares. When we talked it over a second time, he said, "You're young, and you're only an employee. But if you bought shares in your bank, you'd be a kind of partner; you'd have more of a voice in the operation."

That appealed to me. But I didn't have the $80 to buy the stock. When I left Manufacturers Trust, I had paid off my bank loans. I'd arrived at Franklin Square free of debt, but also unburdened by any cash.

Mr. Weisberg offered to buy the Franklin Square bank stock for me and to let me pay him back when I could save the money. I took him up on it, and saved the $80 within a month. Those ten shares, the first I owned, would have been worth close to $250,000 when I resigned my executive responsibility thirty-four years later.

Naturally, as a result of this generous action, I had a more than average regard for Philip Weisberg. So when he came over to see me at the bank in June 1934 to talk about the Federal Housing Act, I was willing to listen. His idea was simple: Why not pay for replacing coal furnaces with oil burners via the modernization loan program under Title I of the act, "Housing Renovation and Modernization," which permitted such loans up to $2,500? It would help him—since he was short of capital—and it would help us, by giving us more lending leverage.

The way he put it to me was "How would you like to get some government paper that would pay the bank about nine percent?" Of course I was familiar with the act and with Title I, having attended a seminar of Long Island bankers at which it had been explained by a federal housing executive. This had made little impression on my fellow bankers, I might add; and similar orientation sessions hadn't convinced many bankers anywhere of the soundness of Title I. Their consensus was expressed in the *American Banker*, one of our trade papers: "Good borrowers can get the necessary credit anyway, and the FHA program is not needed by them."

This did not seem to me to jibe with the facts. There were plenty of good risks—if by a "good risk" you mean someone who will do everything in his power to repay a loan, someone you are certain is honest—who couldn't get credit simply because they had no collateral. Under FHA the government was going to hold 20 percent of the loan in a reserve fund—which meant that against loans of $1 million, we could take losses of $200,000. In banking practice this kind of loss was so remote that the reserve amounted to virtually a 100-percent guaranty.

I took Phil Weisberg's plan to President Phillips, at his office in Hempstead. I told him about this 5-percent discounted guaranteed loan that assured the bank of 9.7-percent interest. But Mr. Phillips was a conservative gentleman. He pointed out that the directors had not approved our participating in FHA loans. Later that day he called a banking colleague, Dr. Clarence Cohen of the Second National Bank of

Hempstead. He learned that Weisberg had already approached the Hempstead bank, and had been turned down. Nevertheless, Mr. Phillips was prompted—perhaps by my enthusiasm for the business, perhaps by the fact that Phil Weisberg was a valued customer—to present the idea to our board of directors. And they approved it for a trial period.

Weisberg, now a leading investment banker with an office on Park Avenue in New York City, looks back on that decision as the beginning of the phenomenal rise of the Franklin Square Bank.

We could see that if putting in oil burners created sound modernization loans, there were other kinds of home improvement that could easily be justified as the basis for sound bank lending.

There was a community adjacent to Franklin Square called Elmont—you might have called it almost a shantytown, a cluster of tiny bungalows, or shacks, built by Italian workmen who lived in Brooklyn and the Bronx. They used to come out on weekends in their ice wagons and their coal wagons and tend their gardens. Some were stonemasons, which you could see in the construction of their houses. Their plots were tiny, many no more than 30 by 80 feet. But these were serious, hardworking people who were following what you might call an almost atavistic instinct to get back to the soil. They lived in tenements in the city, but their *homes* were these shacks.

When the depression hit, many of the Elmont people were forced to give up their city flats and move out to their shacks. But these had been built for summer—they had no heat, no indoor toilets, many had no running water. These people needed help to make their shacks habitable year-round.

FHA modernization loans were ideal for this. We encouraged the owners to come to us for such loans. I'd go out and look over the property and talk to them about what they wanted to do with the money. These were small loans, averaging about $500, but they would enable these industrious people, unemployed through no fault of their own, to create livable houses out of their shacks.

Then FHA came out with its Title II mortgage loans. These financed new house construction up to $16,000. And under the act existing mortgages could be converted to FHA mortgages.

These new FHA mortgages were really a revolution, making it possible for nearly everyone who wanted to do so to build a house or refinance an old mortgage.

I knew from my own experience that a home of one's own is one of the most important and precious things in a man's life, not just an investment or a piece of property. It's part of ourselves. We'll fight for it, even die for it. Given half a chance, no man will ever let his house or apartment go for debt. And the government was giving much better than half a chance—it was giving an 80-percent mortgage guaranteed by the FHA. I couldn't see the government ever daring to foreclose many homes, especially since they had created the Home Owners Loan Corporation to avoid that problem.

Before FHA, mortgages had run for only five years. They were supposed to be paid off in six six-month installments. But since no one paid their mortgages on schedule, they had had to be renewed. There was a fee for this, economically wasteful.

FHA Title II mortgages were written for twenty years. And they were paid off in monthly installments, which included taxes, amortization, interest, fire insurance. They didn't seem like mortgages at all to most people. When we made our first such loans, the people would come in and say, "Where do I pay my rent?" Yet they were creating equity in their property.

Now Title I had been a success—the figures showed it. We'd made seventy-four Title I loans, grossing more than $30,000. This was part of our improving business picture; it helped attract new accounts. By June 1935, our total resources went above $1 million for the first time since 1930. Our monthly profit, which had been $156.17 when I started, had multiplied by ten to $1,553.50. And the depreciation in the bond account was down to a mere $22,000.

When I'd been hired, one of the directors said later, it had been a kind of holding action, designed for mere survival. But now the bank was moving ahead, and still the same kind of attitude prevailed. My cousin's husband, Fred Schilling, led a conservative board that kept trying to slow our progress.

When Title II came along, the directors permitted only a very limited participation by Franklin. Schilling, like most others in the banking business, did not believe in federal guaranties of mortgages. We were limited to making such mortgages only up to $250,000 in the spring of 1936. But the board had to double the figure when we reached the quota within a few weeks. By September that year, our monthly profits were over $2,500, plus another $1,000 from the FHA business. Starting in 1935, the board began declaring small stock dividends, staring with 1¾ percent; and these grew larger as profits mounted. Actually, they were rather large when measured against the 2-percent interest earned by "Special Interest" (savings) accounts at that time.

We began to get the name and reputation of being liberal lenders. One reason people came to Franklin was because we would talk to them face-to-face and make the decision right then and there. In other banks, loans had to be submitted to a committee the board of directors, who weren't always around, so there were long delays. People don't like being delayed when they need money.

I converted as many of our existing three-year mortgages to twenty-year FHA mortgages as possible, and then went around to see builders. At first we used a broker but an old friend, Mack Kanner, a big builder who'd built the Hotel New Yorker, advised me to get rid of the broker and do it myself.

We were a tiny bank. I handled all these loans until the quantity became just overwhelming. Then we brought in people to help.

We lent out literally nearly every penny we had—80 to 90 percent loaned out—an unheard thing in a bank, particularly then, when others had at most a cautious 20 percent of their deposits in loans, the rest in bonds. They weren't going to be burned twice.

In order to keep on doing more business, we had to find a way out of this capital bind. One obvious solution was to sell our FHA mortgages to other banks.

I took a portfolio of mortgages and tried to peddle them to the biggest, richest banks in New York City: Manufacturers Trust, where I had friends; Chase; First National (now Citibank); and a number of others. They all turned me down. FHA was advancing mortgage money up to 80 percent of the value of the houses. The banks said this was much too high; and they were still certain that the government's guaranty would be declared unconstitutional.

We heard on the grapevine that a Mr. L. Douglas Meredith, vice-president in charge of finance of the National Life Insurance up in Vermont, believed that FHA mortgages were a good investment. It was ironic that New York bankers were afraid of these mortgages, while a life-insurance man from perhaps the most conservative state in the Union was buying them up. I telephoned him and got a pleasant reception.

"I'll be down to visit you soon," he said.

He came, liked what he saw, and began buying our mortgages. He was the bellwether for Vermont. Once he began doing business with us, we heard from the Rutland Trust Company, and the Rutland Savings Bank. There were few places to invest money in Vermont, and these hard-shelled Yankee traders accepted the government's guaranty as gilt-edged, which indeed it was.

Then the word got around, and we began to sell mortgages to local savings banks. They wouldn't originate FHA mortgages, but once we did that, they were glad to buy them from us. They refused to make the loans directly, although they could easily have done so. In fact, they would buy our mortgages as fast as we could write them.

But there were delays that slowed us down. One was in title searches and guaranties. And these were very expensive. Our average new house mortgage was only about $6,000 or $7,000. But even in quantity, we had to pay more than $100 each for title searches. Too, there was an attorney's fee of $100 or $150 for each mortgage. All of which the mortgagor paid. In order to borrow his six or seven thousand, he had to spend at least $250 in cash before he could touch the money.

It was not only slow and costly but inequitable. When one looked into the situation and asked "Why?" the answer was always "Because that's the way it's always been done." No rational explanation.

We got in touch with the Intercounty Title Company, the established firm in the field, and asked them how much they would charge for title searches if we gave them all of our business. The answer was the usual fee of $100 plus.

So we contacted a new company, Security Title, and they said they could do the work for $35, a clear saving to each borrower of $65, equal to an average month's payment on a mortgage.

We'd been using a local attorney who was slow, expensive, and not very satisfactory. And when we checked into it, we found that the only "legal" work was filling out a set of FHA forms. No skill or knowledge, other than penmanship, was required. Why, then, pay a lawyer $100 or more?

The question answered itself. I began doing the work. Some lawyers accused me of acting as an attorney; I wasn't. Just filling out a form, and not charging for it.

A large builder, Mott Brothers, came into Nassau and bought a huge tract of land in Garden City. We spoke to them about handling the mortgages on the houses they planned to build. They asked the size of our closing fee. I asked them how much they thought we should charge on the large volume of business they were going to have.

Mr. Mott said, "A hundred dollars."

This was less than half of what most people were paying to other banks, but I readily assented. Since we were doing all our own closings, and our only expense was the $35 title search to Security Title, $100 represented a $65 profit for the bank.

Our perennial problem was that we were doing too much business, originating mortgages each year that totaled more than our entire assets. So we had to find a way of turning them around as fast as possible, to keep the bank liquid. If we could have a representative of the title company in the bank, we could save days or weeks on each transaction. I proposed this to Tom Quinn, president of the Intercounty Title Company.

He owed us a favor. His company had been affiliated with the Floral Park Bank, which had failed to reopen after the bank holiday in '33. At that time, title companies guaranteed mortgages and were subject to examination by the state insurance department examiners. Tom had told me that he expected that the bank examiners, who were due soon, would ask him to charge off a number of mortgages. His company didn't have enough cash in their reserve fund to absorb this, and might be forced out of business.

I said, "What do you want me to do?"

He said, "Can you take a look at these properties?"

There was a house in Bay Shore, and other properties. Although the mortgages might seem shaky to the examiners, the real estate looked good enough so that if there had to be foreclosures, the bank would not lose any money.

Although Intercounty was technically insolvent, I had been confident that it would become solvent if given enough time. I had told Tom Quinn we'd take the properties off his hands temporarily; but that when his company become a little stronger, in a year or two, we expected him to buy them back. And he'd justified our faith in him, and had taken the mortgages back later.

Now we needed a man from his company full-time in the bank. Tom Quinn assigned Edward Bordeau.

Title reports used to be inordinately complex, twenty or thirty sheets of paper. They entailed a great deal of paperwork, which meant more delay, yet in all the papers they gave you, nowhere was there a direct statement of a clear title. Why? Again, it had always been done that way.

"This is what we want," I told Quinn. "A single sheet of paper that states simply that the bank has a good and valid first lien on the property covered by the mortgage, and it is to state a clear description of the property."

Quinn said he'd have to take it up with the New York State Insurance Department. And they agreed that there was no reason not to.

The next move was speeding up certification by the FHA. The steps of getting your title policy, having a reported mortgage returned, and having it certified by the FHA required three months. This meant tying up hundreds of thousands of dollars of our bank's assets, and this in turn prevented our doing more business. Since we were almost alone in this field on Long Island, it also meant that scores of our customers who wanted to buy homes were delayed in doing so.

Well, we'd gotten two steps speeded up: the mortgage form and the title search. Now it was time to face the FHA with their part of the problem. So I went to see them. To expedite things, I suggested to FHA executives that we would give them a letter with each mortgage that stated clearly that we had conformed to all requirements of a guaranteed FHA mortgage. In the event that they later disagreed and couldn't underwrite that particular mortgage, we guaranteed to buy it back from them and replace it with another. With the letter, we gave them a list of the papers enclosed, and those that could be expected later.

They accepted this package as the basis for an immediate mortgage. Thus, we were able to lop three months off the transaction. In effect, this multiplied our capital by about 1,200 or 1,300 percent. For now we could do in a few days, at most a week, what had taken more than ninety days to process. Thus, the money that had been turned over, say, four times a year could now be turned over fifty-two times a year, providing we could find that many mortgages.

And there was no dearth.

In 1934 and 1935, we were handling about 75 percent of the FHA mortgages in all of Nassau County, one of the most rapidly growing sections of the United States.

By 1936 we had loaned out more than $1,200,000 under FHA. We were the leader among the nation's small banks in this type of mortgage, and our volume compared favorably with that of many of the very largest in the country. Among the big bankers, only A. P. Giannini of the Bank of America in California saw the true potential in FHA.

This was the cornerstone of Franklin's subsequent growth, and an important part of the growth of Nassau County. At a rough estimate, Franklin financed about one out of every four houses built in the county since 1934—between 20,000 and 30,000 houses. That's housing for nearly 100,000 people, a small city. We were helping people who wanted what I wanted when I left New York City to work at Franklin

Square: a house of their own, a plot of ground for a garden, a place to bring up their families.

Of course, communities made many mistakes during this rapid growth.

Nobody had had experience with such swift proliferation of housing before. There was zoning in many places, but authorities didn't know much about planning. It was left to individual builders, some of whom took the responsibility seriously, and others not—some of them community-minded, but many in it only for what profit they could make.

We went by past experience when communities grew slowly, and developed services as needed. In older days, there had been time for this to evolve. And those places grew, and developed, and prospered—and then began to go downhill. There's a human ecological pattern of growth and decline of communities that once seemed inevitable and uncontrollable.

But we know now that this isn't so. What problems we create, we can solve. And what problems we can solve, we can anticipate, and plan for, to shortcut the social dislocations and disorganizations that accompany unregulated growth.

Long Island learned a lot from its mistakes. Some of them have been rectified. And there's no need to repeat them. We know now that it's not enough to build sewers and streets to go with houses; we must plan for every aspect of community life—education, religion, commerce, industry, shopping, transportation, police, fire department, recreation, parks, all the rest. It's the only way you can create a harmonious and stable community quickly.

I learned these things the hard way. First I learned how to build a house from my father and brother. Then I found out something about building groups of houses. But this was far from enough. And as time passed, I learned something from our experience, and when it became possible, I encouraged the new young people who came along in building and development to put into practice what I had discovered, and tried to help them to plan intelligently for the future.

3 • Turning Franklin Around

When I left Manufacturers Trust, I sold every share of stock I owned—about $2,000 worth—to pay off my debts. And made a personal vow to myself that I'd never again read the newspaper from back to front—i.e., I'd give up starting with the stock market quotations.

However, when I joined Franklin I was told that part of my duty was to ride herd on our bonds. It was considered essential for banks then to have the major portion of their assets in such solid-sounding securities as "gold bonds." Yet it was the depreciation in these securities by some $200,000 or more that nearly destroyed the Franklin bank as bonds had destroyed hundreds of others.

Now, as the New Deal primed the various economic pumps through the RFC and the FHA, the nation's sick businesses; felt the rush of energy and began trying to get out of bed; they found that they were healthy. The bond market recovered and much, but not all, of our loss was recouped.

It seemed a good time to raise the question with the board of directors: Why, when we were earning money in commercial and mortgage loans, should depositors' money be put into bonds, which lost money, instead of into more loans?

The board had appointed a new bond advisory service, Bernstein Macaulay, Inc. Mr. Bernstein, at the board meeting of November 17, 1936, recommended that we hold all our current bonds; he also spoke of our FHA business as good "short-term investment."

With the profit picture now so healthy, I felt it was time to challenge his basic assumptions. So I said, "Gentlemen, you've heard Mr. Bernstein's position. Now let me present mine. You have placed these bonds under the supervision of one investment advisory service after another. With all respect to Mr. Bernstein, Franklin's bonds have proved to be one cat and dog after another." I said, "If we make a loan, we'll know soon enough if it's a good loan or not. But I challenge Mr. Bernstein to predict what's going to happen to our bonds from one day to the next.

"Let us break from these traditional moorings, gentlemen. Let us make Franklin into a vital institution that builds our community and our island." And I proposed the revolutionary idea of disposing of all of our bonds, except U.S. governments and municipals.

This was a shocking thing to say in front of Mr. Phillips, to whom having bank funds invested in foreign and corporate bonds was as fundamental as Gospel. He said, "I'm completely aware of Arthur Roth's contribution to the prosperity of this bank. I support everything he's done. But I can't go along with his proposal." He shook his head as he repeated twice, "I never heard of a bank having no corporate bonds." And there were actually tears in his eyes.

But the youngest board member, Herbert Mirschel, who'd served as volunteer interim cashier just before I arrived, got up and strongly supported the idea of disposing of our bonds. He made a very good speech, pointing out that when bonds defaulted, court actions ate up any crumbs that might have been left for the holders.

What we were asking was permission to sell $250,000 worth of bonds, or about 20 percent of the bank's resources, at a loss of about $20,000. The board was split almost fifty-fifty on the idea, but we won by one vote.

Herbert Mirschel said about thirty years later that that bold demand had increased my stature with the board. But, much more important, it set us apart as "the bank that was different." Very simply, it made us a lending bank at a time when most banks were squeezing their borrowers for repayment of loans. Word about this spread fast; we got business from a radius of twenty miles around.

I meant what I said: We ought to orient ourselves toward building our community, to provide all the banking services needed. Our FHA business burgeoned; we were servicing more than a million dollars of such business for the National Life Insurance Company of Vermont alone, at a service charge of .5 percent—or $5,000.

By mid-1937 we were 100 percent loaned out; and this at a time when other banks were content to lend only 20 to 30 percent of their assets. Naturally, those bankers questioned our methods; but we had the support of banking authorities.

At a board meeting only four months after we'd closed out our bonds, in March 1937, we could report that our bank's profits were almost 200 percent greater than the average of all other banks with assets of between $1 million and $5 million. We were earning 19.7 percent on capital funds as against an average of 6.8 percent.

A good part of this was the direct result of FHA. Yet most other banks were reluctant to participate. We would make mortgages, and sell them and service them to many savings banks such as the Dime and Willamsburgh of Brooklyn. Any bank could have done what we did in making FHA mortgages. But because of the innate conservatism of bankers, and because they wouldn't take the trouble to learn how the papers were handled, they turned to us. We would make a $10,000 mortgage on which we would net about $100 for the paperwork. Then we'd sell that mortgage to a bank or insurance company for $10,200. There was a $200 profit to us. Then we would service it for about 5 percent a year, or another $150. The service charge was not, of course, pure profit, but it was profitable—that is, it did not cost us $150 to service the mortgage, but we netted probably $50 out of that. So each $10,000 mortgage brought us a profit of about $350 the first year, plus an annual profit of $50.

When FHA was started, Jesse Jones offered to match dollars with private capital in setting up national associations to buy mortgages. There were such companies in the private market, but none came forward to take advantage of the government offer of partnership to purchase FHA paper. "Nearly four years went by without our getting a single offer of cooperation," Jones said later. The government was forced to enter the mortgage market.

In 1938, the RFC set up a wholly owned subsidiary called the Federal National Mortgage Association, which offered to buy FHA mortgages at 99 percent of their face value. They were then sold at par. This went over so well that "Fannie Mae," as the agency came to be known, began buying at par and selling at a premium.

"Before Fannie Mae was a year old, it had authorized and purchased 26,276 mortgages aggregating more than $100,000,000 and had found it necessary to start foreclosures on only twenty-five," according to Jesse Jones.

I mention these things to show the almost total resistance of bankers to this innovative financing. They had a kind of neurotic compulsion to sound and reject the new, even though it might be profitable and to repeat past self-destructive behavior.

In 1937, President Roosevelt, who had never understood modern deficit financing, opted for a balanced budget (which he never attained). He decided to reduce spending on the Public Works Administration, which had been attacked as a "boondoggle," and to balance this with an order to the RFC to stop lending money to business. There was, of course, no sensible reason to link the two: The PWA was a direct *spending* program, designed to give employment and build public works; the RFC was a *lending* operation, which was actually taking in more in repayments than it was lending at this period. Yet for Roosevelt's political purposes both types of economic activity had to be curtailed. Too, the Supreme Court had recently struck down two other New Deal agencies: the National Recovery Administration (NRA) in 1935 and the Agricultural Adjustment Administration (AAA) in 1936. These, coupled with the desire of bankers to pay off their RFC preferred stock and get back to a comfortable liquidity—which meant lending no more than 20 to 30 percent of their assets—all combined to put a brake on the economy, which had just began to move ahead.

Suddenly, in the fall of 1937, all the economic indexes showed a marked slowdown: Industrial production, carloadings, steel production, heavy goods and automotive production all fell while unemployment rose. The stock market dropped, and so did the commodity market, the latter because of bumper crops of corn and cotton.

It added up to a sharp recession.

In 1938, Jesse Jones wrote to 14,000 banks telling them that "if banking is to remain in private hands it must meet the credit needs of the country." His hope was to pump $3 billion into small businesses. But only 1 percent of the banks responded—although, Jones reported bitterly, "at least half had been directly assisted by the RFC, and all had been indirectly assisted."

Among the 1 percent who responded was one of the very biggest, the Bank of America, and one of the smallest, Franklin Square National. I asked the board for permission to participate in the RFC small business loan program, and was allowed to place "one or two advertisements in a local newspaper." We went after this business as vigorously as we had FHA mortgages, and soon we were able to report that we were the leading bank in the United States for our size in this type of loan.

On an RFC business loan, the government guaranteed 75 percent and set the interest rate. It was about 4 percent. On the other 25 percent that was not guaranteed, the interest rate had to be higher: 6 percent.

Since we were paying 2 percent for time deposits, there was a large enough spread here to earn the bank a decent profit.

We continued to build all these types of business, and to push for installment loans as well. And a third type of FHA mortgage (Title I, Class 3), up to $2,500, designed to help create low income housing, fitted into our program.

At the end of 1937, we could report another boom year for the bank, in spite of the recession. Our total assets were nearly $1.7 million, of which $438,000, represented FHA mortgages and $317,000 installment loans. The only other bank in the country with a similar proportion was the Bank on America, on whose aggressive community-building we had deliberately patterned ourselves.

I had been raised to $6,000 in salary and was elected to a newly created seat on the board of directors in January 1938.

Just about the only industry on Long Island (except for Grumman and Republic aircraft companies, neither of which did business with any of the forty-three small Long Island banks) was the building industry. As a commercial bank desirous of lending money to business and industry, we naturally loaned mostly to people who built houses on speculation. This fitted with my early experience in the family building business; I could talk builders' language, and was able to judge the value of their projects. Hence, I had no hesitancy in backing my judgment with loans.

But because we were restricted to this one field by the nature of our community, we ran afoul on the banking examiners who were sent out by the comptroller of the currency. Deputy comptroller E. H. Gough, a tough, tobacco-chewing bureaucrat, was a literal-minded enforcer of the banking regulations. These had been drawn up in response to the numerous bank failures that had plagued our industry. They were so protective they defeated the very idea of banking as a creative economic force.

Under the regulations we were restricted to loans no greater than 50 percent of our capital in any single business category. Since our capital totaled $135,000, and surplus was not counted in with capital, we could loan only $62,500 to builders.

At the examination of June 8, 1938, the examiners found that we were carrying $87,600 in builders' loans, a clear violation. We were told that we must reduce these to the legal limit. In answer to our protests that this was the only industry in the area, Deputy comptroller

Gough wrote, "You are advised that the only way this matter can be remedied would be by Congress."

If that was the only way, we would have to pursue it. I wrote to the American Bankers Association and requested that they present this change to our legislators, and got a positive reply from their assistant general counsel.

We wanted to buy back our preferred stock out of profits. We were told not to buy back our preferred, but to increase our capital to support our lending policies.

We were hit with another criticism. According to the Federal Reserve Act, direct real-estate loans by any bank were restricted to 60 percent of its "time" deposits—i.e., savings accounts. We had $917,000 of such deposits, and $660,000 of real estate loans—or 71 percent of the deposits—which meant we were 11 percent over the ceiling. Again, we were told to cut back, and we made an effort to do so.

It was galling, because it defeated the very purpose of banking. The most progressive national leaders saw this. Marriner Eccles, chairman of the Federal Reserve Board, and Jesse Jones of the RFC wanted more liberal bank-examination policies; and they were supported by the liberal Michigan Republican Arthur H. Vandenberg, who got loan classifications changed from "slow," "doubtful," and "loss" to categories, I, II, III and IV. A small change, perhaps, but one with large psychological impact on bank examiners.

Secretary of the Treasury Henry Morgenthau was the main roadblock. He had President Roosevelt's ear—they were both Dutchess County, New York squires, and old friends—and he was not a banker, either by training or inclination. And the people he appointed, Comptroller Preston Delano, Roosevelt's cousin, and the chief deputy Cyrus B. Upham, were extremely conservative.

Upham, particularly, harassed and impeded us incessantly. He never concealed his dislike for Franklin's banking methods, and has since said that he tried to block us at every turn. Even when we later applied to change our name from Franklin Square to Franklin National, he opposed us; as he said recently, "I wasn't about to go along with anything that they wanted."

But back in the late Thirties and Forties, we had no choice but to knuckle under.

However, it didn't restrict our growth. We made and sold and serviced mortgages to all the big Brooklyn savings banks, and many life-insurance companies. We steadily built up our installment-lending department—people were being gouged for as much as 30 percent annual interest by finance companies; we lent them money for the same purposes at only 12 percent.

In 1938 our business had grown so that we had to build a 20-foot addition to our bank—which cost us $50,000 including the land. We felt flush enough to invest in a director's table and ten walnut chairs: total cost, $425. By June 30, 1939, our total assets had passed the $3-million mark.

But what was more important, 95 percent of our deposits were loaned out—nearly $2,400,000. The average ratio of loans to deposits was 32.5 percent for all banks; the Bank of America was considered extremely daring at a 48-percent total! But we kept on rolling up more and more loans; in the first six months of 1939 alone, we'd loaned nearly $1.8 million, excluding mortgages.

Our bank examiner was highly critical: "Advances to speculative builders alone aggregate $280,067.75, an increase of $117,000 since last examinations, which amount appears disproportionate and hazardous and to represent a substantial and unreasonable degree of risk." He said that our loan policy "which permits unwarranted concentrations of credit [is] unsound and requires the attention of the directors for correction." He added that our management hadn't been able to keep up with our growth, and that the bank was "too dependent on Cashier Roth," and encouraged the board to take out a $25,000 insurance policy on my life.

We were still a small bank, but less small: We'd moved up from forty-third in Nassau County to seventeenth and we had accomplished this during a serious economic recession.

And the FHA told us that we were doing the best job in the United States in financing Title I Class 3 loans.

To expedite these loans, we brought in a young attorney named Samuel Spitzbart on a fee basis. He closed 375 such loans by September 1, 1939; he earned more than any regular employee in the bank, including me, and was worth every penny.

Those loans totaled $750,000; we split them with the Dime Savings Bank on an odd-even arrangement—each of us would take every other loan. Only one of those loans defaulted, and that because of a devastating illness that made it impossible for one mortgagor to repay.

This was a new kind of banking. Our only surety was the integrity of our borrowers, and the 10-percent insurance granted by the FHA.

It was still unaccepted by more than 90 percent of bankers, however. To try to change some perspectives (and minds), we prepared a booklet on Title I FHA loans in 1939. This got so much attention that the FHA followed through with their own promotional mailing to banks.

It all brought in business. In 1940 we were able to pay off the entire $50,000 we had received from the RFC for Class A preferred stock; this stock was retired. We increased capital by selling our own preferred stock to shareholders.

Over the years, I borrowed money from Manufacturers Trust to buy whatever shares of Franklin stock came on the market. Our own president, Arthur Phillips, had little confidence in the bank's future, and sold his stock. I bought it; I considered I was investing in my own future. In 1940 I held 210 of the 1,000 shares of common stock, or 21 percent. The par value had been increased from an initial $40 to $60. My cousin's husband, Fred Schilling, was the largest owner of our preferred stock.

In 1940 we invited 175 local builders to a meeting at the bank to tell of the easy mortgage money available through the FHA. The idea was to inspire them to enlarge their vision and their operations. Nassau was wide open; there was so much open land in those days that if you hadn't seen it, looking at the urban sprawl of today you wouldn't believe it.

One of the first large developments resulting from this meeting took place in Elmont. Worthmore Homes, Inc., started there in March 1940 to build fifty houses selling for from $2,650 to $3,000. Albertson Estates started nearby at nearly the same time—150 houses, four rooms and bath, costing $2,700 each.

These multiple-house developments for low-income people were a shot in the arm to our local economy, and gave people a real stake in our country. The Roosevelt administration had capitalized on the importance of owning your own home by coming to the aid of people who were about to lose their houses. And now it was carrying the idea the logical next step by helping wage earners to buy new houses.

But for every action there's an equal and opposite reaction in society as well as in physics. Our own board of directors had a conservative faction, led by the builder George Estabrook, that opposed our helping builders to put up a lot of cheap houses for ordinary folk. Estabrook actually started a move in the board to cut off our Class 3 loans. His reasons were that these inexpensive houses would depreciate the value of the more expensive houses already built, and that the influx of families requiring more city services such as schools and police would force the tax rate higher.

It's the perpetual fight between the haves and the have-nots that's still going on in our suburbs.

I opposed the conservative board faction on this. I said that these houses could be located so as not to depreciate existing houses, or property reserved for expensive construction. And these new homeowners would carry their share of taxes. I agreed to talk the problem over with Estabrook and local officials and other bankers, and it was worked out. The board agreed to back me on continuing the Class 3 loans; but on condition that all such loans had to be eligible for sale to the RFC mortgage company.

Besides informing builders of the mortgage possibilities, we did everything we could to aid builders. For instance, to inspire Skillman Homes to do some construction, we actually bought up some farmland that was zoned for dwellings and resold it to the builder at exact cost. This is the sort of thing that we feel a banker should do to build his community, because when he does this he also builds his bank.

The *New York Times* took note of our activities in Nassau County, reporting the enormous surge in building in Queens, Nassau, and Suffolk, "especially in the marginal areas between existing communities."[2]

Among the FHA Title I modernization loans we made, the largest number were to builders. And two of those builders turned out to be violators of the law.

One was the Brownie Lumber and Supply Company of Brooklyn. Simon Brown, the owner, made 107 modernization loans through our bank. A few of these were fraudulent, we later found out. A typical fraud went like this: A borrower would qualify for a $1,000 FHA modernization loan. Brownie would do the work; they would bring us the loan. We would make it. But the actual job would be for only about $500; the rest of the money went for personal use, such as buying automobiles.

As soon as we found out about this we went to the government with the information, and, of course, immediately stopped making loans to the Brownie Company early in 1940.

There was a grand-jury investigation, and 17 of the 107 FHA loans made to Brownie were found to be in default, under circumstances that indicated fraud. Brown and others were tried, and Simon Brown went to jail.

The other large customer who had violated the regulations was John Schmidt, a builder with an excellent reputation. He was responsible for 112 modernization loans to his customers. But it seems he would get this business by telling his clients that if they couldn't pay up in three years—the FHA modernization-loan period—he would let them go for a longer time. What he did was ask them to sign two notes: one for three years to FHA for the loan; and one to his company for from five to seven years. He would repay the FHA loan within the specified time. But the customer would pay him over the longer period. In effect, he was using FHA money to go into the private lending business.

When a young clerk named Stephen Hayes reported that this was going on, I called Schmidt in and asked him about it. He tried to dodge it, but confessed that he was violating the law. He was an excellent contractor who did fine work, but what he was doing was neither ethical nor legal. In fact, on investigation it turned out to be criminal. Like Brownie, Schmidt had been conniving with clients to borrow government-guaranteed money fraudulently. And all the money wasn't being used for the intended purpose.

Both of these violations, following as they did one after the other, put the bank in more jeopardy in March 1941 than it had been in since the problems with the early cashiers. The Dime Savings Bank of Brooklyn, to whom we had sold scores of mortgages, lowered the boom by canceling its agreement to work with us. Mr. Jay Keegan of the FHA sent a letter by hand to our board on March 21, 1941, saying, "You are hereby notified that effective as of the close of business March 27, 1941, you are to discontinue accepting applications . . . under the provisions of Title I."

That was a nearly fatal blow. I made an appointment to see Keegan on the following Tuesday, March 27.

Also very serious was a letter on March 24 from Deputy Comptroller of the Currency Upham, demanding that a committee of officers and directors including me and Joseph Clayton, the man who handled our FHA loans, come to see him in Washington. President Phillips and Fred Schilling went along as counsel. I pointed out that we had notified the FHA of the Brownie frauds early in 1940, and that as a result Brown tried to involve us in his confession. We were asked to make a deposition, which we did. But it had been more than a year since we had severed relations with the Brownie Company. And we had reimbursed the FHA for losses on two fraudulent Brownie loans.

At the same meeting, we explained the Schmidt matter, which we had thought in the beginning was not a question of fraud. But we offered to the FHA to interview all of the 112 people who had made modernization loans through Schmidt, and to pay all those that the borrowers could not pay.

The government asked us to do more than that. They wanted all that paper to be removed from FHA insurance, because these people had signed two notes and, as far as they were concerned, the FHA note was not the amount that they borrowed. And they had obligated themselves to Schmidt to repay not in the usual three years but in five, seven, or ten years.

I said, "All right, we'll transfer all those loans to bank loans." And we did. And as a matter of fact, every one of those loans was repaid. Not only did we suffer no loss, but we even made a profit—far more than we would have earned if they'd remained as FHA loans. Because we charged Schmidt a 5-percent discount, and an additional 2 percent as a security fund.

We needed desperately to reinstate ourselves with the FHA not only as a matter of immediate business but for the reputation of the bank. To convince the agency, we presented a summation of the pioneering work we had done with FHA mortgages. For seven years we had vigorously promoted their programs, while other bankers had held back. We were doing the spadework and later we persuaded other bankers to accept some of the profit. Under Title II we had originated more than $7 million of mortgages, and there had been precisely twelve foreclosures. We had serviced mortgages for forty-nine other financial institutions, all of them much larger than ourselves. Among these were New York Life, National Life, Schenectady Savings Bank, and the Home Savings Bank of Albany. We had also initiated $1.5 million in Class 3 loans.

We put into the record Keegan's own letters of appreciation to Franklin for the services we had rendered and a report of his own deputies, who had found that our bank had FHA insurance for over $2 million of Title I loans, of which 25 percent went to individuals and 75 percent to ninety-two large builders. Out of all this, only the Brownie and Schmidt transactions were questionable.

When FHA suspended our right to make these mortgages, they eliminated the greatest part of our business. More, they called into question our veracity, our good faith, our honesty—the cornerstones of any banking business.

I put everything I felt into a plea to let us continue in the work, pointing out that we were in an area of growing need for building and modernization, because of the thousands of new people streaming into the area to work in war industries.

The ban on our Title I mortgages went into effect on March 27. Five days later, on April 1, it was lifted, due, in large part, no doubt, to the enormous services we had rendered in pushing FHA programs since the beginning.

The five-day FHA suspension had been the most serious setback the bank had had since the bank holiday of 1933. The fact that we were reinstated in the agency's operations so quickly defused this potentially explosive situation. Our board backed us to the hilt by a unanimous vote of confidence.

We set to work to find a replacement for the Dime Savings Bank in our mortgage program.

At the same time, we agreed with Upham to reduce our unsecured builders' loans, which we did by 50 percent within the year; and we balanced this with an increase of about 100 percent in our secured loans to builders.

One way we managed to do this was to work out an arrangement with the Marine Midland Bank. They put up 98 percent of the loan and we put up only 2 percent. Thus, a $10,000 loan, which was made in our name, required only $200 of our money. Marine Midland liked this arrangement because they were getting 5 percent on their investment. In those days, banks made few loans; most of their money was in government bonds, which paid only 2 or 3 percent. Hence, the 5 percent was very attractive to them. And we liked the deal because we earned the service charges on the loans.

However, the arrangement didn't last. They eventually pulled back, and left us with the choice of reneging on commitments to builders or making the loans ourselves. Actually, a great many of these were housing mortgages under Title VI of the National Housing Act. But the comptroller's office was staffed by men who'd had little or no practical banking experience. They went by the book, instead of applying common sense; and they called all these loans "builders' loans," because the builders' names were on the notes, and lumped them together as though they had been made to the builders. On this basis, they could find that we had gone beyond the legal limit even though the mortgages were 100 percent guaranteed by FHA. This was changed later, but at the time they tried to make it stick.

Deputy comptroller Upham said that we were the most heavily loaned-out bank in the United States—we had ten times our capital outstanding. I tried to explain about our arrangement with Marine Midland: that actually we weren't that heavily loaned, but that Marine

Midland was taking from 90 to 98 percent of each loan. These notes had our name on them, to be sure, but we had to carry 100 percent of a loan only for a short time after it was made. He wouldn't listen. All he could say was that we were doing too much business for a bank our size. I think that's what irritated him—we were going contrary to the rules. But we were making more money than all the banks that did go by the book. Our profit position was impregnable; that's what saved us.

The fact was, we were in an excellent liquid condition. We had cash and government securities equal to 50 percent of our assets. Today in a comparable bank that would be only 30 percent. But this was just after the depression, and the bank holiday, when so many banks had closed; people in Washington were scared stiff.

But Cyrus Upham was unhappy about our general approach to banking. He wanted us to go back to the ways of the past that had got so many banks in so much trouble. One thing that brothered him was that we were servicing mortgages for other banks. He felt that this was not a bank function; or that if it was, it ought to be under a trust department. We didn't have a trust department, and didn't want one. It would be too expensive for the amount of real trust work available to us. A trust department requires highly paid experts to make judgments on investments; they are needed to advise clients on where to place their money, when and what to buy and to sell. We argued that no judgment was called for in servicing mortgages; that this wasn't properly a trust function. Servicing is a simple matter of billing people and collecting monthly payments. But for years Upham stubbornly argued that we had no right to do it without a trust department. We never gave in, however.

4 • The People's War and The People's Bank

Between 1934 and 1941, the American economy moved from recovery to recession to preparation for war. The Franklin Square National Bank responded to the challenges in the changing situation, riding the waves of the present while other financial institutions kept their eyes resolutely on the past.

The bank's recovery and growth had been predicated as we have seen in good part on New Deal agencies designed to improve the domestic economy. Roosevelt's foreign economic policies, much less effective, were no concern of a bank as small as Franklin Square.

But, of course, international events were having some impact even on that largely residential community. The United States had begun to rearm, even before threat of war. Roosevelt, always dedicated to sea power, had begun to build the U.S. Navy up to parity with Great Britain, using $238 million of emergency relief funds to construct thirty-three new ships. His excuse was that shipbuilding was a kind of public works project that would give employment to people in almost all of the forty-eight states. The impact of this program on Long Island, which had no shipyards, was minimal.

But when Hitler's imperialism affected U.S. foreign policy, Long Island knew about it. Their two aircraft builders, Grumman and Republic, began expanding their facilities to build warplanes.

The Franklin Bank wasn't important enough to finance them, or other large manufacturers, such as Sperry Gyroscope of Brooklyn. But when these firms hired more workers, the workers needed houses. These the bank could and did finance. And when houses were built, local retail businesses came along to service the new inhabitants—which created more need for bank loans.

Franklin, alert to these developments, profited by them more than most other banks. It did this by anticipating people's needs and devising means of fulfilling them. Its service-oriented approach to banking encouraged fresh thinking and innovation. Arthur Roth probably created and furthered more new attitudes and services in banking during these years than any other banker in America, with the possible exception of the Bank of America's Giannini. What made his performance the more remarkable was that Franklin, although growing fast, ranked about number 1,700 nationally; while Giannini's multibillion colossus, sprawled out over the state of California and nine other states (including a substantial interest at that time in New York's huge First National), was the largest in the country. Roth had a simple point of view that was the key to his methods.

I had always believed that banking was a business. That doesn't sound like a very revolutionary statement, but in 1940 it was pure heresy. Bankers insisted that banking wasn't like other businesses. It was a profession; it was garlanded with traditions, taboos, shibboleths, veiled by conventions, protocols, and other kinds of mumbo jumbo, all knotted up with an Old School Tie. It was a gentlemen's game, played according to rules that made as much sense in the 1940s as the court etiquette of Louis XIV.

I hadn't gone to the right schools and didn't belong to the right clubs. I'd been hired by a practically moribund bank to put it on its feet. This meant, very simply, making money. And to make money you have to be businesslike not only in the internal efficiency of your organization; you have to use all the tools that other businesses use to make themselves acceptable to the public. By this I mean service, advertising, showmanship, public relations. You had to give the public what they wanted, not just what you thought they should have. And most basically, you had to be responsive to community needs—to people's needs. A large percentage of our customers earned an average of only $2,400 a year. The typical client was forty-one years old and had two children. To the average banker, such folks were poor risks. And they were small potatoes, too unimportant to bother with much less cultivate.

But we felt, and our experience proved, otherwise. Those people would take a $1,500 Title I modernization loan and they would improve their property by much more than that amount. They would build a $2,500 house—that was the average price of the development houses we were financing via FHA—when they found that it didn't cost much more than paying rent. And when people build a house, they care for it. I knew that from my own experience; after all, I'd only recently built a house for my family and it wasn't long since I'd been earning around $2,400 a year.

Twenty-seven percent of our borrowers for low-cost houses were mechanics; 18 percent were civil-service employees, 5 percent utilities workers, and so on. In an article for the FHA I wrote, "Many of these borrowers pay their monthly installments in advance, and more than half of them have greatly increased the value of their properties by improvements and additions made since they first built them. This they do out of their own pockets. In all my experience, I have never seen people so attached to their homes as these."

Not only didn't other bankers encourage such borrowers, the authorities didn't appreciate them either. I recall one woman—and she wasn't alone—who'd had her house foreclosed on a tax sale for nonpayment of one-half of a year's tax. All subsequent taxes were paid. The tax people were brutal about it; they gave you two years to pay your taxes, and if you didn't, they auctioned your house off from under you. And they would do this on the shortest notice. They were supposed to notify you by registered letter, but most little people didn't know the regulations. A lot of politicians and others were involved in these tax sales because they made a good deal of money that way. Sounds almost unbelievable, but that's the way it was.

Well, this poor woman who'd lost her home in Elmont, a widow in her fifties, came to see me and asked if there wasn't something we could do. She could barely speak English, and it was obvious that she was not capable of fighting for her rights.

I found out the name of the man who'd bought her house, a builder named Mike Forte, and called him up. I said, "You can't take this poor woman's home away from her." He said, "I bought it legally, it's mine." I said, "You just can't do things like this." He said, "Of course I can—it's done all the time." So I said, "I just can't allow this to happen."

I got in touch with Harry Hedger, the Nassau County treasurer, and told him the story. He said, "I don't know what we can do." I said, "I think you should get in touch with Forte and tell him that the woman should be allowed to repurchase the house. If he insists on a profit, tell him to take a hundred dollars over what he paid."

Well, this is what happened. The woman was able to repurchase her house, but only after I threatened to give the matter wide publicity.

This happened so many times it was sickening. I tried to publicize it so that the people would know and then the laws could be changed.

Eventually the press did get interested in this situation—not in this particular woman, but in the general problem. I don't cite this tale to demonstrate that we were public benefactors. We were bankers, but perhaps we did have a different attitude toward the people who came to us than some other banks.

And perhaps this is one of the reasons why our bank grew. But there were others. Thinking of ourselves as a business, we used business methods.

It was obvious that our growth didn't depend on Franklin Square customers. We were attracting people from a twenty-mile radius, or more. And transportation was poor. Most of our customers drove in. It was logical for us to do what other local businessmen did: provide a parking space.

A simple enough notion. But we were a national bank, regulated by the comptroller, and the only real estate a bank was permitted to own was its banking house. The Second National Bank, in Hempstead, had tried to break through this interdiction. Their president, A. Holly Patterson, who was supervisor of Nassau County, had bought a piece of land behind the bank to turn into a parking lot. But the comptroller's office had forced him to sell that land, and not to take a loss on it either. The Second National was very chagrined.

I read the law, and it seemed to me that the property restrictions to the banking house meant that you were supposed to own property to enable you to conduct the banking business. It was obvious in 1940 that to do that in Franklin Square, you needed parking space.

We negotiated with the Hoffmann family, who had a house and land behind our building, for their property. And I went to see Chief National Bank Examiner Gibbs Lyons and was able to persuade him that a parking lot was a necessary requisite of banking. The Washington people listened when I repeated this and I offered to write off the property and carry it on our books for $1. They said to put it in writing, and I did; and they approved it. A small enough item, but a major breakthrough—the first time they'd ever permitted a bank to own a parking lot. The next step was to go to the town board of Hempstead and ask permission to build the lot. And this was granted.

Once we could offer parking, the logical consequence was to create an outdoor banking facility. I'd noticed that in summer many women wore shorts and were walking their babies in carriages. Dressed like this and encumbered with an infant, it was natural for them to feel shy about entering a formal bank building. So we built a pergola just off the parking area, where they could write their deposit and withdrawal slips, and cut a teller's window into the rear wall of the bank. Later we glassed in the pergola and the area was heated so it was serviceable the year-round. It became a trademark, a symbol of the bank, and was the beginning of our use of the Williamsburg colonial style of architecture that later distinguished our bank from so many others.

We decorated the parking lot with a dozen or so wrought-iron signs, each of which carried an amusing design and the name of a particular banking service. They were the result of a forced layover in Florida, where my wife and I had been on vacation: Not wanting to waste the time, we made some trips and, on one, found the sign company in Little River and ordered those signs. Our signs for dental loans had a dentist yanking a tooth; for professional loans the symbol was a stork; for modernization loans, a hammer and saw; and so on.

I mention these details because they all helped to create part of the image of what Franklin was—a different bank. If you are different, you ought to look different. We always did.

I was known as the "wonder boy" in those days—and lest you think I'm boasting, the line went "Wonder whether he'll make it, or whether he won't."

That helped, too, in a way. When people wonder about you, they pay attention. It makes you and your institution stand out from others. When you're on people's minds, they're more apt to come to you than to some competitor.

When we opened our parking lot and pergola in April 1941, we attracted a lot of notice from other bankers, and from Washington, too. And, of course, from the townspeople.

Later that summer we petitioned the town board and the banking authorities in Albany to create a kind of cooperative parking district behind a row of shops. It was to be paid for by the merchants in a four-block area. We ran into a lot of opposition on that one, especially in Albany, where they accused us of trying to expand our own parking facilities. But it went through.

Then we decorated the bank basement, and added a kitchen; this provided a meeting place for various community groups, like the Red Cross. It was good for the town, and added another bit of luster to the image of Franklin as a good neighbor.

We got involved with the commuting problem. Working with the Association of Long Island Commuters, and my good friend John Rath, we were able to persuade the Public Service Commission to franchise three new bus routes to serve Franklin Square, which was not on the railroad.

We felt that our bank should be used by the Nassau County government, and made a bid to get more deposits of county funds. So we did an unprecedented thing in 1941: We outbid all the big New York banks and bought an entire issue of Nassau County bonds, totaling $826,155. That was an enormous sum for us to put into a single venture, but it paid off in two ways. First, we resold the bonds at a profit. And second, we began to get county deposits. Government funds are plums for banks; they are usually large amounts, and the balances remain for long periods of time. We became the main depository for Nassau County funds.

We set up a speakers' bureau of our officers. They would go out and lecture on topics having to do with banking and finance. They weren't selling anything, just informing people, but of course they helped to create an authoritative image for the bank. And we set up a business library where people could come and look up information. It was a small service, but added something to our reputation for being of help. And, of course, it brought people into the bank.

So far as we knew, these activities were unique among banks. Other bankers just didn't do such things.

One of the other new things we had done in the bank was to institute service charges. That is, we would charge an account for service if the balance wasn't large enough to pay for the activity—the checks and deposits. This was a rare thing in banking in the Thirties and Forties, and I had a lot of trouble with it. We were such a small bank, so local and personal that if a customer didn't like paying a service charge he would complain to one of the directors whom he might know, like my cousin's husband Fred Schilling a local storekeeper. Fred would assure them that they didn't have to pay the charge, but I would insist that they did. And they did. This created some tension between Schilling and me. This had begun even earlier, when I went out and solicited accounts and got people to bank with us who had never banked with Franklin before.

When you institute something new like the service charge, especially when it costs customers money, it creates resentment. But it was a needed and logical things. To explain this, it seemed like a good idea to persuade the depositors through their children. That is, to educate their children into the realities of banking so that they could explain to their parents that our service charges were honest and necessary.

To do this we started a program of letting senior high-school students in business administration, with grades above 85 percent, work in the bank for up to six weeks; this was considered part of their school work. The advantage to them was that they would have an employment record: We would keep track of what they did, and give them a letter saying that they had so many weeks of training, describing their work and rating their performance. Then when they graduated and looked for work, they would have something to answer prospective employers, who always asked for experience. It would give them a big edge in the labor market because at that time young people were having a tough time finding jobs.

We proposed this to the directors, and many were against it. Their reason was that they didn't want a bunch of kids looking over depositors' accounts. But I insisted that there was much more potential good than harm in it. These youngsters would tell others about the bank, and would inform their parents, and in general they would be a source of accurate information about banking, which at that time had a very bad name. It might bring in some business. And it would help explain the reason for service charges.

So I got a reluctant go-ahead, and went to the local Sewanhaka High School. The idea was favorably received, and we began getting student volunteers. They were the finest group of youngsters we could have asked for. And at first it was entirely without pay. Then we began paying for carfare, and then lunch money. As the program went on through the years, we paid them the minimum wage. Many became bank employees, something we hadn't expected.

Then the program was extended to Hofstra College, in a more serious way, as a scholarship. It came about because Hofstra asked us for financial help. I asked Dr. Matthew N. Chappell, the head of the psychology department, to survey his graduating class and find out what careers the students were seeking, and what they had done to prepare themselves for these careers in the way of summer work. We learned that none of them had done any kind of work that would help them get a job in their fields.

So I told the college that any students interested in banking would be given a $500 scholarship; we would pay for their tuition for the year. In return for this, they would have to promise to work in the bank during their Christmas and Easter vacations and during the summer. We would pay them; at the time the salary was only $15 a week, but this was a fair wage for unskilled work. And they would get invaluable training in banking, their field of interest.

The idea was enthusiastically accepted by the students, and we reaped a large bonus in trained employees. At least fifty of these youngsters took permanent, full-time employment with the bank, and several of them rose to become officers. As time went on and the nation entered the period of full employment, banks were hard put to hire enough efficient people. Franklin was helped to overcome this problem because of the student training program. Yet the whole thing started initially as a kind of educational idea.

When I began working at Franklin Square, I was disturbed at the very bad image that banking had in general. There was real reluctance on the part of many people to deal with any bank. I used to try to think of things that might get them to feel favorably toward our bank, hope that other banks would see this and do the same or similar things.

This was the birth of our Christmas pageant. I have always liked children, enjoyed children, and wanted to make the bank attractive to them. I wanted them to feel that it was a friendly place, where you could have fun.

On a trip I'd seen some attractive dolls dressed in native costumes of different countries, and I'd bought a dozen or so. When it came toward Christmas in 1937 or '38, I thought it would be a nice idea to have a diorama of the Nativity set up in the bank with the theme "These Are All My Children." The crèche would be surrounded with the dolls representing all nations. We found out who made the dolls and bought an international assortment of twenty-two.

To express the theme of the Christmas diorama, we used a verse whose author was unknown. It went like this:

> *These are my children on every land and sea.*
> *Black, white, red, or yellow, all have their life from me.*
> *Each child of any color, of any race or land,*
> *For all my children I do care.*
> *Would that man, too, this love would share.*

The last line was my own addition.

Along with the display, we had marionette shows twice a day, run by professionals. Children came from all over Nassau County to see the shows, many with their parents, and others brought by their schools in scheduled groups. They talked with Santa and received a small present.

In this activity we established another link between ourselves and the people, as a bank that cared about something besides making money.

At first we had to advertise the shows, but they quickly became known on their own. They practically caused us to shut down banking for most of the month of December. There would be huge lines outside the bank. But the net effect was nothing but good for banking, and for Franklin. The only complaint I ever heard came from an Irishman: He wanted to know why we didn't have an Irish doll. We got one.

Along with these public-service activities, we left no avenue of potential business unexplored. In talking to the National Life Insurance Company of Montpelier, Vermont, we learned that the Federal Reserve Act, which regulated national banks, had a clause permitting banks in communities of less than 5,000 inhabitants to write life-insurance policies. The rationale was that in small towns there might not be enough life-insurance agents to do the job.

Franklin Square was a small town. As an unincorporated village, it did not appear on the 1940 census rolls. The school-district figures as of August 30, 1939, showed a total population of 4,575 people. On that basis, we opened a life-insurance department in the bank in the fall of 1941.

Once again we brought the wrath of Upham on our heads. What did we think we were doing? Well, we were doing what the law said we could, and he was appointed to enforce it.

This tiny affair became a *cause célèbre* in insurance circles. Was banking going to step in and take business from agents and brokers? There was a stream of mail to congressmen from insurance people all over the country. And then congressmen got in touch with the comptroller's office. It enraged Upham to have this problem on his neck; he called us in and berated us. Eventually the comptroller determined that Franklin Square now had more than 5,000 people and on that basis we were told to shut down our insurance business. Actually our purpose, as we told our shareholders, hadn't been so much to sell insurance as to counsel our depositors on setting up their estates.

Although we had taken advantage of a technicality—the law was intended for banks outside metropolitan areas, in very small towns, where they would be performing a necessary service—the insurance companies found we hadn't harmed them or their agents. When they added up the sales, and followed up the new policyholders we had procured for them, they found that we had educated people to the need for insurance and had in fact opened a new market for them. These new policyholders came back to the insurance companies for much more insurance than we had sold them.

We also got involved in a totally new kind of insurance that appealed to us very much: medical insurance. Even in 1941 there was a crisis in medicine, with people not getting enough medical care and there was talk of the government stepping in. I felt that doctors should do something about the problem. It was a doctor, Dr. Elliott, one of the founders of Blue Cross Hospital plan, who brought us the idea in 1941.

His plan worked like this: Any depositor could authorize the bank to deduct a fixed amount from his account, about $5 a month. And for this he would be entitled to receive up to $500 of medical treatment in any one year. He would get a special checkbook that we designed with a picture of a doctor driving a horse and buggy, and a card showing he was a member of the plan which was called the Medical Expense Fund of New York, Inc. approved by the state Department of Insurance. We were the first bank to go into this.

When a plan member went to a doctor, he or she would show the card, and the doctor filled in the service performed and the dollar amount and he and the patient signed it. This became a draft on the insurance fund. It was deposited immediately to the doctor's account; he was paid as soon as the check came into the bank. But the doctors didn't like the plan; they wanted to be paid in cash. And after a year or two, we dropped the plan.

We tried a dental plan, too. This was a kind of professional loan to patients who wanted to spread out their payments over a year. Many dentists went along with this. They would get paid immediately by the bank; we would take over the account as a loan, with the patient the responsible party. Our fee was five percent, which the dentist had to pay. It is the same way today with credit cards: When you charge a meal to American Express, the restaurant gets paid as soon as it turns in your signed slip; but American Express deducts a percentage for their financing and service charges.

The dental plan patient would be given a coupon book for his payments; he paid no interest, just paid off his treatment in monthly installments over a year's time.

But we found that when dentists had patients they considered reliable, they would carry them for a year; but when they treated someone who they felt would not pay, they would put him in the plan. In other words, they turned over only their deadbeat clients to the bank. I tried to convince them that they ought to give us all their accounts who wanted to pay in installments. But the dentists didn't want to pay 5 percent for this service; they wanted to give us only their nonpaying clients. That made it uneconomic for the bank, and we were forced to drop the plan, too.

When in December 1941 our country was attacked by Japan and then the Axis powers declared war on us, our directors showed their spirit in many ways. One was in a resolution.

> The Bank will endeavor to provide employment for some member of the family of every member of the staff who enlists or is called for War Service, in order that the family shall not lack support. In the event that the employee goes to war service, the Bank will endeavor to employ the wife, sister or some member of the family and see that funds are adequate to meet the support of his family regardless of whether the position taken by that person warrants that much salary or not.

Not many employers in or outside of banking were that generous. But we felt that the least we could do was to reassure our servicemen that their families would be protected financially, and that their jobs would be waiting for them when they returned. All of our employees subscribed to War Bond deductions.

Nobody was thinking much about business after Pearl Harbor in December 1941. But it had to go on. And the year had been a phenomenally successful one for the bank. We had far surpassed our goal of $5 million in assets—we were up to nearly $6 million. And we felt that this was the product not only of our business methods—but of a new approach to banking. Our basic aim was to serve people, whether there was an immediate profit or not. And we tried to make it easy as well as pleasant for them to use bank services. This extended to planting flowers around our walks and the backyard banking area; there was always something blooming there, from spring right up until frost, starting with forsythia and ending with marigolds and chrysanthemums.

To cap 1941, we borrowed another idea from business: accountability. It had been the bank's custom to publish semiannual financial reports in the form of simplified balance sheets. Now we did something that no banks were doing: We wrote out in simple language what we had done during the year to build our community and our business: In other words, an annual report such as every large publicly held corporation publishes annually to its shareholders and for the public.

This was as heretical in banking as Luther's ninety-five theses.

Bankers just didn't like the idea of accountability. Their customers, the businessmen to whom they loaned money, had to publish annual reports. And the banks from whom businessmen borrowed demanded of their borrowers the same sort of information. But bankers felt that they were exempt from such disclosures. It destroyed the mystique behind which they practiced; it lifted the veil of secrecy from the countinghouse.

I have always believed in full disclosure of everything connected with the business, consistent with the privacy of the individuals with whom we dealt. In other words, I was always ready to disclose the bank's part in any enterprise, civic or whatever it might be.

But to most bankers, the idea of an annual report was repellent. Many told me, or told my friends, that I would rue the day I had embarked on this dangerous mission. One major bank said I'd feel foolish the next year, boasting about what a good year we'd had; because we'd never be able to repeat it. But our shareholders liked the report. So did our customers. It showed good faith, they felt, that we didn't hide behind the technical requirements of the law that demanded only that we publish a financial statement in the newspaper, which most people never saw or read. And it was noticed by the press; editorials were written about what an innovative bank we were. None of this was bad for business.

5 • Growing with Nassau

With a war on, there was no question that we could perform a lot of new services to help out. But first we had to increase our capital base. We did this in two ways. After repeated attempts and arguments, we won permission from Upham to issue $150,000 worth of preferred stock. And we increased our common stock from $87,500 to $300,000 by means of a 300-percent stock dividend. It wasn't easy to sell the preferred stock; the richest director on the board subscribed only $10,000. I was able to put up $3,000 by borrowing from my parents. In 1942, in spite of our sharp and continued rise in profits and deposits over the preceding seven years, we hadn't eradicated in many peoples' minds the memories of bank failures and of shareholders being assessed double the value of their stock to bolster their banks' capital. That was under a law that was repealed in 1936. But people were still wary of bank stocks, and we had to beat the bushes for customers.

Once we had the capital, however, we could go into a number of new enterprises both locally and even outside the state. There was no law that forbids out-of-state banking, it just wasn't usually done; banking authorities expect that local businesses will receive the necessary support from local banks. If a business can't borrow locally, it's assumed that local banks regard it as a poor risk. Hence, if a business has to go out of its community, or out of state, for a loan the authorities look at the loan very hard.

But when our good friend Philip Weisberg proposed taking over a ladies' handbag factory in Turners Falls, Massachusetts, and converting it into a war production plant, he came to Franklin Square for his financing. And knowing his record and reputation, we were glad to oblige. Before the end of 1942, Weisberg and his associates were running two shifts at Turners Falls, turning out gas masks, haversacks, jungle bags, and pack carriers for soldiers. Closer to home, we financed the Brown-Taylor Engineer Company, headed by my friend Stanley Brown, which made high-precision parts for aircraft. We also helped Mobile Refrigeration, Inc., to convert its production to calibrating and testing chambers. And Jaeger Brothers, house builders, converted to aircraft parts and communications instruments. L. Potter & Company switched from upholstering to making engine and cockpit covers, blind-flying hoods, and other military aircraft equipment. Even the local Square Deal Garage became a war industry: the Elmont Machine and Tool Company.

In that single year we went all out to support the Federal Reserve program of guaranteeing small subcontractors up to 100 percent of the amount borrowed. By the end of 1942, 76 percent of our commercial loans were in war-related enterprises as compared to only .6 percent the year before. Even our installment loans reflected the war: Most of them were for the purchase of machinery and equipment.

Our deposits went up by $2.5 million in 1942 to total more than $7 million, an increase of 50 percent. As a reflection of the impact the bank was making in the wider community, only 31 percent of our deposits were from Franklin Square itself. We bought more than $3 million in war bonds for our own account, and sold nearly another $2 million to depositors.

FHA started a new program, Title VI, to supply defense housing. The FHA didn't want to make this available on Long Island, in spite of the fact that we had two huge aircraft companies with an enormous influx of workers. But we went to Washington with Harris Brothers, the builders, and persuaded the authorities to include our area in Title VI loans. They gave us the right to finance fifty such houses.

Under Title VI, a builder could construct homes selling for up to $4,500. FHA guaranteed 100 percent of the cost with no down payment and gave the purchaser thirty days in which to make a 10-percent equity payment.

We had to face opposition from people with more-expensive houses. I appeared before the Hempstead Town Board and told them, "The man who buys a forty-five-hundred-dollar house has to have at least forty dollars a week in income. And this will probably soon go up to fifty. Don't you consider that someone earning this much money is a desirable citizen for Nassau County? Or are we trying to make Nassau a second

Westchester, with all of its white elephants and unsold houses [as it was in those days]? The future of the bank I represent depends on the sound growth of this county. I would not make this recommendation that we permit these small houses to be erected in certain areas unless I felt it was sound."

The town fathers voted, somewhat reluctantly, to permit a small amount of defense-housing construction.

As I mentioned earlier, we had gone in with Marine Midland as our coparticipant in building loans under the National Housing Act. They had replaced the Williamsburgh Savings Bank as our co-lender. The basis was anything from 98–90 (Marine Midland) to 2–10 (Franklin Square).

Not only did this arrangement clear up the lending-limitation problem with builders, it gave us great lending power under Title VI. In 1942 we two banks made nearly $2 million of such loans together in Long Island.

As with other FHA programs, bankers in general were reluctant to participate. This left an enormous vacuum, not only in Long Island but in other states. We suggested to some of our leading builders that they help fill this vacuum in Connecticut—counting, of course, on Marine Midland's commitment.

One of these builders, Sokolov Brothers, formed Sylbert Homes in Connecticut. But then Marine Midland's Connecticut correspondent banks began to complain: We were encroaching their territory. And we were under running fire from the comptroller's office. A new deputy comptroller, L. H. Sadlacek, brought up the old complaint about our being overloaned in building. He wrote to our board in 1943 saying, "The condition of your bank is very unsatisfactory" and "Your bank is being placed on the special list for closer supervision."

He wanted to reprimand us. And the biggest reprimand he could give was to increase the number of examinations. These are mandated by law at twice a year; now the examiners would come in three times a year.

I felt we could work our way out of this bind given time. In spite of the comptroller's criticisms, our record spoke for itself. We had almost no foreclosures. The loans were guaranteed by the government. We were earning a large profit—larger in relation to capital and to operations than any bank in our Federal Reserve district. Thus, the comptroller's criticism was vitiated by the reality of our growth.

Still, we were under his jurisdiction and had to heed his strictures.

Our board responded to Sadlacek by saying that our experience with Title VI was completely different from Title II. Under the older program, a builder would construct only the number of houses he thought he could sell in a limited period of time. He had had to be cautious because he could only borrow 50 to 60 percent of the cost of construction. But under Title VI, he could borrow up to 90 percent; hence he was tempted to take longer risks and build more houses than he could immediately sell. Even though those were fully insured by the FHA, their aggregate had mounted up to a sum more than the legal limit of 10 percent of the bank's capital and surplus. Of course, with the pent-up demand for housing, these loans were "safer than houses." But the comptroller never exercised judgment in assessing these loans; it was strictly a rule-book determination of regulations that were out of step with the great need for wartime housing. To be blunt about it, the men in the comptroller's office were not practical bankers.

Our board wrote to Sadlacek that "we did not willfully disregard the provisions of the National Banking Act in regard to excess loans." Once again I had to go to Washington to explain, this time accompanied by lawyer Sam Spitzbart, who had handled the closings for the bank.

Then Marine Midland gave in to their correspondent banks' pressure and pulled out of their joint agreement with us. This left Sokolov Brothers committed, on our say-so, to building houses in Connecticut. And there were other building deals in Long Island and Connecticut predicated on the same cooperation.

We could have pulled back ourselves, reneging on our commitments to these builders. If we had, we'd have forced some into bankruptcy, since they had borrowed money from us to buy land and materials and were already into construction and had nowhere else to turn for financing.

We couldn't, in conscience, do this. I felt we had to shoulder the responsibility, even though we were overloaned in the comptroller's assessment, and try to fight it through. Ethically, this seemed the only correct stance with our customers; and it was the right thing from a banking point of view: These were not ordinary mortgages, but government-guaranteed.

This was the second time that a bank with whom we had a commitment had abrogated its agreement with us—first the Dime, now Marine Midland—and each time we had to suffer the comptroller's criticism.

Fred Schilling, who had been Franklin's president (Phillips had moved up to the newly created post of board chairman, and I was executive vice-president), lost no time in blaming me. "Another case of Roth misadventure and mismanagement," he said.

We were faced with another regulatory crisis, even though we were in a very sound financial condition. Albert Sacco, a very bright ex–FHA employee who had joined us in the architectural division in 1943, and Sam Spitzbart had had an idea. They went to see Joseph A. Kaiser, the thirty-six-year-old executive vice-president of the Williamsburgh Savings Bank of Brooklyn. That bank had resources of $350 million, nearly forty times our own. But we had an advantage over them in that our charter enabled us to perform certain kinds of banking services, such as construction loans to builders, that they could not. Before they could lend money to a builder, he had to have the foundation and rough framing of a house completed; but we could lend him money to buy land and materials.

Sacco and Spitzbart made an enthusiastic pitch to Kaiser, pointing out how beautifully his resources and our abilities meshed.

Kaiser's bank was bursting with war deposits, which he was investing mainly in government bonds paying 2 or 2½ percent interest. FHA mortgages were paying twice that. But there was little building, and we had the inside track with builders.

Kaiser and I met and liked each other. We agreed to undertake joint mortgage financing without any written agreement, merely a handshake. And on that handshake over the following ten years we financed more than $40 million of mortgages together; we worked so closely that the banking authorities charged us with being a branch of the Williamsburgh, and vice versa.

Actually, we had foreseen the need for expansion, and would have established branches if given permission to do so. One opportunity to branch out was presented when Edgar C. Newell, vice-president of the First National Bank of Bellerose, a community near Franklin Square, approached us in 1942 about a merger. Their assets were almost entirely in bonds and securities. We applied to the comptroller for permission to merge and were refused on the grounds that the merger wasn't essential to the war effort; we didn't need a branch in Bellerose.

What the comptroller was really worried about was that if we increased our assets, we'd expand our activities. We were already into many things he didn't understand and he was worried about our going into more.

However, if we couldn't add Bellerose as a branch, we could approach the problem from another direction. We spoke to Frank Krippel, the regional director for the comptroller, about merely taking over the Bellerose assets and liabilities. We argued that purchasing assets was no different from making loans; and taking over liabilities the same as accepting new accounts. Krippel and Franklin Peterson of the Federal Reserve could find no legal objection to our reasoning. We hoped that once the takeover went through, we would be permitted to establish some kind of banking service in Bellerose to serve the people there. With gas rationing and no transportation between Bellerose and Franklin Square there would be no other means of banking left to those folks.

But the authorities claimed we didn't have sufficient capital to support the branch, so the other bank was closed. We moved all the furniture, cash, and so on to Franklin Square. Those employees who wanted to join us were also made welcome.

To take care of the Bellerose customers, we made an arrangement with three local drugstores in that town to cash checks, up to $50 each. We guaranteed the checks, providing the druggists would assure us they knew the people cashing them.

James Smith, who came to us as a teller from Bellerose and later became president of Franklin, recalls filling the trunk of his car with trays of coins and driving to the drugstores each day. He'd pick up their deposits, and bring them the receipts the next day with more change. "I was running a small branch office from the trunk of my car," he says.

We tried to get permission to open a branch office in Bellerose to handle this business, but instead were ordered to close down all our operations in the town.

Still, the purchase had been a good one. About two-thirds of the more than $2 million of Bellerose deposits stayed with Franklin, in spite of the fact that a bank in Floral Park was much closer.

But this incident was further proof to President Schilling that I was an unsound fellow. He wrote on a ledger sheet that I'd had to be helped out of trouble for running a branch office by Franklin Peterson of the Fed. And he predicted that the regulatory agencies would "get" me one day.

Meanwhile, we carried on with what we could do to support the war effort through banking. A large part of our contribution was to sell war bonds, which of course brought no pecuniary profit to the bank.

We wanted to show what our county was doing for the war, so in April 1943 we staged a weeklong exhibit and demonstration at Adelphi College in Garden City, called "Nassau at War."

Attended by 60,000 people, the exhibit showed in every way we could devise what our county was doing to further victory. There were exhibition bouts among boxers who had been recruited into the army: Private Sugar Ray Robinson led the card. There was music from the Grumman Swing Band. And there was an exhibit of what Nassau industry produced. We also covered every branch of the armed forces; victory gardens; the Red Cross and other volunteer organizations. All in all, 1,500 volunteers worked to put together this event whose main purposes were to sell war bonds and to recruit women for industrial war jobs and volunteers for the various organizations that were serving the country.

In 1944 we put on a television show, the first telecast from any bank. The well-known correspondent Lowell Thomas was master of ceremonies of the program over the National Broadcasting Company. One of the participants pointed out that Nassau County produced more warplanes than any other area in the world. Every plane and ship that took part in the D-Day invasion of France was equipped with instruments made in our county. Our products had taken part in Guadalcanal and were effective in knocking out enemy submarines.

Looking ahead to the postwar period, we offered our depositors a chance to save for the things they wanted: television sets, automobiles, washing machines—all the things that had "gone to war." We displayed the coveted items in the bank, and worked out the approximate price of the purchase; and set up a plan whereby the prospective buyer could save for it in 100 weeks. We called it the Purchase Club and offered the idea, free, to all the banks in the country. If each of the then 15,000 U.S. banks opened 1,000 such accounts averaging $200 each, we calculated that $3 billion in purchasing power could be diverted from the omnipresent black market and stored up to go to work when industry reconverted to peacetime manufacture. Actually, our own bank attracted 600 customers to participate in the plan, and 300 other banks around the country picked it up.

By October 1943, Sadlacek was giving grudging approval to our activities. "Considerable improvement in the condition of the bank's assets," he wrote. In January the even more grudging Upham noted the "encouraging trend" in loan reductions. But when we tried to retire 10 percent of our preferred stock, $15,000 worth, Upham refused permission. We bought government bonds at a slight premium because we felt the Federal Reserve would not permit them to sell below par; while high-premium bonds, we thought, would be allowed to float with the market. As it turned out, we were correct.

We were fortunate in hiring a brilliant public-relations expert, C. W. Green, who planned the Nassau at War week and the telecast from the bank. We paid him $4,500 a year; I was by then earning $10,000. As far as we knew, it was the first time a bank of our size had a full-time P.R. man on the staff.

With Green, we worked out a plan to persuade our local merchants to modernize their storefronts. We had designs drawn up, showing what they would look like; and we arranged five-year-loans at low cost to finance the work. And when a vicious hurricane struck Long Island in 1944, we asked the Federal Reserve for permission to run a special advertisement:

> Notice: The 3,000 families on Long Island who have their mortgages with us are insured with very few exceptions against hurricane losses. Money is available to homeowners who have to make property repairs as a result of the hurricane, FHA terms, up to three years to pay. We have available contractors and suppliers for immediate work.

It may seem strange to those not familiar with banking, but even so innocuous a thing as that helpful advertisement had to be approved by the authorities. We ran into the same problem when we wanted to advertise outside our community, in *The New York Times* and *Herald Tribune*, two papers read by our local businessmen. Our own local papers' readers were largely housewives. We had to reassure the banking authorities that we were not encroaching on other banks, we were not seeking business outside Nassau County; we were merely trying to reach the local businessmen who read those papers.

By 1944, I'd been with Franklin for a decade. During that time our assets had grown from less than a half-million dollars to more than $15 million: Deposits were $14,144,814.61 as of December 31, 1944; capital, surplus, and undivided profits were up to $760,431.27, an increase of about 500 percent.

We continued to publish annual reports in detail of all our operations, ideas, plans. The '44 report was an attempt to look ahead to the postwar future of Nassau, which we felt would be tremendous. And we were making plans for a greatly enlarged bank building—the third time we'd had to expand in the decade.

We concluded: "Businesses succeed when they operate on a sound philosophy and deliver a good product. . . . Banking is a business. And there is nothing peculiar about it which exempts it from measurement by the same sort of yardsticks which measure other kinds of businesses.

"In particular, ours is a community banking business. In its operation we perhaps come into closer contact . . . with our customers than does the large metropolitan institution. And this imposes on us a definite obligation to know our community thoroughly—to be concerned with many activities which have to do with the welfare of the community. . . ."

This pretty well sums up my philosophy. And it was, I think, the reason behind Franklin's rapid growth which, now that the war was beginning to come to an end, with the return of normal business, could begin to accelerate even more.

6 • The War Ends

Franklin's activities often made local news. This began to spill over into the New York dailies. Advertising magazines wrote up our promotional aspects. And then in 1945 the *Reader's Digest* condensed an article from *Advertising and Selling* about us, which suddenly made us not only nationally but internationally famous (when it was reprinted in their Portuguese edition for South America).

The *Digest* article, by Roger William Riis, was titled "Here's a Banker with Imagination." It was too flattering; I preferred the original title, "This Bank Is for People." It told how we created business by getting all the local businessmen of Hempstead Avenue together and showing them video projector photos of their dingy storefronts on a screen. And then, suddenly, we flashed on the screen an architect's drawing in color of how their shops could look if they were renovated. There was a gasp from the audience. "To make our town look like this will cost $15 a foot," I told them. "The bank is prepared to lend you the money on a five-year basis at a low rate."

Everybody signed up. Then we helped them by getting a glass manufacturer to handle all the renovations as a unit at low rates. We set up discussions with other manufacturers of building materials and store fixtures. "There's no use in sewing a clean collar on a dirty shirt," I told the shopowners. And they agreed; they began planning new interiors, too. This was to be a postwar activity; but one of the shops had a fire, and when the owner rebuilt, he followed the new master plan. His business increased immediately, and the other merchants took note.

None of this was the activity or the responsibility of the traditional bank. But we felt it was our job to originate business, to stimulate business, and to follow through in helping our borrowers use their loans wisely and economically.

We took the same approach with our individual borrowers, not only in lending them money, but taking responsibility to see that they got full value for it especially when they followed our advice in spending it.

After the war it was difficult to find contractors who would do reconstruction. We advertised that if someone wanted to modernize his house, he should get in touch with us and we would find him a contractor to do the work.

I remember a woman coming to see me one day and saying, "We hired your contractor, and we've overpaid him, and he's left the job unfinished. We were going to convert part of our bathroom into a kitchen, and the toilet bowl is still sitting there in the middle of the kitchen. When someone has to use the bathroom, everybody has to get out of the kitchen."

This sounds funny, but it was serious to her, and we felt responsible. So I asked how much she had overpaid. It was about $600 or $700. I said, "We'll find another contractor to finish the work, and we'll take care of paying him."

We did that in a number of similar instances even though one could say we were not legally responsible. We were certainly morally responsible. These people had taken our word and we felt we had to make good.

In another instance we were much more directly involved. A large law firm in Rockville Centre had gone into the floor-waxing-franchise business. They were selling the floor-waxing equipment and a so-called franchise, which included the names of about three or five customers, for $600; and our bank was accepting these purchase agreements as loans. The lawyers' total investment was $125 for the equipment.

I learned about this when I saw a number of these so-called loans on the delinquent list, and asked the loan officer in charge about them. I asked if we had many more of these delinquent accounts, and the man said yes. The bank had put a 5-percent reserve aside for these loans, but the officer hadn't charged the loans against the reserve—he was suing the signers.

I ordered him to drop all these suits and to charge the bad loans against the reserve, and to stop accepting any more of these agreements.

A member of the law firm came to see me. "Your bank has promised to take up to $1 million of these notes," he said, "and we've built a big business on that understanding."

I said, "We're not buying any more of your paper."

He said, "Then we'll take you to court."

I said, "I'd welcome that."

Of course they never dared to go to court with this fraudulent scheme.

We exhausted our reserve account on the paper we'd bought, and lost another ten or twenty thousand dollars, but we never sued any of those people who'd been fooled into signing up. They should never have been in business; how much could they have made doing a few waxing jobs a month?

Our loan officer protested that the law firm was a very important account of our bank. I said that made no difference; we weren't going to be involved in any rackets like that.

From almost all points of view, the bank was doing very well—growing, making money, accepted as the unofficial center of the community, and getting national recognition. But Fred Schilling managed to view all this through a very dark glass. He took our success as a criticism of himself instead of, as president, glorying in it. He looked for plots against himself, and made board meetings a test of my ability to sustain his ill will and constant criticisms.

Finally, in May 1945, he resigned as president. But he carried with him a large burden of personal animosity against me.

When Schilling left, Arthur Phillips was elected president, and Franklin continued on its path of growth and expansion.

The ending of the war in 1945 unleashed an enormous pent-up demand for every kind of consumer goods; which meant a sudden rise in all kinds of credit and borrowing.

Our business loans went up from $821,000 in 1944 to more than $7 million in 1946. Deposits passed the $20-million mark, and capital, surplus, and undivided profits rose from $760,441 in 1944 to nearly $1.3 million in '46. Every department and activity of the bank showed the same sort of quantum leap, the most dramatic was in new mortgages. Since private building had been almost at a standstill in '44, it was no wonder that we loaned less than $1 million that year for 170 houses. Those figures had multiplied by about ten in 1945—to 1,481 mortgages totaling $11.8 million; now in 1946 we were servicing $23 million in mortgages in our portfolio. The tiny bank of 1934 with four employees was bursting at its seams with 142 employees in 1946. There was, of course, no difficulty under these conditions in rehiring all the former service people who had been discharged and wanted to return to the bank. We weren't only glad to have them, we were anxious to welcome them back.

With our expanding resources, we were able to help returning veterans go into business. Two who had read about us overseas in the *Reader's Digest* started with Franklin loans, respectively a camera shop and a pharmacy. Another veteran opened a barbershop. Some larger enterprises—such as a packaging plant, a machine-tool manufacturer, an electronics plant, and a charter fishing fleet—were also started or expanded with money from Franklin.

Telling these stories, along with a detailed account of our growth and a full financial statement such as other businesses (but few banks) did, in our 1945 illustrated *annual report*—won us an "Oscar of Industry" award from *Financial World*. It was to be the first of a number of such awards as Franklin continually tried to show its accountability to its community as well as to its shareholders. Our purpose wasn't self-aggrandizement but an attempt to demonstrate to other banks that such an attitude was appreciated by the public. We hoped that all banks would shuck their traditional posture of mystery and secrecy and look their communities in the eye and talk common sense. That way, banking might recoup some of the respect it once had.

On the twentieth anniversary of the founding of the bank, at a private party given by the directors on October 17, 1946, Arthur Phillips tendered his formal resignation as president and was elected to the new post of chairman of the board of directors. I was elected president.

It had become obvious that our rapid growth had made it increasingly difficult to do business in our present quarters, which had once been much too large. Now, with the ending of the war and the relaxing of building restrictions, we were able to plan for a new building. We hired a firm of architects and asked them to draw plans for a second story on the original corner structure, and to design another building next door. The new structure would give us a chance to dramatize a new idea in banking that had been developing at Franklin. We called it "department-store banking."

We'd tried to popularize the idea that we sold credit, just like a store. And to do this we eliminated the physical barriers erected around credit transactions as a means of breaking down the feeling of shame that most people had when they borrowed money.

People who wanted a loan could stand up at a counter just the same as those making deposits, withdrawals, or doing other bank business. It didn't have to be done in cubicles the way other banks and finance companies did it. By making it an open transaction, we helped people become proud of the fact that their credit was good, that they could borrow money. We made a point of saying that we were "selling credit," which made them buyers, not people coming in and pleading for a loan. Of course, if anyone insisted on seeing an officer in private, this was arranged. But the new procedure appealed to hundreds of people, and we like to think that it helped to build our consumer credit department, which became about three times as large as our business-loan department.

Now, in our new building, we could carry the idea a step further. We weren't just selling credit, we were a department store of 100 banking services. And to make the point, we built an addition that had a huge storefront type of window. This could be slid out of the way to admit large items for display. This was to be our "family bank." We had always gone out of our way to provide a banking atmosphere in which women felt comfortable, and they appreciated it—80 percent of our customers were now women.

I asked the contractor to build a strong hook in the ceiling of the new building, and to make sure it was well supported so that it could hold very heavy objects weighing several tons. But he thought I was kidding. When I examined the construction of the ceiling, I said, "I'm afraid it won't support more than a few hundred pounds. You'll have to tear out some of this and put in a very strong beam; I want that hook to be able to hold several tons."

He looked at me aghast. "But I didn't think you were *serious*," he said.

I'd never been more serious. He had to remove part of the ceiling and install a girder capable of supporting heavy equipment.

When we were ready to open, one of the things we brought in through the sliding window was a small, private airplane manufactured by Republic. There wasn't room for both wings; one had to be removed. The plane hung from the hook in the ceiling. On it was a card giving the price and telling how the bank would finance it for purchase.

The *Christian Science Monitor* reported:

Other merchandise on display includes household equipment, such as washing machines, radios, vacuum cleaners, heating plants, air-cooling equipment [the entire bank was now air-conditioned, something brand-new in 1947], home furnishings, silverware, jewelry, toilet articles, layettes for prospective mothers. . . . Exhibits are mounted on velvet- or satin-draped pedestals in cork-lined niches, in built-in wall display cases and two-purpose hexagon showcases.

These showcases also are used as tellers' counters. They are patterned after the newer type of detachable units used in department stores. . . .

We installed a music system with 1,085 selections; a public-address system with thirty-five loudspeakers; and a carillon with loudspeakers in the clock tower. A closed-circuit television unit—revolutionary in 1947—was built for us by a local technician to speed identification of signatures and avoid bad checks with a minimum of embarrassment and lost time. There was a travel department, a real novelty in banking then.

One of our innovations was a children's bank. Each child who made a deposit received a free lollipop—which gave us a new nickname, "the Lollipop Bank."

A columnist wrote, tongue-in-cheek:

If I had any money on deposit with the Franklin Square National Bank of Franklin Square, N.Y., I would take it out and hide it in a well-darned sock under the third hearth brick from the left. Because the Franklin Square National Bank is about to undertake an experiment that bodes no good for its future security.

The bank, so its annual statement says, is going to install children's banking facilities with a counter low enough so they can see what goes on, and invite the small fry to do their banking just as adults do.

Either the directors of this bank know absolutely nothing about children or else they are trying to start a riot. Because most children's knowledge of banking comes from watching daddy operate on their own piggy bank with a hammer, and, as far as their limited experience goes, this is the accepted practice everywhere.

So the first day the bank throws the doors open to its juvenile customers, the place is going to be flooded with a couple of thousand opportunists, armed with hatchets and mallets, eager to do a brisk day's banking business. . . . As for overdrafts on children's accounts—well, let's just not go into that.

When the new addition opened, on June 23, 1947, we received national attention from newspapers and magazines, including *Newsweek,* which noted in a column titled "How to Sell Banking" that in thirteen years we had gone from "a shaky 43rd place to first place among Nassau County banks."

"By advertising, promotion, and 'doing business the way the people like to do it' Roth has actually attracted more business than he can handle, and passes some along to others," *Newsweek* wrote.

We won a bronze award for our 1946 annual report from the highly regarded *Financial World* business weekly. In 1947 we won again, plus another "Oscar of Industry"—a silver award for producing the best annual report of any financial institution in the country. That was quite an honor for a still small country bank.

But the real accolade came when we were recognized by *Fortune*, the magazine of big business.

Arthur T. Roth, forty-one-year-old President of the Franklin Square National Bank . . . that last year gave away 25,000 lollipops, has emerged as a disquieting phenomenon in U.S. banking. In a white-cottage, white-collar suburb with no industry, no railroad station, and very little money, he has developed a way to triple normal banking profits. His bank acts as if it weren't a bank at all. On the simple proposition that a money retailer ought to use retail-merchandising techniques, F.S.N.B. . . . has made a net profit that for the past ten years has averaged 2½ percent. Average net profit of all U.S. banks for the same period, 0.7 percent. . . . Franklin Square is perhaps the only community in the country where children go to a bank to see Santa Claus.

In developing his banking style, Roth has been a thorough eclectic. Department stores have furnished his chief inspirations, but he has also drawn ideas from theaters, filling stations, drugstores, and occasionally, other banks. Perhaps his best idea came from remarking the way a local pastor was merchandising his church with a flower garden. . . .

Such shenanigans obscure the fact that essentially F.S.N.B. is an extremely hard-headed operation. By making intensive time-cost studies, for example, F.S.N.B. has reduced mortgage-processing time from the usual three to four weeks to three days. . . .

Like his customers in Franklin Square, Roth is still somewhat unestablished. Bankers of the old school think he's pretty fresh. They conceded that he is a "remarkable operator," "sound investor," "wonderful cost man," but deplore his violations of "accepted banking behavior."

Other bankers attributed our growth partly to "sunny banking weather" and said we ought to be thinking about retrenchment. But as *Fortune* noted, we were just starting a $1-million "Let's-Get-Better-Acquainted" campaign with "among other things twelve singing canaries as prizes for employees bringing in the most new business."

More than fifty national publications had taken notice of little Franklin Square. Our deposits leaped more than $5 million in 1947 to over $25 million, and our capital, profits, and undivided surplus were approaching $2 million.

We issued more stock in 1947 to help finance this rapid growth. In a special report to shareholders about this, we showed how $1,000 invested in Franklin stock in 1934 would have grown to $28,000 in 1947 through stock splits and increased book value. And this did not include the nearly $3,000 in cash dividends paid during the preceding four years.

Wall Street, too, was beginning to become interested. Grimm & Company, members of the New York Stock Exchange, issued a financial report about the bank in January 1948 indicating our deposits since 1934 had risen six times as fast as the average of the New York City banks—and was now up eight times. Grimm mentioned the nationwide interest in our new methods of operation. They "do not require detailed discussion here. The fact remains that these methods have been unusually successful." They strongly recommended our stock because of this fact, and because Franklin "shares offer capital appreciation probabilities as the growth of the bank and the community it serves continues."

This kind of notice from the financial community provided a much wider market for our shares. And this was very important since we were about to issue another $125,000 of capital stock to keep pace with our growth; each current shareholder had the right to purchase one share for every five he or she owned.

Grimm also said, "The present dividend policy of the bank affords an adequate return which should be supplemented by stock dividends and the issuance of rights. . . ."

I had always believed that stock dividends were a much better way to increase capital. In that way, you did not disburse profits in the form of cash, but kept it and gave bonus shares to shareholders instead of cash. I saw it as very advantageous to us, and to our owners. If you distributed cash dividends and then wanted to sell more stock they had to consider whether to buy that stock after paying the federal income tax on the money. But if you retained earnings and issued new shares against them, there was no immediate tax to pay—it would be payable only when the shares were sold.

To determine our policy, we surveyed brokers and the dividend practices of other banks in New York City. And just about every bank analyst said we should pay about one-third of our earnings in cash dividends. The reason they gave was that savings banks and the trust departments of commercial banks would invest only in stocks of banks that paid cash dividends.

So we began the practice, against my better judgment; and I'm very sorry that we ever took that route.

Now it was becoming obvious that as the number one bank of Nassau, we had more demands than we could handle from one location; we could not service the entire county with just the Franklin Square office. We could no longer attract people from wide areas, because the roads were too congested; it took too long to drive to Franklin Square. And Meadowbrook National and other competitors had started to create mergers. We wanted to stay ahead of them. So in 1948 we applied to Frank Krippel, the New York deputy comptroller of the currency, for permission to establish branches in Elmont and in Levittown.

Krippel liked us, and treated us fairly, but he had his own ideas about banking that were 180 degrees opposed to ours. He looked at me sorrowfully and said, "Arthur, I've always held up your bank as the shining example of what a bank could do without branches. And here you're asking for a branch."

I said, "No, Frank, not a branch—*branches*. I wouldn't think of going into branch banking with a single branch; we're going to need at least ten or twenty branches. It's necessary because of the county's rapid growth, and the congestion on the highways."

Also, I pointed out that the big New York City savings banks and commercial banks were eyeing Nassau hungrily (as they were eyeing Westchester). They were beginning to exert pressure and use their political muscle to persuade the banking authorities that they should be allowed to "follow their customers to the suburbs," by setting up branches there.

I was getting ready to fend them off (see chapter 11, "Second Front"), but it was apparent from the beginning that this would be a rearguard battle. We were fighting for time, not victory. And I wanted to use that time to make Franklin big enough and strong enough to take on the competition when it poured in.

But Krippel was adamant: No branches in Elmont or Levittown, said he.

The next year we were instrumental in saving the independence of the comptroller's office against the recommendations of the Hoover Commission. (See chapter 10.) And when we reapplied for permission to establish the branches, it was granted from Washington.

Krippel complained that it was our "reward" for fighting for the comptroller. He just couldn't see that it was the logic of events that made it inevitable for a bank offering Franklin's unique range of services, with the demand for those services from the public all over Nassau—and farther away (as evidence, even an ever-increasing number of shares of our stock were being bought up by investors in other states, as far away as California). Access was so difficult by road that we had only one choice: If depositors and borrowers couldn't come to us, we had to go to them.

Elmont, which had always counted heavily on us and was only two miles away from Franklin Square, was the largest Long Island community without its own bank. Thus, it was the logical first step in our expansion.

The branch was built in the same style as our home office: Williamsburg colonial, with a cupola, a clock, and a weather vane, a form of architecture that was to become our trademark. I've always taken a great interest in building, and the style of buildings, and it seemed to me that this particular architecture mirrored perfectly our approach to banking. It gave us a setting that bespoke our interest in and commitment to a certain style of life. It is an honest kind of architecture, capitalizing on balanced proportions and simple materials such as brick, wood, and glass. It evoked our past, so seemed appropriate to a bank that likes to create the atmosphere of stability. And at the same time this kind of building is homelike, welcoming—not like the old banks, which were massive fortresses of stone and concrete.

When the new branch opened in Elmont on Saturday, March 4, 1950, it attracted 7,000 visitors—there were long queues outside waiting to get in. And they liked what they saw; 2,500 opened accounts. Our belief that Elmont had truly needed its own bank was immediately justified.

In fact, there was so much unfinished business at the end of the first day that we had to keep the bank open every night for a week, and with a staff of fifteen—double what we expected for normal operations. Actually this, our first branch, was larger than the original Franklin Square building had been when the bank started.

When the Levittown branch opened, I got a letter from Bill Levitt, the builder, enclosing a list of contractors who worked for his company, and saying, "I think you should tell them that we consider your bank one of the most progressive in the United States and that we have opened an account with you."

We'd worked with the Levitts from their early prewar projects.

Levitt's father was a short, stoop-shouldered lawyer, a fine person. He got into the building business by chance: He'd financed a builder in Lindenhurst in the 1930s; the man was unable to pay, and Mr. Levitt was forced to take some property instead. He started to build on that land.

His first real development was in Rockville Centre during the depression. He built some $8,000 houses, with a first mortgage of $4,000 and a second mortgage of $1,500 or $2,000. Before FHA this is how people had to borrow to build a house—the second mortgage always carried a higher rate of interest than the first. I was impressed with the construction of his houses, and also by the fact that he landscaped them beautifully with roses.

He decided to build Levittown before the war. I lunched with him and his sons: Arthur was the architect, William the builder and promoter—he did all the advertising. They'd optioned almost 1,000 acres—that's more than two square miles—of potato land for $400 an acre. It was known as the Great Plains area of Long Island. The old man described how he was going to build a self-contained community there, an entirely new concept then, with walkways, bicycle paths, local shopping areas. Then the war came, and he lost confidence in his plans and dropped the options. When his sons returned from the service, they were much upset by his action. They reacquired the land for $800 an acre. We helped them buy it; since it was potato farm; we were able to arrange a farm mortgage, equal to 50 percent of the price. (In those days, it was impossible to give builders mortgages on unimproved property.) On this farmland they built Levittown.

Now we had two branches, and our deposits were increasing very fast. But we were barely keeping pace with the growth of Long Island. By this time we were engaged in the fight over the word *savings* with the savings banks—a fight that we felt was necessary for our own future, as well as the future of other commercial banks (see chapter 10, "Savings"). We were servicing about $50 million of mortgages for savings banks, but we had to risk that business against our need for time deposits to finance the skyrocketing demands of our communities. In the long run, we'd be better off being able to advertise for savings—which we were then not permitted to do except through the use of circumlocutions that most people didn't understand—than to retain our mortgage-service business with the savings banks.

We began to think of other ways of expanding our bank. Setting up our own branches was expensive. We had to buy land, build and furnish the building and hire and train new employees. To open a branch meant an investment of about $100,000.

But if we could work out a deal with another bank whereby we could exchange their shares for ours on the basis of market value, we could bypass the heavy investment of building branches—yet we could add branches with a ready-made clientele, trained employees, deposits, physical plant.

The year 1949 had been a banner one for the bank; we'd gone over $44 million in total resources, up more than $10 million from the year before. But the first six months of 1950 were our most active ever; by June 30 we had passed $52 million. It was the first time that any bank in Nassau had risen above the $50-million mark.

There was a regulation that the city in which the head office of a bank was located had to be part of its title. We had to print on checks and stationery, "The Franklin Square National Bank of Franklin Square, L.I." For many years I'd been writing to the comptroller of the currency asking permission to shorten our name. We were steadily refused permission to simplify our ponderous title, but this didn't keep us from continuing to keep the question open.

Now we were no longer a single-branch bank, we had branches in two other towns, so we brought up the name again. It no longer made sense to repeat "Franklin Square" twice in our title. We were permitted to shorten the name to the Franklin National Bank of Franklin Square. Actually it would have been more reasonable to identify our location as Nassau County. But that was too much of a change for the comptroller. Eventually, as we grew and acquired many branches in Nassau and later in Suffolk County, we were permitted to call ourselves the Franklin National Bank of Long Island.

A month or two after our first name change in 1949, we were approached to consider a merger with the South Shore Trust Company of Rockville Centre, a longtime rival of ours, I had collided head-on a number of times.

A couple of years earlier, after we'd set up a great many FHA mortgages and had financed developments such as the one in Garden City, South Shore took advantage of a drop in mortgage interest to write to homeowners informing them of that fact. The mortgagors were paying 5 percent; Loft got them to attend a meeting where he suggested that they should write to us and ask to have their mortgages transferred to his bank. He would issue new mortgages for only 4.5 percent.

In one day we got thirty or forty letters from Garden City homeowners asking that this be done. Loft's purpose was to make these new mortgages and then sell them to other institutions at a two-point premium. He was seemingly within the FHA regulations, which were so badly written that the mortgagor had the right to demand that the mortgage be reassigned at any time.

This seemed inequitable, and we flatly refused to transfer these FHA mortgages. We were servicing most of them for the Dime Savings and the Williamsburgh Savings banks. I got in touch with George Johnson, head of the Dime, a rather hotheaded man, and told him of the attempted raid by South Shore. I suggested we get up a delegation and go to Washington and tell the FHA if they allowed this kind of thing we'd just refuse to make any more FHA mortgages. After all, we'd pioneered this business; it was totally unfair that we should lose the mortgages overnight because the regulations were so sloppily drawn up.

A half-dozen of us went to Washington and told the FHA they'd better change their regulations to protect mortgage holders. They said they'd consider it and could probably give us an answer the next day. We'd wait, we told them. The next day they issued a new ruling saying that a mortgage could be transferred only when it was satisfied, and then only on payment of a premium. That made it uneconomic to switch and settled the issue in our favor.

Another time, South Shore began running ads saying they were the largest bank in Nassau County. Franklin ran ads saying *we* were the largest bank in Nassau County. The newspaper asked if we had proof. I pointed out that this was a fluctuating situation—one day they might have more assets than we; the next day we'd be bigger than South Shore.

The newspapers went to the Better Business Bureau, who told us to cease and desist this advertising. I said, "We will if they will." And that's how it was resolved.

There were other run-ins. George Loft, South Shore's president, was a short man who liked a fight. He was a loner, and his bank was not even a member of the Nassau County Clearinghouse, but he had fine political connections. His bank carried a large sum of public funds on deposit. This helped his growth; also, the fact that he had no service charges was a big help.

Then he died, and the attorneys for his widow came to us and asked if we could take over the South Shore Trust Company. Mrs. Loft owned about 70 percent of the stock. They set a price that seemed equitable, so we made the deal based on an exchange of stock. U.S. Bank stocks sell at a multiple of their book value*—usually double or triple book value. But Franklin stock sold at a much higher ratio—higher, in fact, than any bank in the country. This was simply because investors valued it much more highly. They had seen our rapid growth, year after year, and they were anticipating that it would continue.

This high market price on our stock made it most attractive to other banks seeking a merger. Because of it, we could outbid competitive banks who might want to make the same merger we were after. And we always made money on a merger, because the merged stock had a higher book value than the separate stocks before the merger.

Since the South Shore merger was to set a pattern for many subsequent mergers via exchange of stock (we had to resort to cash only twice in mergers), it is worth detailing briefly: Through two underwriters— Blair, Rollins & Co. and W. C. Langley & Co.—we issued 26,650 shares of $10 par-value capital stock at the market price of $55 a share. This was to exchange for shares of South Shore, or to pay South Shore shareholders in cash.

The consolidated bank would have 125,000 shares of $10 par-value capital stock, an increase of about 36,000 shares. Each current Franklin shareholder would receive an additional $27/890$ of a share. The shareholders in South Shore Trust would receive 33,300 shares on a ratio of $1\frac{4}{5}$ shares of $10 par Franklin for each $20 par share in their former bank or the equivalent in cash. After consolidation our board of directors anticipated paying $3 a year cash dividend on our stock, or 75 cents a quarter.

South Shore Trust Company would become the South Shore branch of Franklin. We invited all South Shore employees to remain with the bank. This offered them the advantages of working for a larger institution with a greater possibility for advancement, greater scope of training, a wider range of salaries with a larger opportunity of earning more money and getting more frequent raises.

At the end of 1950, Franklin showed a 75-percent increase in its total resources, up to $78,363,000. Of this, $15 million came from increased deposits in our own branches, and $18,600,000 represented the added resources of South Shore. We held over $25 million of U.S. government securities; our loans and mortgages had gone up by 50

---

*Book value is the total of assets over liabilities

percent to more than $35 million, and we were servicing $87.2 million of mortgages for seventy other financial institutions, including many large life-insurance companies and savings banks. Our total capital had gone over $5 million.

7 • Charge Accounts and Credit Cards

When we took over South Shore, we gave its building a face-lift. Then we asked the employees to move all the unused furniture into one room. We found there was more than twice as much equipment than was needed to run the branch. Paper and files were stacked up all over. It was quite a job of housecleaning. This was typical of many later mergers—we were usually able to increase profitability simply by introducing efficient methods.

The merger with South Shore also led us toward two new types of banking: charge accounts and credit cards.

As we were new in Rockville Centre, we made a survey of local shopping habits. And found that most of the inhabitants didn't shop in their own town. They went to Hempstead, Jamaica, Garden City. The reasons they gave were the poor selection of merchandise in Rockville Centre, the local merchants not as pleasant as they could have been, the goods poorly displayed and the like.

At a meeting of the local chamber of commerce, at which Rockville Centre merchants were present, I discussed these reactions and showed pictures of some areas of the town's shopping district that looked almost like slums.

A local jeweler jumped up and said, "Some of this may be true, but it doesn't explain why people don't shop here. The real reason is because we're not big enough to carry charge accounts. Our customers go to department stores in other towns because they can charge there."

Several others got up and said pretty much the same thing. I think they had organized it before the meeting.

But what they were saying seemed reasonable, so I said, "All right, we'll allow you to operate your shops so you can compete with department stores. You'll have charge accounts, which we'll carry and collect for you. You can deposit your charges with us the same as checks.''

I hadn't thought it through; it was off the top of my head. This sort of thing had happened to me before: Faced with a challenge, I would sometimes respond in a way that boxed me in. And then I'd have to find a way to make good.

I went to our attorney and told him what I'd said, and he told me a bank could buy only a negotiable instrument—and a sales slip wasn't any such thing.

"What do we have to do to make it negotiable?" I asked.

"The customer has to sign the slip," the lawyer said. "Then, in effect, they've signed a promissory note."

I thought of using this idea in selling fuel oil, because these were large sales. But often deliveries were made when no one was home and nobody could sign. And people questioned why they had to sign; they'd never signed before.

Our attorney suggested getting powers of attorney from customers, and one of our officers tried—but was refused most of the time.

I called Thomas Patton, author of a lawbook called *Patton's Digest*, published by the American Bankers Association. "When I was collection clerk at Manufacturers Trust," I said, "book publishers used to send us batches of drafts drawn on customers to whom they'd shipped books, and we'd put them through for collection. Were those drafts negotiable instruments?"

"Yes, they were," Patton replied, "but you'd be crazy to buy any paper like that."

I said, "Thanks, you've answered my question." If we could get the fuel-oil dealer to write on the sales slip that he was drawing this draft payable on Franklin National, for the sale of the article to the purchaser, then it ought to fulfill the banking requirement.

I asked our lawyer to send it to Gloyd Awalt, a Washington attorney and former acting comptroller of the currency. Awalt took it up with the comptroller's office, and their answer was that this would be a legal draft, we could buy it. But, they added as they so often did, this was not the sort of business a bank should engage in.

I said, "I didn't ask for their advice. If it's legal, I'll decide whether or not we'll engage in it." And Awalt repeated that it was legal.

I decided to go ahead and do it. We set up a department to buy sales slips from merchants. We kept the charge-account department open as late as the stores; they could call us and get an immediate approval or disapproval over the phone. We had files on most customers, and could check on others through the Nassau County Credit Clearinghouse. At first we allowed a purchase up to $10, then raised it to $25 for good risks, with the notion of checking later. There would be some small losses, but we'd charge that to advertising and promotion—the cost of initiating and promoting a new service.

Since we were the first in this business, we applied for a patent on the form and tried franchising other banks. But few bought it.

The lawyer for *Gourmet* magazine, which had a small but very select readership, heard about our charge-account business and came to us with the suggestion that we go into a fifty-fifty partnership with *Gourmet* in issuing credit cards to their subscribers. The card would be good for dining in the fine restaurants that advertised in the magazine.

This was just about the time when Ralph Snyder invented the credit card and started Diners Club. But he was running into heavy weather. Diners Club had very little capital; they had to borrow from finance companies at high rates. To save interest they delayed paying restaurants sometimes a couple of months, which, naturally, the restaurants didn't like at all.

This gave us a selling point. We told restaurants that if they accepted the *Gourmet* credit card, they would be paid the very same day that they presented the signed slips. We would give them an envelope and a checkbook. Every time they deposited $100 in slips, they would write a check for $95—the 5 percent difference was the bank's service charge.

We began opening accounts all over the country, with *Gourmet* subscribers. The cards were sent out automatically to the subscriber list, about 2,000 people. We'd checked them out and felt there was no risk. Most of the people never used their credit cards.

The restaurants were very happy with the arrangement. Most of them advertised in *Gourmet*, and they were delighted to be recognized as worthy of being noticed by the magazine, which had a top reputation.

A few months later *Esquire* magazine came to us and asked if we'd make a similar arrangement with them, and we said we would. They had hundreds of thousands of names of their subscribers and mailing lists they used. We had these checked out and found that 50 percent weren't worthy of having a credit card. But even among the 50 percent that were approved, there were a number of bad accounts. Our credit-card business became quite sizable with the addition of the *Esquire* names; but as the gross mounted, so did losses. Ninety-nine percent of the cardholders might be honest, but there was no limit on what they could charge, and the 1 percent of bad risks could run up many thousands of dollars of debt. We had the problem of trying to find attorneys all over the country to try to collect for us.

One of our directors, Judge Hooley of the state supreme court, used to take a particular interest in this business, which was showing a loss. And I was very involved in the activities of our fast-growing bank, and couldn't give it much attention. So I decided to get rid of the credit-card business. I told *Esquire* we were discontinuing, and they sold their accounts to Diners Club.

Mr. Howard L. Clark, president of American Express, came to see us to inquire about credit cards. It seemed like a perfect idea for them. They had offices worldwide. "But don't repeat our mistake of thinking that because ninety-nine percent of the people are honest, you needn't be very careful," I told Clark. I counseled them, on the basis of our experience, to use the network of traveler's checks sales they'd already set up with banks. Let the bank originate the accounts—the credit-card holders—and pay them $10 for each name. You would then have the guaranty that the bank found that person a good credit risk. And then if there was a collection problem, American Express could send it back to the bank which originated the account and ask them to collect it. The banks could receive a one-percent fee for their service. Then there would be no problem of hunting up attorneys all over the country.

"If you set it up this way," I said, "we'd like to handle the accounting and bookkeeping for a fee. And we'll start you off with a nucleus of excellent accounts." The *Gourmet* cards, which we still had.

American Express came back and said that the people in charge of their traveler's checks felt that credit cards would be damaging to their check business, and probably not profitable. I thought this was exactly the opposite of the truth: Credit cards would build up their traveler's check business. It was logical for them to get into credit cards; with their reputation and network of offices, they could charge a fee for the card.

They got into it slowly. I gave them the *Gourmet* accounts without charge, but I suggested that they advertise in the magazine. They still run a full page in each issue, as far as I know. And I offered them the services of Ed Donahue, who had run the business for Franklin.

But business came in too slowly for American Express, and so they took some full-page advertisements in the search for new accounts.

They got them in droves; and along with them they got all the problems and losses we'd tried to help them avoid. They lost millions of dollars in bad accounts.

Some time later I spoke with Mr. Clark and asked him why he hadn't tried to profit from our own costly experience. He said he didn't know why. They'd had no problems doing business through banks. But business had been coming in too slowly, so they decided to hype it up.

Not long ago at some banquet, someone delivered a speech and said Arthur Roth had started the credit-card system in banks and charge-account banking fifteen years too soon. That's partly correct; timing is vital when you try innovations. But more than that, size is important, too. We were too small—we did it on too small a scale.

I tried to patent the bank credit card, but the patent was denied. We did franchise some banks around the country with the idea; the franchise was turned over to our employees' profit-sharing fund, which got a small income from the idea for about five or six years.

8 • The Fight for the Comptroller

Wrote Hugh McCulloch, first U.S. comptroller of the currency, in 1863:

Bear constantly in mind, although the loyal States appear superficially to be in a prosperous condition, that such is not the fact. That while the Government is engaged in the suppression of a rebellion of unexampled fierceness and magnitude, and is constantly draining its mechanical industry from works of permanent value to the construction of implements of warfare; while cities are crowded, and the country is to the same extent depleted, and waste and extravagance prevail as they never before prevailed in the United States, the nation, whatever may be the external indications, is not prospering.

. . . Manage the affairs of your respective banks with a perfect consciousness that the apparent prosperity of the country will be proved to be unreal . . . and be prepared, by careful management of the trust committed to you, to help to save the nation from a financial collapse, instead of lending your influence to make it more certain and more severe.

. . . Let no loans be made that are not secured beyond a reasonable contingency. Do nothing to foster and encourage speculation. Give facilities only to legitimate and prudent transactions. Make your discounts on as short time as the business of your customers will permit.

Distribute your loans rather than concentrate them in a few hands. Large borrowers are apt to control the bank . . . Pay your officers such salaries as will enable them to live comfortably and respectably without stealing; and require of them their entire services. If an officer lives beyond his income, dismiss him . . . Extravagance, if not a crime, very naturally leads to crime.

If you have reason to doubt the integrity of a customer, close his account. Never deal with a rascal under the impression that you can prevent him from cheating you.

In business, know no man's politics. Manage your bank as a business institution, and let no political partiality or prejudice influence your judgment.

Every banker under the National System should feel that the reputation of the system, in a measure, depends upon the manner in which his particular institution is conducted . . . There are few items that have a better look upon the balance sheet; and none that is better calculated to give aid and comfort to the managers of a bank, and to secure for it the confidence of a people, than a large surplus fund. Create, then, a good surplus, even if you have for a time to keep your stockholders on short commons in the way of dividends to do it.

The office of comptroller of the currency was established in the National Bank Act of 1863 to supervise the new national banks. These were supposed to replace the many state banks that had been set up during the years 1832–63 when the United States had no central bank or banking system. During that period there had been two types of money. One was notes issued by banks, which circulated like cash—although usually at a discount, depending on how far away from the bank of issuance they were and how long it might take to redeem them. The other form of money was checks issued against bank deposits.

One purpose of the 1863 law was to replace state bank notes with a national system of currency redeemable at par in any state. In this it succeeded; but in its other purpose, to force state banks to take national charters, it did not. State banks continue to exist.

It's amazing how many of the rules laid down in that 1863 letter by the first comptroller of the currency are still applicable to sound banking today: A bank's officers must live within their means . . . spread loans among many borrowers . . . create a surplus, and don't try to build prestige with shareholders by paying them large cash dividends.

All these criteria were basic to our way of doing business at Franklin. And they were all proved sound in practice.

Even the first comptroller's assessment of the state of the Union during the Civil War can read, with little editing, as a description of the problems and challenges the country faces today: our seeming prosperity based on enormous deficits; our overwhelming expenditures on weapons of war; our overcrowded and decaying cities; the waste and extravagance in government.

This underlying belief in the rightness of the first comptroller's assessment of the country and of banking's role and principles not only guided our efforts to build Franklin National, but was a reason why—in spite of the fact that we had had many direct run-ins with the comptroller's office—when the independence of the comptroller's function was threatened, it seemed unquestionably right to come to its defense.

The comptroller's office has always been a rather special branch of government. It was set up by Congress to be independent from the beginning. The comptroller is appointed by the president, subject to approval of Congress, but he reports to Congress. His term of office was deliberately set at five years so as not to coincide with that of any elected member of Congress or the Senate or the president; the idea was to keep him as much out of politics as possible.

Although the office is part of the Treasury Department and thus under the general authority of the secretary of the Treasury, the comptroller is self-supporting.

The way it works is this: The comptroller is in charge of all 5,000 national banks; he issues their charters; his deputies examine their books regularly. The banks pay fees for this, which are large enough to cover the salary of the comptroller and the 1,100 members of his department, as well as all other expenses of the operation. It costs taxpayers nothing. Moreover, the income of the office is large enough so that the salary scale of comptroller personnel is considerably higher than that paid in other Treasury departments. The comptroller sets his own budget and is not subject to control of the Bureau of the Budget. His fiscal independence guarantees administrative independence.

High salaries and a self-controlled budget created great resentment and envy among other bureaucrats, particularly in the Bureau of the Budget.

But the system worked the way Congress and the bankers had hoped. During nearly a century, the comptroller had achieved a record of honest independence, integrity, and sound judgment that had won the respect of bankers all over the country.

After World War II, President Harry S. Truman, concerned with the sprawling bureaucracy of the federal government, appointed a presidential commission, headed by former president Herbert Hoover, to examine the structure of the executive branch of government and to make recommendations for improving efficiency. Serving on the commission were such highly regarded public servants as Dean Acheson, James Forrestal, George D. Aiken, and Joseph P. Kennedy. There were six Democrats and six Republicans.

Besides the prestigious steering group, Hoover enlisted some 300 experts in government activities, organized them into task forces to look into specific problems, and gave them the assistance of professional researchers and management consultants.

The Hoover Commission (as it came to be known) created twenty-one separate reports and submitted them to Congress between January and April 1949. The first of these, *Reorganization Plan No. 1 of 1950*, recommended transferring "all functions of all other officers of the Department of the Treasury and all functions of all agencies and employees of such Department" to the secretary of the Treasury. This would have shifted the powers of the office of the comptroller of the currency (along with Internal Revenue, Customs, Narcotics, and four other departments) to the secretary. It would have destroyed the independence of the comptroller's office.

In March 1950, I visited our attorney Gloyd Awalt in Washington, and he told me what was being done to the office of comptroller. As former acting comptroller under President Roosevelt, Awalt was particularly concerned. He said, "This is going to go through, and the public will suffer, and all the banks will suffer, and nobody is doing anything to stop it."

This was news to me. I had thought that the American Bankers Association had taken a stand against this move and were actively opposing it.

"They've taken a stand," Awalt said, "and that's all. They're still standing there."

"But this can be stopped," I told Awalt.

"How?"

"By writing to all the small banks in the country and asking them to protest to Congress. This is what the Bankers Association should be doing. If they aren't, I'll be glad to try."

"In that case," Awalt said, "you had better meet L. K. Robertson, the acting comptroller."

I found Mr. Robertson upset over the proposed change. But he wasn't taking an active part in opposing it. He said, "In the government, we're all members of the same official family. The president is for this; we can't be squabbling among ourselves."

I told him of my desire to stop the Hoover Reorganization Plan No.

1, and asked him why Hoover had taken this position against the comptroller.

"Hoover doesn't know anything about it," Robertson said. "His staff went to the Bureau of the Budget for information. The bureau is envious of our department because we're completely self-supporting and because our salary scale is higher than that of other Treasury personnel. This is why the Hoover staff investigators were given the type of information that would lead to dissolution of the comptroller's independence."

In this country we have two competitive commercial banking systems. National banks are regulated by the comptroller; and state banks, which operate under state laws, are regulated by state banking commissioners. There are about twice as many state banks as national banks; but national banks have the edge in assets—they control more than half the commercial bank assets in the country.

All national banks are part of the Federal Reserve System. Many state banks are members, but their membership is optional. Both groups insure deposits with the Federal Deposit Insurance Corporation.

If the comptroller's function was merged under the Federal Reserve and the FDIC, as the Hoover Commission had proposed, it would have effectively ended much of the healthy competition between our two banking systems.

There was little time to act. The president had published his intention of implementing Reorganization Plan No. 1 on March 13, 1950, in the *Federal Register*. If there was not a majority of negative votes from one of the houses of Congress within thirty days, the plan would automatically go into effect.

There had been an adversary relationship between the comptroller's office and banks. This had been particularly true under President Roosevelt. And this was a good thing: You can't control an industry if you're too friendly with its members.

Few bankers had had as many arguments or problems with the comptroller as we had; the comptroller was always opposing our attempts to move banking forward. I felt that very often we were discriminated against; and I felt that we suffered because the comptroller's people always went by the book, instead of taking into account the needs of practical banking.

Still, I respected the comptroller's office for its honesty, and because it stood for the independence of national banks.

I believed that other bankers would feel the same way. William B.

Gladney, president of the American Bankers Association, had sent a letter to all member banks on March 23, 1950, explaining the seriousness of Reorganization Plan No. 1. In an accompanying memorandum, he analyzed the plan and asked that bankers get in touch with the senators from their home states, and with the chairman of the Senate Committee on Expenditures in the Executive Departments, to oppose it.

But the ABA, like many trade associations, was only as strong as its weaker members, and there was no enthusiasm in the leadership to oppose, head-on, President Truman, former President Hoover, and Secretary of the Treasury Snyder. Without an aggressive attempt to block Reorganization Plan No. 1, it was likely that it would go into effect by default.

Two Senate resolutions had been filed against the plan, by Senator A. Willis Robertson of Virginia and Homer F. Capehart of Indiana. Hearings on these resolutions were scheduled for April 11.

Awalt counseled that the most effective way to stop the plan was to concentrate on the (then) 96 senators rather than on the 435 representatives. On April 2 we sent a telegram to the senators, and to representatives from New York State:

WE URGE YOUR SUPPORT OF THE RESOLUTION INTRODUCED BY SENATOR H. WILLIS ROBERTSON, OF VIRGINIA, REQUESTING THE DELETION OF SECTION ONE OF THE REORGANIZATION PLAN. THE OFFICE OF THE COMPTROLLER OF THE CURRENCY HAS OPERATED EFFICIENTLY FOR 86 YEARS AS A SEMI-INDEPENDENT AGENCY AND SHOULD BE SO CONTINUED IN THE BEST COMBINED INTERESTS OF BANKING AND OUR PEOPLE. NO ECONOMIES COULD POSSIBLY RESULT FROM THE ABOLISHMENT OF THIS EFFICIENT OFFICE.

We received personal replies from most senators, many reacting positively. One especially touching letter came from Senator Arthur H. Vandenberg, then recovering from cancer surgery. With typical candor and open-mindedness, he wrote:

I think the Hoover Reports are entitled to a strong presumption in their favor. However, in a program of [this] magnitude it is expected that there may be occasional proposals which invite legitimate controversy. Furthermore, there is always the question whether the President's recommended Reorganization Plans accurately reflect the intent of the Hoover Report. . . . I shall be glad to advise you of my own ultimate decision when the matter comes to final issue.

On April 4, the Senate Banking Committee issued a resolution opposing the president's Reorganization Plan No. 1. This would undoubtedly have a strong influence on the senators who were to hear testimony for and against the plan.

The same day, I sent a letter to every national banker in the United States, as well as to the heads of six savings-banks associations and forty-eight state secretaries, urging that they let their senators know how they felt about retaining the comptroller's independence. This unleashed a flood of letters and telegrams; banking opinion was almost unanimous in supporting the Robertson-Capehart resolution.

I remember Ray Gidney, later comptroller of the currency, saying how surprised he was by the support we had helped to rally for the comptroller. It certainly helped to change the feeling that the comptroller's office had toward the Franklin National Bank.

My letter had the opposite effect on Senator William H. Benton of Connecticut, however. Senator Benton was a strong supporter of the Hoover reports, and he regarded them as a unit. If you disturbed the package, to his way of thinking, you might start a process that would destroy all the reports. He pleaded with the Senate committee to defeat the Robertson-Capehart resolution. He said that this was the first recommendation of the Hoover Commission before us. If it went down to defeat, the other recommendations might follow. Benton was the most vocal questioner among the committee that held the hearings on April 11 and 12.

Before the hearings started, the chairman inserted a potent letter into the record from Treasury Secretary John W. Snyder, opposing the change in the comptroller's status. Dated April 7, it spoke of the "trust and confidence" that bankers had in the comptroller's office, which served as "a coordinating, steadying and vitalizing force in the entire banking system. If Reorganization Plan No. 1 of 1950 becomes effective," Secretary Snyder wrote, "I would use my full powers thereunder to preserve the continuity of this Bureau in all possible respects. . . . However, it must be borne in mind that my policy . . . would not necessarily be maintained by future Secretaries of the Treasury." In short, for these and other reasons "I doubt the advisability of the proposed transfer of the functions and powers of the Comptroller of the Currency. In all other respects the plan has my unqualified endorsement."

Until then the administration had preserved a united front behind all of the Hoover reorganization plans. Now here was the key official, who would have benefited from Reorganization Plan No. 1, rejecting it and pointing out the future dangers to the country.

On the other hand, the incumbent comptroller, Preston Delano, refused to issue a statement or to testify about the plan.

The *New York Times* wrote on April 4:

> Banks throughout the country are rallying in opposition to President Truman's Reorganization Plan No. 1. . . . Although the proposal primarily affects national banks, the National Association of Supervisors of State Banks, it is understood, has joined with the American Bankers Association, state banking associations and other interested groups in an effort to arouse resistance.
>
> The drive will reach its peak intensity . . . this week, when hearings are scheduled . . . before the Senate Committee on Expenditures in the Executive Department. . . .
>
> Although [the Robertson and Capehart resolutions] might be expected to allay concern, bankers are not relaxing the fight, at least not in this area. Despite the resolutions . . . Arthur T. Roth, president of the Franklin National Bank . . . mailed out a 7-page statement to all national banks. . . .

At the April 11–12 hearings, thirteen bankers, officials of banking associations (including state bankers), and senators testified for the Robertson resolution. The only testimony against it came from Frederick J. Lawton, assistant director of the Bureau of the Budget.

On April 14 the powerful *Washington Post* came out against Reorganization Plan No. 1. And on April 17 the Executive Expenditures Committee voted 8–3 to uphold the Robertson-Capehart resolution, only Senators Humphrey, Leahy, and Benton opposed. The opposition asked for time to prepare a dissent to the committee's report.

That won them some delay. But by May 9 it was clear that a majority of at least forty-nine senators was ready to uphold Robertson's and Capehart's resolutions; the only problem was whether it could come to a vote in time. There was a southern filibuster going on against a fair-employment-practices bill. If this was allowed to continue past the May 23 deadline, the president's plan and the Reorganization Plan would be adopted by default.

Our only hope of breaking the filibuster was in an unrelated situation. President Truman had proposed an executive revision of the Taft-Hartley Labor Act. Senator Robert A. Taft of Ohio, one of the authors of this important piece of legislation, felt very proprietary about it and wanted to bring the president's proposal to a vote, for he felt he could defeat it.

In order to do this, he would have to interrupt the filibuster. If he could manage this, not only the Taft-Hartley Law but the Robertson and Capehart resolutions could be voted on. But if the filibuster continued, the deadline for opposing the Hoover report would pass and the comptroller's office would lose its independence.

Taft was a very powerful senator, and he felt that his personal prestige was deeply involved. He appealed to the Senate that President Truman was trying by administrative action to "reverse a major policy decision of the Congress less than three years ago." It was calculated to rally the pride of the senators, and it worked. He was able to get his vote (and to get it his way, too—53 to 30 against the administration).

There was still time to vote on the Robertson and Capehart resolutions before the deadline. Our majority was overwhelming: 65 for, 13 against. The *New York Times* headlined it as a rebuff for Truman; but to bankers it was a victory for the dual system of banking in this country.

9 • "Savings"

258. Prohibition of unauthorized savings banks and use of the word "savings"; exceptions as to school savings.

No bank, trust company, national bank, individual, partnership, unincorporated association or corporation other than a savings bank or a savings and loan association shall make use of the word "saving" or "savings" or their equivalent in relation to its banking or financial business, nor shall any individual or corporation other than a savings bank in any way solicit or receive deposits as a savings bank; but nothing herein shall be construed to prohibit the use of the word "savings" in the name of the Savings and Loan Bank of the State of New York or in the name of a trust company all of the stock of which is owned by not less than twenty savings banks. Any bank, trust company, national bank, individual, partnership, unincorporated association or corporation violating this provision shall forfeit to the people of the state for every offense the sum of one hundred dollars for every day such offense will be continued.

—New York Banking Law of 1893

The world of banking has more than its share of social lags and vested interests. One lag and interest led to a long and costly fight over a single word, a semantic battle that trekked through all the various layers of New York State jurisprudence and up to the Supreme Court of the United States of America.

All this legal activity was inspired over the simple word *savings*. To understand why, and how precious this noun was, you have to know a little bit about mutual savings banks.

Concentrated in seventeen northeastern states, they are theoretically "owned" by their depositors, who supposedly share in the banks' benefits, for there are no shareholders in any mutual institution. Savings banks are assumed to be nonprofit.

The first one in the United States was the Provident Institution for Savings of Boston, founded in 1816. That name tells you a lot about its original purpose. It was not called a "bank," although it was one. It was founded by wealthy, successful people to provide for the poor. That is, it was a means for the rich to help the less affluent to safeguard themselves financially by encouraging thrift, a worthy if paternalistic purpose, with the useful corollary that it would relieve the burden of giving alms to the needy. The goals were typical of other such banks. The Bank for Savings of New York was founded (in 1819) by the Society for the Prevention of Pauperism.

Knowing the background, one can understand that such worthy institutions were given a number of special safeguards and privileges. They had to be safe. At first their investments were restricted by law to U.S. government bonds. Later they were permitted—in fact encouraged—to go into local mortgage lending. The idea was that since their money came from "little people," it ought to go to help their neighbors at the same economic level to build houses.

The original philanthropic purposes of mutual savings banks have long since been dissipated. They are now well-established banks, no longer run by philanthropists for poor people but by professionals to make money. Their powers have been greatly enlarged; no longer restricted to local mortgages, they can invest in both bonds and preferred stock of corporations (N.Y. State laws of 1949 and 1952), and in Canadian securities (laws of 1937). They can also rent safe-deposit boxes (laws of 1926), sell life insurance (laws of 1939), sell traveler's checks (laws of 1938), permit depository to write checks and undertake a number of other banking functions, some of which have been denied to commercial banks. In other words, they are powerful competitors of other banks in offering a variety of banking services.

The mutual savings banks, in the seventeen states where they exist by law, are now frank and powerful rivals for the depositor's dollar, vying with commercial banks, life-insurance companies, credit unions, and all other forms of banking. They enjoyed an edge on commercial banks in the higher interest they were permitted to pay thrifty depositors for savings accounts. This is why their share of deposits was steadily rising, while time (savings) deposits in commercial banks had been dropping for years.

In spite of the changes that have obliterated the original purposes of savings banks, these banks profited from several special dispensations granted to further their early social goals. One of these—in New

York, Maine, and Minnesota—was that the word *savings* was restricted to savings banks—no other banking institution could use the word *savings* in any way to describe its deposits.

Seven years before I joined the Franklin Square Bank its president, Arthur Phillips, knowing that the National Bank Act had recently been amended to permit national commercial banks to take in savings deposits, wrote to the comptroller of the currency to ask if he could advertise "savings accounts." Deputy Comptroller of the Currency E. W. Stearns replied that "the law . . . empowers a national bank to receive and pay interest on savings deposits and the request to advertise and solicit such savings accounts is necessarily incidental to the exercise of that power and cannot be interfered with or denied."

Phillips began advertising Franklin's "Savings Bank Department."

Immediately he was warned by New York State banking officials that an 1893 state law restricted the use of the word *savings* to mutual savings banks and loan associations, chartered by the state. Although commercial banks could take in time deposits, they couldn't call them "savings" but had to resort to such euphemisms as "special interest accounts" or "thrift accounts." Most people didn't know that these meant savings. The restriction thus hampered the bank's activities, and this was still true when I joined Franklin.

During and after the war, with the shortage of goods, people were piling up surpluses of cash and they wanted to save it. Naturally, they went to savings banks—particularly as the latter were able to advertise their savings accounts. Which means that a growing portion of bank deposits were going to those banks.

There was only one savings bank in Nassau County. But the big New York savings banks had large advertising budgets. All of them—Bowery, Manhattan, Dime—went after depositors' savings in Nassau County. And we were fighting with one hand tied—we weren't supposed to use the word *savings*.

I could see that in the near-future our borrowers would be clamoring for loans—justifiable, good loans—that we wouldn't be able to make for lack of deposits.

When I first came to Franklin, I felt that savings accounts were a vital part of the bank's assets, and that we should do whatever we could to attract more of them. I had done some research in the law. It seemed clear that although New York State banks might be prohibited from using *savings* since they were under a state charter and state law, a national bank like Franklin could not be restricted since we had a national charter and were governed by federal law.

Almost from the beginning, when I entered the bank in 1934, we used the word *savings*. Above a group of tellers' windows, we had a lighted sign that said "Savings Accounts." As mentioned earlier, we had also put up decorative wrought-iron signs in the parking lot, each with a kind of cartoon character, and each advertising the bank's various services. One of these, showing a thief entering a house, carried the word *savings*. And we advertised for savings accounts in the local newspapers.

We were so small then—under a million dollars—that nobody paid much attention. But as we began to attract more deposits—over $3 million by 1940—we began to receive more notice.

One day that year we got a letter from Charles Schoch, deputy superintendent of the state banking department, advising us that we were violating the state law—and that the penalty was $100 a day for every day in which we violated that law.

That began a long correspondence. I replied to Schoch, stating that as a national bank we had the right to use the word *savings*. A state commercial bank could not use that word, it was true, and I urged the superintendent to recommend that the legislature and the governor change the law, which was giving us an unfair advantage over the state banks. It was an old law, and obviously out-of-date.

This correspondence with the state Banking Department went on in a rather desultory fashion for several years. No action was taken to stop us from using the word *savings*.

Then in 1947 (by then we were a $28-million bank) I received a telephone call from Frank Krippel, the assistant comptroller of the currency in New York. He had been phoned direct by Preston Delano, the comptroller of the currency in Washington. Delano was inspired to make this call because of what he was told by Elliot Bell, the superintendent of banks of New York State. Bell had warned Delano that the state was going to take legal action against the Franklin Square Bank to stop us from using the word *savings*.

Obviously, we weren't important enough to be called direct by either Delano or Bell; but the situation was serious all the same.

Krippel said, "Is using the word *savings* important enough to you to make it worthwhile to accept a suit by the state of New York?"

A lot of things flashed through my mind. For one thing, about 50 percent of our business had been with savings banks—on FHA mortgages. Going to court would put us on a collision course with our best customers.

Then there were political overtones. The Bell–Delano call was no accident. This was 1948, an election year, and anyone who could read the polls could see that President Harry Truman was going to lose his bid for reelection and Governor Thomas E. Dewey of New York, his Republican opponent for the presidency, was going to win, hands down. Bell was managing the Dewey campaign; it was as certain as taxes that he was going to be Dewey's secretary of the Treasury. And the secretary of the Treasury has authority over all national banks.

It didn't seem politic to antagonize Elliot Bell at that point, so I said to Krippel, "You know we have the legal right to the word *savings*. But we don't want a court battle. I'll agree to discontinue using the word for a year."

I didn't want to make it permanent; I felt that our consent should be limited to one year to see what effect not using the word would have on the growth of our savings accounts.

And I thought that had settled the matter for the time.

Then, six or eight months later, I heard from a builder, Sol Atlas. He told me that a friend of his in the state attorney general's office had told him they were going to take legal action against Franklin. (We were now known as the Franklin National Bank, having dropped the *Square* the year before.)

I asked what legal action they were going to take.

Atlas said, "I don't know. But my friend says that if you'd like to come with me to his office, he'll show you the file."

I went to New York with Atlas, where an assistant State attorney general, showed me the file. In it was a letter from Edward Barrett (later president of Long Island Lighting) in which he said that at the National City Bank, where he then worked, he had been warned never to use the word *savings*. They called their savings department the Compound Interest Department.

The attorney told me, "What you're doing at Franklin is illegal. You promised to stop using the word *savings* and you're still using it."

In spite of our careful attempt to keep our pledge, the word had crept into our annual report, not widely circulated or read, and one or two other documents of about the same level of importance.

"Look," the attorney said, "I'm not being pressured on this. Think it over. Make up your mind."

I said I had made up my mind, and had given instructions to

everyone in the bank not to use the word, and that this was sincere. These "violations" were just small mistakes that could happen in any organization.

I said, "I'm not the one to start a battle with the savings banks. Almost half the profit of our bank comes from the mortgages we originate and service to the savings banks. Why, that's the biggest single block of our business."

He repeated, "Why don't you decide?"

"I have," I said. "We don't want to fight it."

"Then why not go to the state Banking Department and tell them?" the lawyer suggested. "I'm sure they'll instruct me to withdraw the case."

So I went to see Schoch and said, "This is all wrong. I'm sure I could win a legal victory in the Supreme Court of the United States. But I'm not the person to undertake that battle. We do too much business with savings banks."

"If you feel you can win, go ahead and test it," Schoch said.

I said, "No, I told you I'd discontinue using the word for a year, and I meant it. If it crept in a couple of times, that was inadvertent."

He sent me to see their attorney, who told me, "Now you understand you cannot use the word *savings* in any way."

I said, "In our parking field we have a small wrought-iron sign that says 'Savings.' Does that have to come down?"

"Absolutely."

"And it's on our deposit and withdrawal slips."

"They will have to be changed."

"And at the tellers' windows, we have a sign that says "Savings.' "

"That, too."

"But that's inside our own house, inside the bank."

"Makes no difference."

I said, "You seriously mean that if we don't take down that sign, you'll go to court against us?"

He said, "Yes."

I said, "Well, you've just pushed it too far. Go ahead with your suit."

I really hadn't wanted this, and had not planned for it. But I was sure we were correct, and on a matter of principle it didn't seem right to yield—especially as our effort to be conciliatory got nowhere.

Sure enough, we were served with a Summons and Complaint by Nathaniel L. Goldstein, attorney general of the state of New York. He had filed suit in the state supreme court for an injunction to stop the Franklin National Bank from using the word *savings* in any way. Without intending to, our tiny bank was put in the position of carrying forward a test case that affected the interests of all the banks in New York State.

There were two sharply contradictory legal points of view about this. As far back as 1907, the American Bankers Association had issued an opinion that national banks had the right "to receive savings deposits, and to pay interest thereon." Various state court decisions had taken the opposite view, and even the U.S. Treasury Department, which oversees all national banking, had opined that where state law forbade "savings" to national banks, that law would probably be upheld.

Suddenly, we felt like David taking on Goliath. We were a small bank, and this was going up against the entire state, and would cost a lot of money. If we lost, it would be even more expensive.

The suit was assigned to a Nassau County supreme court, and the trial was set for late fall.

In September we found allies. The Nassau County Clearinghouse appointed a special committee to look into the case. Augustus B. Weller, head of the Meadow Brook National Bank, one of our strong competitors but a good friend, was the head. The committee drew up a resolution supporting our fight.

I had been convinced for years that most people were confused by the different terms used to describe savings accounts, and weren't too sure of the various types of institutions involved. I asked one of our vice-presidents, Bill Green, to go out on the street and ask people if they knew what a thrift account was, or a compound-interest account. Perhaps one person out of twenty that he polled gave a correct answer.

Then I suggested to Matthew N. Chappell, a friend who was professor of Psychology and ran the Psychological Workshop at Hofstra College in Hempstead, that he take a scientific poll of the public on these questions. Make it a project for his students, and use them as investigators.

Dr. Chappell, who was an expert in this field, was enthusiastic about the idea. He and thirty students worked out a scientific "probability sample" of 1,000 people, and did 928 interviews. The results were what we hoped. Eighty-five percent knew what a savings account and a savings bank were; Only 40.8 percent knew what *compound interest* meant; a mere 24.4 percent knew what *special interest* meant; and just

19.5 percent recognized the meaning of *thrift accounts*. Nor did they know where to find such accounts. The clearinghouse retained the workshop, but we paid for the work.

The case finally came to trial in May 1951. The night before, I received a phone call from Judge Thomas Cuff. He was a neighbor and I knew him, but not well. He invited me to come over to his house and play pool with him and a few friends.

I'd never been to his house. I said, "The bank has a case coming up in the supreme court tomorrow, and it may be assigned to your part, and I wouldn't like to have it said that we played pool the night before." Judge Cuff said that didn't make any difference, but I said I'd rather not.

As it happened, the case did come before Cuff, for a simple reason: He was literally the only supreme-court judge in our area who was not on the board of any bank. (Judges were permitted to be bank directors in those days; they no longer are.)

When they offered him the case, Cuff said, "I want you to know that Arthur Roth is a friend of mine, and I would not take offense if you transferred the trial to another court." But they left it with him.

We brought the thirty Hofstra students who had done the survey to court to testify. The state tried to have their testimony thrown out because it was "hearsay," so we had to prove that random sampling was a scientific technique that gave answers accurate to within 2 or 3 percent. This was the first time that this had been done in court; we were a test case for the pollsters, as well as for banks.

Sidney Friedman, later chairman of the board of the National Bank of North America, was our attorney. The trial lasted two weeks. Then, on Tuesday, May 29, 1951, Judge Cuff issued a twenty-page decision, which read in part:

> To deny the defendant the right to invite the public, by all proper means of expression at its disposal, to make "savings deposits" with it, is to curtail the power to receive such accounts, to reduce its effectiveness as an agency handling that kind of financing—in short, to defeat one of the main purposes for which it was created by Congress.
>
> Under such conditions, one law or the other must give way. The State Law must yield to the Federal Law—the supreme law of the land. . . . The New York Statute is unconstitutional.
>
> Judgment with costs in defendant's favor dismissing the complaint will be entered.

Naturally, we were happy with this decision, and made preparations to start advertising for savings accounts.

The public-opinion poll had really been the keystone of our testimony: The judge had been most impressed by it and actually incorporated the finding into his decision:

"The public understands the meaning of the term 'savings account,' " he wrote, ". . . far better than it understands the meaning of any substitute terms. I am also satisfied . . . that the word 'savings' when used with the word 'account' in relation to a bank, provokes a much stronger appeal to the eye and understanding of the public than do the substitutes. . . ."

The public-opinion poll had cost money; the defense had been expensive. I had no hesitancy in composing a letter to the commercial banks of New York State, pointing this out.

> The expense of preparing and presenting our case, which we believe is also the case of all the commercial banks in New York State, has been quite substantial . . . more than one hundred people, over a number of months, have worked together in amassing the evidence for defense of this case. Many banks acquainted with the situation have made unsolicited offers to contribute to the expense. We feel that, since all commercial banks will be directly benefited by this successful conclusion, they would like to be given an opportunity in helping to defray the cost.
>
> We do not know what the total cost of establishing our rights will be. . . . In the event, however, that the contributions received are insufficient, we will ourselves make up the amount of any shortages, in addition to our own assessment. If, on the other hand, the contributions exceed the final cost, it is our purpose to refund the excess. . . .

The letter produced some moral but very little financial support. Over the next few years—a few small banks eventually put up about 25 percent of what the court actions actually cost us—that is, they subscribed about $38,000 or $40,000 of the $160,000 expense.

But many banks were afraid to be seen in our company. The large New York City banks suffered from divided loyalty. They had savings-banks officials on their boards of directors, and vice versa; and even more important, they had large deposits from savings banks. There were millions of dollars at stake.

First National City never gave us any help, although they lost no time in advertising for "savings accounts." They used to sponsor a news announcer on television, John K. M. McCaffery, who had had a small sign announcing "Compound Interest Accounts" on his desk in the TV studio. The bank had a substitute sign reading "Savings Accounts" prepared and put it to use the very day that Judge Cuff's favorable decision was announced.

Chase Manhattan supported us—under the table. They sent an officer out to see me with $5,000 in cash; they didn't want any record of the transaction, which could have damaged them with their savings-bank customers.

It certainly damaged us with ours. Before the suit started, I'd gone to see Joe Kaiser, president of the Williamsburgh Savings Bank, our best customer. I told him what had happened in the office of the superintendent of banking. I asked, "How do you think your directors would feel if we went through with this suit?"

He said, "It's going to hurt a good deal. We hold this word *savings* very sacred."

I liked and respected Joe Kaiser. But I felt we had to go through with that suit; it was a matter of principle. And I felt that if we were forced to give up our mortgage business with savings banks, which amounted to about $55 million a year, we would find other business to replace it. We were growing very fast; there was no reason to be fearful.

There have been many times when I was forced to take a decision like this, sometimes on the spur of the moment without any contingency plans. But I felt that I had control and understanding of the general situation; problems create challenges, and challenges create opportunities—that has always been my philosophy.

However, Judge Cuff's opinion did not end the litigation. It went on for two more years and cost us a lot of business. But the longer it continued, the more talk there was about the bank. When there is conversation about you, people think about you; and when they have business to do, your name is on their minds, so they come to you rather than to some other bank. Thus, it also brought us a lot of business.

If I hadn't had complete confidence in the ultimate rightness of our cause, the lawsuits could have been very depressing. The State attorney general appealed to the New York State appellate division and won a reversal of Judge Cuff's decision, on a split verdict. Then we appealed to the next-higher state court, the Court of Appeals. We lost there, too, on another split verdict, 5 to 2, on July 14, 1953. In this case the New York State Bankers Association, representing 650 bank and trust companies, supported us strongly as *amicus curiae*.

These two decisions could have shaken our confidence. But in a fight I try never to be on the defensive. There were about 125 savings banks in the state of New York. I sent each one of them a check for $100 and asked them to open an account in my name.

Savings bankers held special meetings to figure out what I was up to. Fifteen banks returned my checks, refusing to open an account. Several who had opened an account wrote me and said that, as I was the archenemy of savings banks, they wished to cancel my account, and would I please return the passbook. A public institution is not allowed to do this. But I never answered any of them. In fact, I never said a word. When people asked me what I was up to, I would just say, "I have something in mind. They'll be shocked when they find out."

They held meetings with their attorneys to figure out what I might do. I had no purpose in mind—it was just a form of psychological warfare to worry them. I never did a thing, just kept the passbooks for a few years, then closed them all out. I'd invested about $11,000. Got it all back with full legal interest.

We were forced to take the case to Washington, to the Supreme Court of the United States. We continued with the same law firm, Alley, Cole, Grimes & Friedman; but we added expert Washington attorneys Gloyd Awalt and his associate Samuel O. Clark, Jr., to help us. And the New York State Bankers Association filed a very strong *amicus curiae* brief. The acting head of the office of the powerful comptroller of the currency, Ray Gidney, permitted us to include a supportive letter he had written on the subject. And the Treasury asked the Justice Department to support us, too.

The New York Court of Appeals had justified its restriction of *savings* with the claim that the use of the word by a national bank would be "misleading . . . deceptive verbiage," and other such phrases.

The Court of Appeals had said that "special-interest account" and the other descriptions of savings by commercial banks were "synonymous" with *savings*. "If these expressions are actually synonymous with the word 'savings,' then it is difficult to perceive how harm can result from the use by national banks of the word 'savings,' " said the Bankers Association brief. "Since Section 258 (1) of the New York Banking Law applies not only to the use of the word 'savings' but to its 'equivalent,' it would seem that the state recognizes that the statute cannot be validly applied as written. Otherwise, the synonymous expressions would come within the ban of being equivalent."

Sidney Friedman pointed out that in the three New York decisions, there had been five different opinions, for and against. None of them used the same reasoning, or was based on the same issues. Friedman felt that this showed much legal confusion, and it made him feel secure in the rightness of our basic contention: that federal law superseded state law in the case of a federally created institution, like a national bank.

First, of course, we had to convince the nine justices of the Supreme Court that the case embodied not only an important constitutional issue that should be heard but one of substantial size. The Bankers Association made a strong case for us here: They stated that their interest was very substantial, since in New York State the savings deposits in commercial banks amounted to nearly $2 billion. In Nassau County, where Franklin did business exclusively, they nearly equaled the total of demand deposits.

Our Supreme Court brief stated that the appeals-court decision "leads to the extraordinary result that the mere verbatim quotation by a national bank of the relevant language of the Federal Reserve Act [to receive time and savings deposits] in the course of its business subjects the banks, without more, to civil penalties under a state statute. This statute . . . encroaches on the power and interferes with the operations of national banks and discriminates against them. We believe that the question is substantial and of public importance. . . ."

The Supreme Court decided that it had jurisdiction, and agreed to hear the case in February 1954. We invited all the bank's directors and their wives to Washington to the trial.

Arguments before the Supreme Court are limited to one hour—and this includes the questions that justices ask. They asked so many questions that our counsel never had a chance to finish. But we weren't discouraged; the fact that they interrupted so often showed the depth of their interest, our lawyers explained.

Besides the points made in the early briefs, the lawyers brought out that both legislative and administrative history supported our position; that no state\ can impose its banking standards on national banks; that national banks are a necessary instrument in carrying out the nation's monetary policy, through the Federal Reserve System; and that savings deposits are an essential element of any national bank's business—thus interference by the state was, in effect, interference with the purpose of national banks.

We returned to New York confident of our cause. On April 5, the Court announced its decision: 8 to 1 in our favor. The majority opinion by Justice Robert H. Jackson stated: "We think the Federal and the state statutes are incompatible and in such circumstances the policy of the state must yield.'' He said that the constitutional right of the federal government to create and govern national banks within states was not ''open to question.''

The *New York Times* headlined the story

NATIONAL BANKS IN STATE ALLOWED
BY COURT TO USE WORD "SAVINGS"

It was an expensive victory, cost us another $120,000 out of pocket. But the bank was growing fast—by 1954 our capital and surplus were nearly $16 million; we had $278 million of deposits. Our profits were soaring; the price of our stock was going up. So none of our directors ever questioned the rightness of our carrying the burden and brunt of the battle. Of course, I don't know what they might have said had we lost.

10 • Second Front

New York State is the center of power of the mutual savings banks. Controlling assets of about $16 billion in the 1950s, the New York savings banks were and are able to exert control over much of the state legislature. The public is unaware of this; it is the product of the present legal-political structure, which not only permits but encourages conflicts of interest.

It works this way: A majority of state senators and assemblymen were, and are today, lawyers. The savings banks do business with many of them, mainly in mortgage closings. Legislators receiving legal fees from savings banks are apt to be at least sympatheic to their clients' legislative problems.

The savings banks have also controlled many, if not most, of the superintendents of banks of New York State through a simple and well-worn device: A superintendent could count on a well-paid job as president of a large savings bank whenever he left government. This has happened to almost every man who has been superintendent until quite recently.

It is understandable then that savings bankers were permitted to expand their activities while retaining their special privileges. The law gave them a perpetual advantage in seeking deposits; commercial banks were forbidden to pay as much as savings banks did for savings deposits—although commercial bankers could and would have paid as much if given the same tax and credit advantages. These were two: while commercial banks paid the same income tax as corporations (52 percent), savings banks paid close to nothing (in 1955 their taxes averaged $154 per bank in New York State). And while commercial banks were required by law to keep 5 percent of deposits in cash reserve, savings banks had no reserve requirement at all. This gave a billion-dollar bank like the Bowery Savings a $50-million edge over any billion-dollar commercial bank. Although we had stripped the savings banks of one unfair advantage, they retained many others. Our fight with these institutions was far from over.

The savings banks won their increased privileges through the superintendent of banks and their powerful lobby, and were able to change the banking law in their favor regularly. Such changes began in 1914, but gained momentum in the 1930s and 1940s. Almost every year the state banking law was changed, or amended, in favor of the savings banks; year by year they were permitted to encroach upon the services of commercial banks, and in one important area—investing in corporate preferred stocks—they had greater powers than the commercial banks.

The number of branches permitted to savings banks had been gradually increased over the years. But in the 1950s they began a drive to greatly expand the number of their branches.

New York State was divided into nine banking districts. New York City is District 1; Westchester is District 2; and so on. The establishment of branch banks had been limited to the cities in which the home offices were established.

During the same period Roth was fighting them for "*savings,*" the savings banks decided to try to change the law to permit branch banking in adjacent districts. Their reason: The suburbs had been growing very rapidly, financed by the suburban commercial banks. There were very few suburban savings banks; only one in Nassau and three in Suffolk. Fewer people were commuting to New York City, more were working near their homes. Although the big city savings banks were advertising heavily for mail deposits, people generally like to bank near where they live and/or work. Savings deposits were growing rapidly in Nassau, Suffolk, and Westchester—and these were flowing into commercial banks and postal savings.

The big city savings banks had been growing, too, but wanted a larger share of suburban savings than they could gather by mail. Branch savings banks in the suburbs were the logical answer, and suburban commercial banks were the obvious target.

This time the commercial banks decided to fight. They did not have the political muscle of the savings banks; they did not have the financial connections with legislators, nor the sympathy of the superintendent of banks. But there were some things in their favor. The majority of legislators were Republicans from small towns. The move into suburbs by large New York savings banks could be seen as a threat to all sorts of small banks everywhere—small savings banks and savings and loans as well. The state Bankers Association of commercial banks was united strongly on this issue, and it found allies among smaller local savings institutions. Together, they set up their own lobby and succeeded in throttling in the legislature the first attempt by the superintendent of banks to give the large savings banks the right to branch into suburbs.

While we were fighting for the word *savings* in the courts, the savings bankers were attacking our legislative flank. Franklin and the other Nassau banks had been so successful in finding mortgage money, and in financing builders, that the county's population had nearly doubled in the 1950s to more than 1 million. Industry established there during World War II had been converted to peacetime production, and new industry had been started, so that people who lived there could work there. The same thing had been happening in Westchester, on a slightly smaller scale.

The volume of savings deposits had also grown. In 1949 they totalled about $124 million, as against about $152 million of demand deposits in Nassau County. And there was only the one savings bank at Roslyn. The New York savings banks' bank-by-mail advertisements were not very effective.

The move to the suburbs was affecting savings banks in other large cities in the state, too.

Savings bankers got together with the superintendent of banks, William A. Lyon, and convinced him that they were being throttled by geographical restriction of their branches. They ought to have the right, they said, to follow their customers and establish branches within a fifty-mile radius of their home offices.

Mr. Lyon drew up a bill to this effect and had it introduced in the New York State Legislature. It was defeated in 1951 or 1952.

In 1953, Lyon came back with a "compromise" bill cutting the radius for branches down to twenty-five miles. This still would have permitted all the big New York savings institutions to branch into Nassau and Westchester—their real purpose. The New York State Bankers Association put pressure on its members to talk to their legislators.

The legislature's Republican majority saw to it that this bill was not even reported out of committee.

In December 1953 John Greene, financial writer, wrote in *Newsday:*

> Twice the city bankers have tried to penetrate [Long Island], once with the aid of an expensive lobby in its backfield. . . . An effort was made to

call the whole thing off if the counties' commercial banks would agree to let them ooze into villages of more than 10,000 population located within 25 miles of the Queens-Nassau boundary. . . . They are frank about admitting it. Old Nassau has grown in stature and wealth in the last 10 years. Thousands of the city savings banks' customers have moved into the area. . . . The savings banks think they have a right to follow their clients. . . .

Mr. Lyon resigned as superintendent of banks and, as naturally as water seeking its level, flowed into the position of chairman of the Executive Committee and trustee of the huge Manhattan-based Dry Dock Savings Bank. He predicted that the next year the legislature would permit savings banks to branch into neighboring communities.

The *New York Times* headlined:

BANK CONTROVERSY
OMINIOUSLY QUIET

The story, on April 5, 1953, by George A. Mooney, told of the savings bankers' threat to go to the public with an advertising campaign soliciting deposits by mail. Commercial banks were warned that they might be required to segregate time deposits and use them only under the same restrictions as savings bankers had to observe (i.e., no business loans). and Earl B. Schwulst, president of the Bowery Savings Banks, stated: "If unreasonable opposition from commercial banks succeeds in continuing to thwart a fair solution of this problem, it may drive some of the savings banks to try to find some way to operate under a federal charter."

They were all under state charters, therefore under state law. If they were able to get the federal government to issue charters, they might be free of the state law (as we were about to prove in court that national commercial banks were in our lawsuit over the word *savings*).

But they decided to try, try again, and on February 16, 1954, introduced a branch-bank bill at the last possible minute. A telegram to members of the New York State Bankers Association warned:

THIS BILL IS EVEN BROADER THAN LAST YEAR'S AMENDED BILL. . . . IN SUBTANCE IT PROVIDES THAT SAVINGS BANKS (IRRESPECTIVE OF EXISTING BRANCHES) MAY OPEN A BRANCH OFFICE IN A CITY OR TOWNSHIP HAVING POPULATION OF 10,000 OR MORE WITHIN 25 MILES OF ITS HEAD OFFICE. . . . YOU ARE FULLY AWARE THAT [THIS] WOULD

SERIOUSLY JEOPARDIZE THE SOUNDNESS OF OUR INDEPENDENT BANKS
THROUGH LOSS OF TIME DEPOSITS TO SAVINGS BANKS . . . DEFEAT OF
BRANCH BILL ABSOLUTELY ESSENTIAL TO SOUNDNESS OF OUR BANK-
ING SYSTEM. . . .

I sent copies of this to all our officers and asked them to contact
their state representatives.

The New York State Bankers Association also published a very
cogent booklet outlining just what this meant in dollars. They showed
that a majority of the fifty-four mutual savings banks in New York City
held well over $100 million apiece in deposits, and one (Bowery
Savings) over a billion dollars. Most commercial banks were very much
smaller—and, what was more important, half or more of their deposits
were in savings accounts. While savings banks had grown by nearly 400
percent (nearly $12 billion) since 1925, the commercial banks were
actually losing demand deposits.

"The big problem presented by the demand of the Mutual Savings
Banks for further branch power is that of the survival of the Independent
Community Banks," the booklet said.

The problem was, the mutual savings banks were richer, stronger,
and more united than the commercial banks. And they had all that
political clout in Albany.

I wrote to State Senator S. Wentworth Horton: "Why should these
tremendous New York City savings banks now want to step into our
territory and take from us the fruits of our pioneering and hard work?
Let them devote their efforts to making New York City a better city in
which to live and work."

But they concentrated on Albany, and got their legislation out of
committee in 1954 for the first time by limiting the branch radius to
fifteen miles. The *Long Island Daily Press* wrote: "The bill is aimed
specifically at Nassau. . . . Nassau's block will oppose it.

"Assemblyman Joseph F. Carlino of Long Beach admitted this
morning that 'we will have a fight on our hands.' "

The state Bankers Association had been effective up to this time.
But the savings banks were making headway. Their 1954 bill got out of
committee, but lost in the Assembly. In '55, they won in the Assembly,
but the bill was killed in the Senate.

Both houses of the legislature appointed a joint committee to hold
hearings on changing the state banking law.

I was a member of the Bankers Association's Legislative Committee. George Newbury, an upstate banker and our chairman, told us: "It's only a matter of time before the savings banks get their way. We all know that they control the legislature and they've been able to get everything they've ever asked from them. We're only fighting a holding action." He urged that we accept some sort of compromise.

It's true that the connection between many legislators and savings banks is a flagrant conflict of interest that existed then and exists today. And it has never been investigated. It's about as close to bribery as you can get.

Now, President Eisenhower made a speech on August 23, 1956, accepting his nomination for his second term, that impressed me greatly. He said that government programs ought to "be based upon principle rather than upon shifting political opportunism. . . . Change based on principle is progress," Eisenhower said. "Constant change without principle becomes chaos."

I wrote a letter to my fellow committee members pointing out that while our chairman felt it would be politically expedient to compromise on savings-bank branches, "other members, who are opposed to any form of compromise, have taken a position that the question should be decided solely on merit and fact . . . in the public interest. Now which course shall be taken by our committee? Principle? Or expediency?" And I enclosed a copy of the excerpt from Eisenhower's speech.

The letter seemed to stop the drift toward compromise. From then on, our committee was united in opposing the expansion of savings-bank branches.

The committee of the legislature was holding hearings on this in cities all over the state, at which we would supply testimony from local bankers. I went to Rochester to hear a typical session, and was appalled at how weakly our position was presented. If this was the best we could do, we were certainly going to lose in the legislature.

I asked the Bankers Association committee if they would permit me to present testimony when the legislators held hearings in New York City. I didn't say so, but if they refused I was prepared to resign and do it on my own; but they gave me permission.

I prepared thoroughly for my appearance at the hearing before the legislative committee, headed by State Senator George H. Pierce, who was also head of the Senate Banking Committee and sympathetic to our position.

One important point was about "flight money." This was money taken from New York depositors by the savings banks, but sent out of the state—mostly to California—for investment. Here was the most blatant disregard of the welfare of the people of their own community; the savings bankers were taking billions of local dollars and sending them 2,500 miles away because they earned more interest—and denying loans to the neighbors of their depositors.

This was only one of the points. There were a dozen or more charts graphically showing the inequalities and inequities between the two types of banking.

I came into the city the night before to get a good night's rest at the Hotel Commodore and be in top shape for the committee. Friday, September 28, 1956, turned out to be a cold, rainy day, the very worst kind for a sinus sufferer like myself. I woke with one of the worst headaches I've ever had. Aspirin did nothing to relieve it, nor did a hot breakfast. I could barely see straight with that pain pounding at my head.

Finally, in desperation, I did something I've never done in my life. At about 8:30 in the morning, I went into a bar and told the bartender to give me a double vodka martini. Straight up.

He looked at me the way bartenders must look at alcoholics early in the morning but said nothing and filled my order.

I took it and drank it down as though it were water. It did not make me drunk but it had a wonderful effect on my headache which disappeared completely. I went off to the meeting at the county Lawyers Association on Vesey Street with the charts. I asked Judge Pierce if I could take more than the usual fifteen or twenty minutes. He said, "Yes, go ahead." I felt so good, I never referred to my notes, but for an hour and twenty minutes gave the committee chapter and verse on why they should not permit savings to branch into suburbs unless they first revised the numerous inequities that gave them unfair advantage over commercial banks, and penalized everyone around—not only other bankers—for their privileges.

If I repeat some of the arguments here, it is because many are still pertinent to everyone with any kind of bank account in New York or any of the other states where savings banks exist. These facts touch your pocketbook even if you have no bank account; they affect the community you live in; they depress the local economy, and the national economy as well; and they even cost you more money in taxes.

First of all, we had a chart that illustrated twenty-nine major banking services, from checking accounts to agricultural loans. Of these twenty-nine, commercial banks offered twenty-eight. The only one not offered is one they are forbidden—selling life insurance. Savings banks performed only five of these services. If a savings bank and a commercial bank served the same community, and the savings bank closed down, the commercial bank would keep the community financed; but if the commercial bank closed down, the community would go out of business. Nationally, commercial banks financed most of the $374.2 billion of credit to industry; none came from savings banks; savings banks loaned a part of the $16.6 billion in private housing mortgages, in which commercial banks also participated.

Yet the savings banks were enormous by comparison; only 2 percent of New York State savings banks were under $5 million, while 52 percent of the commercial banks were this small.

We had photos of slums near savings banks to illustrate how the institutions neglected their job to try to improve their own community through mortgage loans.

Perhaps one of the most telling graphics was one that showed that all the savings banks in the United States, with total deposits over $21 billion, paid a total of only $1.2 *million* in income tax in 1955. The Franklin Bank alone, with a total of only $370 million in deposits; had paid nearly twice as much—$2.3 million—as all those savings banks put together. This was no exaggeration; it was a fact.

Another chart showed that if the New York State savings banks paid their fair share of tax, the government would receive an additional $56 million a year. Nationwide this would be $64 million (about three-quarters of savings-bank deposits were in New York State). This was a real eye-opener to those legislators, to see how much tax subsidy those savings bankers were getting.

We also had a chart showing that Franklin could pay an additional 1.1 percent interest on savings deposits—i.e., more than the savings banks—if it were operated with the same tax and reserve advantages as savings banks.

The facts spoke for themselves more eloquently than any pleading could have done. The *New York Times* next day wrote:

In a presentation that evoked compliments from some opponents, Mr. Roth charged that tax advantages and freedom from reserve regulations now enjoyed by savings banks represented a "double standard" which, he said, siphons money away from the commercial banks and is inimical to the soundness of the economy.

"Come what may," Mr. Roth said, "whether we are hurt or the

savings banks—or no matter who—the issues must be decided on the basis of long-range principle—not short-term expediency.''

A few days later, a Glickman Corporation report, called *Real Estate Review*, said, ''New York money is going afield in greater quantities than ever before to locate sound real estate investments. . . . Soft spots in residential buying and construction [In New York] are being provoked chiefly by tight mortgage money.''

I hoped that what I read in the *Long Island Daily Press* would turn out to be true: ''The consensus in Nassau-Suffolk banking circles is that Roth gave the committee as much to think about that it will put off, for another year at least, approval of legislation permitting the New York City savings banks to set up branches in the two counties.''

That presentation elicited very strong, positive reactions from bankers all over the state. I was asked to give it again and again.

I was heartened by Horace (''Hap'') Flanagan, head of Manufacturers Trust, who set up a meeting for me with the heads of the clearinghouse banks of New York, twelve or fourteen of the most powerful bankers in the state.

The meeting was held in the Great Hall of the City of New York, which holds at least 500 people, and it seemed a bit silly to be facing so tiny a group in that big place.

Instead of sticking to the prepared presentation, I took advantage of having this captive audience of big bankers to tell them that there was a very strong conflict of interest in their relations with the savings banks. They were on the boards of directors of savings banks, and savings bankers were on their boards. They carried millions of dollars of savings-bank deposits. They were allowing their interlocking directorates and these large deposits to cause them to neglect going after the hundreds of millions of dollars in direct savings deposits that they should be getting. And they were neglecting their responsibility to the small depositors who did keep savings in their banks. They would lend money readily to big business, but they were doing almost nothing toward helping small depositors with personal loans, modernization loans, home mortgage loans, because they didn't want to compete with their savings-bank customers. I said that if these matters were brought up before a shareholders' meeting, they might be seriously embarrassed.

I don't think they liked this kind of talk, particularly. But they did react later, in changing some of their lending policies.

Of course, speaking this way did not make me popular. Charlie

Simon, of Salomon Brothers, who ran the investment seminars for the New York State Bankers Association, took me to task on this. "You're always preaching to bankers about how they should conduct themselves," he told me. "You speak to them like a father to a group of children, and I think you should get away from that a little bit."

I hadn't realized that, and I thanked him for telling me.

I made many speeches to bankers on the unfair competition of savings banks. These were greedy financial giants who, under the guise of protectors of the public, were actually harming the public. How?

Although these banks are called "mutual," the basic characteristic of mutuality is the exercise of ownership: Owners elect and manage the organization. "Mutual" savings banks are purported to be depositor-owned. But in effect no one owns a "mutual" savings bank; not the depositors—they have no voice in the management; not the trustees—their powers are limited, e.g., there is no clear-cut provision as to liquidation; not the state—its obligations are confined to enforcing the law. No one.

"Savings banks have been able to pursue ultraconservative policies throughout the years—at the expense of their depositors," I said. "As a result of retaining excess earnings, which could have been distributed to the depositors as dividends, enormous surplus funds have accumulated. These surplus funds, which at the end of last year amounted to $1.6 billion or $154 for each depositor in New York State alone, do no one any good; not the depositors; not the government; and not the public."

Just a few days before, John J. McCloy, head of the giant Rockefeller bank, Chase Manhattan, had said that he was considering asking the legislature to make New York City, Westchester, and Nassau into one banking district. This would have enabled Chase to open branches in any of these areas. And the week before, the other large New York bank, First National City, had announced that they were planning to set up a holding company that would enable them to own banks in other areas, the first of which would be the County Trust Company of White Plains, in Westchester County.

In 1956 the U.S. Congress had changed the national bank law to permit banks to set up holding companies through which they could buy up other banks, just as other businesses can merge. Under this law, First National City applied to the Federal Reserve—as banks must always do in mergers—to take over the County Trust Company of White Plains, the largest bank in Westchester.

L. J. Robertson, the deputy comptroller of the currency (now a governor of the Federal Reserve), told me that I ought to attend the hearing held in Washington by the Federal Reserve early in 1951 and oppose the merger.

I said, "No, I'm getting the reputation of fighting all the time, all over the state."

Robertson said, "You have no choice. If the merger goes through in Westchester, it will be a precedent for New York banks to take over Long Island banks."

So I testified, using First National City's own maps, that their buying County Trust would seriously lessen competition in Westchester. The Westchester bank was doing a fine job, held about half the deposits in the county, and could better serve its customers by establishing its own branches.

The application was later denied, but was still pending when I testified before the joint banking committee of the legislature the next day in New York City. There was a state freeze on bank holding companies, in spite of the new federal law, and even if the Federal Reserve approved the First National City merger the state law would have to be changed before it could take place.

It hadn't been difficult to oppose the merger to an audience of bankers. But now the challenge was to reduce the issues to concepts that legislators who weren't bankers could easily grasp.

The New York banks were making the point that they had grown only 20 percent during the preceding decade; while the Nassau banks had grown 200 percent, and the Westchester banks 100 percent. Of course, the New York banks had taken as a starting date a very high point when the government had sold an enormous quantity of bonds, and the proceeds were on deposit with their banks. But that wasn't so convincing as those percentages.

I went up into the attic and got out an old Chinese checkerboard my children had played with, added some holes, and painted it white. Divided it into three sections: New York, Nassau, Westchester.

At the hearing I said, "The New York banks are complaining that they haven't grown nearly as much, percentage-wise, as the surburban banks. Those percentages bother me. Now let's see what they had. Ten years ago, the New York banks held $37 billion, so we'll give them thirty-seven marbles. Nassau had $700 million, and Westchester $600 million, so we'll give them each a marble, although they're not entitled to a whole one.

"Now, Nassau has increased 200 percent; they get two more marbles, giving them a total of three. Westchester, with a 100-percent increase, gets one more marble, adding up to two. The poor New York banks have grown only twenty percent, but that adds seven marbles. Now they have forty-four. But they aren't satisfied. They want all the marbles.'' And I took the bag and poured them all out on the checkerboard.

The legislators applauded; they got the point.

These experiences with legislators made us realize that they would listen to reason, in spite of many powerful political and economic forces trying to corral their votes. And it was very important that someone keep in contact with them to make sure that they were properly informed.

Our victory in the fight over "savings" we took as a model: Get involved, don't leave it to others.

We began traveling to Albany to see our legislators. We had nothing to offer them except conversation, facts. But we got a wonderful reception, all the same. I was told often that this was the first time that a head of a sizable organization actually had come up there in person to talk to them.

We'd take hotel rooms and see senators and assemblymen. As many as a dozen officers of the bank would be up there at once; we were constantly traveling back and forth on the train. But we didn't lose much time away from the bank business. Actually, legislators do most of their work on Tuesday, Wednesday, and Thursday; they take long weekends. So we could concentrate on those midweek days and then come back to our own work. At the Friday-morning officer meetings, I'd report what had transpired that week.

Rather than interfering with our efficiency, the trips to Albany had the effect of stimulating us; morale was never higher among our people. We managed to cram enormous amounts of work into the remaining days of the week. We were growing at a fantastic rate; we were opening new branches, acquiring other banks, expanding all the while. Of course, the Albany work went on for only a few months of the year, but while it did, we had a lot of fun.

One of the officers who came up with us was Albert Sacco, a very likable person, but very serious-minded. We were going to a restaurant for lunch one day with some legislators, and I bought two hats of different sizes, one smaller and one larger than his regular size. Had the hatbands stamped A.S.S. instead of A.A.S. In the restaurant, I persuaded the hatcheck girl to switch hats.

Al Sacco at first refused to take it, since he had come in with a black hat and this one was brown. But finally he did, and was surprised to see that it fit.

In the hotel, I switched hats to the large hat. Before going to bed, Sacco tried it on. "My God," he said to his roommate, another vice-president named William H. Plock, "it fit, and now look!" It came down over his ears.

He ran out into the corridor to show me what had happened, letting the door shut behind him. He was in his pajamas, running down the corridor filled with schoolchildren who were in Albany to see the legislature adjourn the next day.

The next day we switched with the hat that fit him, but we put paper in the band. Now it was too small, stood up on top of his head. It took him several days to figure out what was happening; for a while he was convinced that his head was shrinking.

We also played more serious pranks on the savings bankers. I would frame my recommendations about savings banks into the form of laws. I would have bills drawn up and give them to Judge Pierce, head of the Senate Banking Committee, and he'd drop them in the hopper. That's a box in the Senate chamber. And he'd advise me whom to go to in the Assembly and do the same thing. This would keep our opponents off balance.

Nelson Rockefeller took office as governor of New York in January 1959, and immediately issued a warning that taxes would have to be raised.

We ran a full-page ad in the *New York Times* agreeing—but with the headline

> WHY TAX THE TAXI DRIVER,
> GOV. ROCKEFELLER?
> WHY NOT TAX ALL THE BANKS?

Instead of penalizing the small taxpayers, "why don't you get behind the proposed laws now before the New York State Legislature to tax the income of savings banks, and to tax 'flight money' investments to other states, as Massachusetts does?"

The savings bankers were confident that they had a real ally in Governor Rockefeller. Because the year before, his brother David, vice-chairman of Chase Manhattan, had come out in favor of an "Omnibus Bill" sponsored by the state banking department, which would permit banks to branch into suburbs—either directly or through establishing holding companies.

The average voter thought the Rockefellers were already so rich that Nelson would be free of the usual financial political pressures. But blood is thicker than votes. What voters didn't realize was that it might not be merely money, but power, that motivates such folks. Having been brought up in the midst of such enormous wealth, on a compound embracing thousands of acres in Westchester, some of the Rockefellers seemed to assume that the rest of New York State was also part of their fiefdom.

Needless to say, Governor Rockefeller did not respond to my ad, nor to a second several days later that showed how he could gain at least $250 million in increased revenues and savings for the state. In addition to $70 million from a tax on the savings banks "flight money" invested in other states, and a franchise tax on their total business, the ad suggested legislation to permit all savings banks to transform themselves into commercial banks, with equity divided between depositors and the state. ("Commercial banks won't like this added competition, but it's good for the economy of the state.") This would bring in about $120 million over the next ten years. The annual increase in personal income for New Yorkers, if the savings banks' capital put to work within the state to finance business and industry, would be incalculable.

The ad also urged additional legislation to force mutual banks to put at least 5 percent of their assets into New York State municipal and school bonds—at an estimated annual savings to municipalities and school districts of $25 million in underwriting and interest cost.

A few weeks later we had four bills to implement these suggestions put into the hopper, the key one being an act for "the conversion and dissolution of savings banks."

A group of savings bankers were lunching in a plush club up the hill in Albany, celebrating what they thought was their progress with the legislature on the Omnibus Bill, when their lobbyist came running in, wild-eyed. "Did you hear what happened today?" he shouted.

"What do you mean?" they asked, astonished. "Everything's going well."

He threw a fistful of bills on the table. "Look at these—there's a move to dissolve savings banks and have them converted into commercial banks!"

There was nothing calculated to cause more acute indigestion in a savings banker. Imagine—being taxed, giving up his privileges, being forced out of his soft berth into nose-to-nose competition with the hard-driving commercial banks. It was a frightful prospect.

This possibility still haunts the savings bankers, and I believe that the logic of circumstances will cause it to happen. There is no question that savings banks are a drag on the economy. They are about as relevant to today's social problems as Confederate money.

11 • Tax Equality

Our biggest battle with the savings banks was over the issue of tax equality. It was a nationwide contest; it went into hearings before the powerful House of Representatives Ways and Means Commmittee, where all tax legislation originates, and on the floor of the House; into Senate hearings and debates as well. It involved the largest bankers' organization in the country, the American Bankers Association, to which just about every commercial and savings bank belonged. The fight had been going on for years behind the scenes, led in the beginning mainly by Shirley Tark, a Chicago banker, head of the Bankers Committee for Tax Equality. But it came out into the open in 1957 and stayed on the national scene for the next twelve years.

As we have seen, savings banks had needed special privileges when they started but retained these long after they had become rich and powerful, especially since World War II. While commercial banks had expanded less than 50 percent during the ten years 1945–55, the savings banks had grown 150 percent.

Their most important single advantage was in paying almost no income tax. In fact, while commercial banks had for decades been taxed just like other businesses, only in 1951 had Congress passed a law designed to partially tax savings banks. The intention was to raise $120 million in taxes. Actually, the law raised a mere $6 million.

The reason was a loophole big enough for the entire mutual-savings-bank and savings-and-loan industry to slip through. The law permitted mutual banks to hold a reserve for bad debts equal to 12 percent of their total deposits, *after* dividends and interest were paid. That is, for every $1 billion of deposits, they could hold out $120 million tax-free. They were supposed to be taxed on their net income, but since this was offset against the reserve and was almost never as great as the latter, their effective tax liability was near zero: one-quarter of 1 percent on the average.

The only tax break commercial banks were permitted was a reserve of about 2½ percent against loans that were unsecured by any kind of government insurance. Above that, they paid the same tax as any other business.

The tax inequity was theoretically a ratio of 1 to 12.

In actual money it was 44 to 1, as follows: In New York State, commercial banks had $36 billion of assets and paid $50 million a year in income tax; savings banks had $16 billion and paid only $600,000 total tax. Many of the largest savings banks paid literally nothing at all.

Not satisfied with siphoning several billion dollars of savings from commercial banks (as we will show later), the savings banks became more aggressive. They took a number of steps to make themselves more competitive with commercial banks, while preserving their nearly tax-free status.

In September 1957 the Brooklyn Savings Bank began making long-term passbook loans. Until then, such loans had been limited by law to ninety days. But in September, when a savings-bank customer wanted to borrow money for a longer time, the bank simply endorsed the loan over to a commercial bank owned by savings banks: the Savings Bank Trust Company, it was called. The customer would pay 5 percent simple interest on the loan, while continuing to collect 3¼ percent compound interest on his savings. The Brooklyn Savings Bank also began another service competitive with commercial banks: savings-bank checks, which the depositor could request to pay bills.

Another, more ominous development was taking place nationally. Mutual savings banks, which were all state-chartered in seventeen states, succeeded in getting Abraham J. Multer, a Brooklyn Democrat, to introduce national legislation that would permit them to merge with savings and loan associations and to operate under national charters in all forty-eight states. They were also talking about expanding their services—as they had been doing steadily—to compete with commercial banks.

I believe in competition. But the essence of competition is equality of opportunity and responsibility. In competing with savings banks, commercial banks were at an enormous tax disadvantage—the mutuals could afford to pay more interest, and to offer all sorts of bonuses and free services. I would have liked nothing better than to see them compete with us completely, but on the same basis of taxation. Of course, the savings bankers did not want this—they wanted the new advantages while retaining their tax edge.

It was obvious that commercial bankers would have to fight back. But the only national organization of commercial banks—the American Bankers Association—also accepted savings banks as members. All of the 500 savings banks belonged to the ABA. The mutuals made up only 4 percent of the membership, but their influence was much greater than their numbers.

The major reason was that the big savings banks were situated in large cities like New York. They controlled huge amounts of deposits, and they kept large amounts with the big commercial banks who controlled the ABA. Further, there were often interlocking directorships between the two, so they could influence many ABA members to support their position. In some states, like Massachusetts, savings banks could own stock in commercial banks; they actually owned a controlling interest in some of the largest.

The Savings and Mortgages Division of the ABA had written to President Eisenhower back in 1955 that tax exemption "did and does give the Savings and Loan Associations an *unfair* [their italics] advantage in building up reserves, to meet which the [commercial] banks must either reduce dividend payments or . . . interest."

But the ABA leadership stated that year: "While the law remained most inequitable, the policy of the ABA has not been to actively seek a change, subjecting the Savings and Loan Association to further taxation, but rather to concentrate on the ABA's activities on obtaining more favorable treatment for banks . . . to seek . . . larger reserves for the banks rather than the reduction of reserves for the Savings and Loan Associations."

Now this would mean reducing the tax paid by commercial banks. The Treasury was interested in doing just the opposite. So this policy declaration was in effect a vote for tax *in*equality.

In their policy discussions the ABA mentioned only savings and loan associations, which were not members, but not the mutual savings banks which had the same unfair tax advantage but were members of the ABA.

I got in touch with Mr. Joseph C. Welman, the president of the ABA, a very honorable and decent individual, and pointed out how having savings banks as members weakened our organization. I suggested that since savings banks had their own exclusive national organization they should stick to that and not belong to ABA.

Welman said that in order to accomplish this, the ABA constitution would have to be amended by two-thirds of the voting members at the next ABA to bar the savings banks.

It was clear that the leadership of the ABA was not going to undertake this. It would have to be done from the outside. And since nobody else was attempting it, I decided to try.

On November 20, 1957, I sent an open letter to the chief executive officer of every one of the 13,407 commercial banks belonging to the ABA. In it I pointed out that savings banks were preparing national legislation to get themselves national charters.

> Who will lead our cause in Congress against the unfair tax-favored *national* competition that lies ahead? THE AMERICAN BANKERS ASSOCIATION. Naturally. BUT IT CANNOT DO THE JOB EFFECTIVELY AS LONG AS THE MUTUAL SAVINGS BANKS ARE ABA MEMBERS. . . . The savings banks have their own state and national associations *solely for savings banks*. COMMERCIAL BANKS NEED AN ASSOCIATION SOLELY FOR COMMERCIAL BANKS.
>
> There is but one answer. AMEND THE ABA CONSTITUTION TO MAKE THE ABA AN ASSOCIATION WHOSE OBJECT IS THE GENERAL WELFARE OF COMMERCIAL BANKING.

Along with the letter went two questions:

"Do you favor having the ABA an association whose object is the general welfare of commercial banking?

"Do you favor having article II of the constitution of the ABA amended to exclude savings banks from eligibility for ABA membership?"

This made news in the financial press. The next day, Mr. Welman felt compelled to state his position on the Multer bill that was pending in the House of Representatives. Welman said that "there was no doubt in my mind" that the ABA would oppose a bill to establish a dual-charter (state and federal) system for savings banks. According to the *New York Times* of November 22, 1957, "Mr. Welman's observation was in response to a call by a commercial banker, Arthur T. Roth . . . to expel savings banks from the ABA." (Of course, Welman's statement was only his personal opinion. The ABA had taken no position and no action on the Multer bill.)

"Mr. Welman disowned the Roth survey, declaring that the ABA had no connection with it and had not approved its questions."

The next day two savings bankers, Daniel T. Rowe of Brooklyn and Charles R. Diebold of Buffalo, weighed in with an attack. Rowe said that I was "the greatest single obstacle to the sorely needed revision of the banking law of the state of New York." And Diebold said (correctly) that I "feared the expansion of savings banks and New York City commercial banks into my area."

But while drawing fire from Welman and the savings bankers, my letter was attracting nearly 100 percent support among commercial bankers all over the country. Many took the time to write letters expressing strong support for expelling the savings banks from the ABA.

One letter writer—H. Clyde Holmes, president of the Edgewater National Bank—was certain that "the big city banks had not and would not do anything for the county banks if such action would in any way be construed as favoring those correspondent banks over the mutual savings institutions." And he enclosed a $25 check as a contribution to our campaign.

Within a few days we had received 352 replies, 351 favoring our position. The only "no" was qualified: One banker wanted first to make sure that mutual savings banks paid taxes, later he would see about expelling them.

Daniel Rowe continued to attack me, saying that my "disregard for the public interest is exceeded only by [my] disregard for the facts." I quoted this in an advertisement in the *American Banker* on November 26, showing that Franklin National's mere $379 million in deposits generated $2.3 million of federal income tax; while the total of more than $21 *billion* in all FDIC-insured savings banks generated only $1.3 *million* of tax.

Bruce Wood Hall, president of the Hempstead Bank, wrote to the *American Banker* supporting our fight, but expressing surprise that we had to go to all this trouble. When the savings banks induced Multer to introduce his bill, "they served warning that they meant to pursue a course damaging to the other 97% of the [ABA] membership. At that moment, they were in honor bound to withdraw voluntarily," Mr. Hall wrote.

R. E. Gormley of the Georgia Savings Bank & Trust Company stated in a letter that he had long recognized the impossibility of getting any useful action out of the ABA and had been working through two other smaller groups: the Bankers Committee for Tax Equality—an offshoot of an organization trying to get tax equality for all types of business—and the Independent Bankers Association, made up of the smaller banks throughout the country. "Frankly, I must say that I think you are shooting at the moon," he wrote. "I am afraid that [the ABA] is too dues-conscious to relinquish any of its membership." The savings banks' dues were $88,000; the commercial banks paid more than $2,100,000 to the ABA.

I didn't believe it was the dues that influenced the ABA; it was the interlocking directorships and the cozy business relationships between the big city commercial banks and the savings banks.

On December 2, I sent an open letter to Mr. Welman, pointing out that 2,832 replies to our poll had been received in one week. Of these, 2,782—more than 98 percent—had voted yes on both questions; only 14 had voted no, and 36 had split their votes. "Never before, to my knowledge, have so many of the banks of America expressed with such unanimity . . . their opinion of matters of such importance," I wrote.

Those polled had authorized submission of the results to the ABA "with the request that the ABA take immediate and appropriate action." I invited an audit of the questionnaires and concluded by saying, "I respectfully request an immediate audience with you or appropriate committee to learn how the ABA plans to carry out the expressed will of its membership. This is a magnificent opportunity to make the ABA the dynamic organization its membership wants it to be."

On December 7, Mr. Welman replied that the Federal Legislative Committee of the ABA had (at last) voted to oppose the Multer bill, and that this committee and the Administrative Committee had considered my proposal to expel the savings banks but "believe [this] is neither necessary nor desirable." If the ABA "kicked out" one kind of bank, this might lead to bickering among other groups. It was a specious argument, as there were no such basic tax conflicts between other kinds of banks.

During the week of December 6–13, we placed the first of a series of advertisements in the *American Banker*, a daily paper. The ads were made up entirely of quotes, identified only by geographical sources, from the hundreds of unsolicited letters received along with the questionnaires.

Welman replied to my request for an appointment with him saying that he would be out of town for several weeks, and suggesting that if I wanted to discuss my proposal I ought to see Mr. Merle Selecman, executive vice-president of the ABA.

I went to see Selecman, asking that top staff people and available committee members be present. But only one other ABA person joined the meeting, as an observer. I was told the ABA planned to do nothing about my poll. I called it a brush-off, which it was, and decided to let the banking world know what happened.

By this time, 3,320 banks had replied, and 3,253 supported our position. There were 24 noes and 43 split votes.

I followed up with a second poll on December 26, using the two original questions plus a third: "Do you favor the ABA taking aggressive action to tax the mutual savings banks and savings and loan associations the same as stockholder-owned banks?"

As the answers began to roll in, we asked the William A. Wood polling firm to analyze them in January 1958. On the basis of the first 3,700 returns, and more than 500 telephone follow-ups of those who had not replied, using standard projection and weighting techniques, the firm concluded that our poll showed that 78 percent of the commercial banks were in favor of tax equality—about 10,000 banks. The total negative vote would be about 2 percent.

It was obvious that the ABA was not representing the will of its members. And this was no academic matter. Tax equality was beginning to become an important issue in the Congress, and the testimony of bankers and their organizations would determine what kind of laws were written and passed. The ABA's position, based on not antagonizing its savings-bank members, was to give lip service to tax equality but to do nothing to forward it. Instead they suggested to some state banking groups who were for tax equality that they soft-pedal the issue, that it could be managed behind the scenes.

They spoke softly, walked softly, and carried no stick at all.

In July 1957, Congressmen Thomas B. Curtis of Missouri, himself a director in his state's largest savings and loan associations for seventeen years, introduced a bill designed to rectify some of the tax inequity. His bill would have reduced the bad-debt reserve provision of the mutual institutions from 12 to 5 percent, and would have limited their tax credit to dividend payments of 3 percent. The net result of the bill would have been not *tax equality* but more *equitable* taxation. And it would have brought in about $165 million more income taxes to both states and federal governments from the mutuals.

It was not a perfect solution, but a sensible one.

This was the relative financial position of mutuals and commercials at the time.

	U.S. Commercial Banks	U.S. Mutual Banks & Savings & Loan Institutions
Dividends:	$616,890,000	$1,802,515,000
Surplus & reserves:	599,835,000	517,555,000
Income tax:	814,636,000	18,448,000
Net income:	$2,031,361,000	$2,338,518,000

(Commercial banks paid 44 times as much income tax as the mutuals.)

Hearings were to be held on the Curtis bill before the House Ways and Means Committee in January 1958. I was to testify, representing a special committee of the New York State Bankers Association, which had made a study of banking in the state. It had been a persuasive, factual study, but experience in testifying before groups of experts on financial matters had taught me that reason and facts did not always prevail. Sometimes you needed a bit of drama.

A few months before, I'd testified at a meeting studying tax questions of financial institutions. All the big government agencies were there— the Fedreal Reserve Board, the comptroller of the currency, the Federal Deposit Insurance Corporation, Treasury Department, and others. I observed that the witnesses read long and complicated statements while the officials sat there and yawned, paying little or no attention.

I determined to keep them awake. When it was my turn, I got up and said, "Gentlemen, you've all heard of the great Bowery Savings Bank, with over a billion dollars of assets. How much federal income tax do you think they paid in the past ten years?"

I took a quarter out of my pocket and flipped it so that it bounced on the wooden table. It made quite a racket at that sleepy hearing— in those days, quarters were made of silver and they really rang out. Instantly, everybody sat up and looked around. I had captured their attention.

"Not so much as that two-bit piece did they pay in federal income taxes in the past decade," I said, "that giant, billion-dollar institution.

"And you've all heard of the huge Dime Savings Bank. Assets of more than $800 million. Do you know how much federal income tax the giant Dime Savings Bank paid during the past ten years?''

I flipped a dime in the air.

"The Dime hasn't paid out one of their thin dimes in federal taxes since 1948," I said. The dime didn't ring as loudly as the quarter, but by this time I had made my point.

The day before I was scheduled to testify before the Ways and Means Committee I sat in the audience and watched the proceedings. Each witness was seated at a table, and the table was some distance below the level of the desk of the committee members. The effect was to diminish the witnesses; the committee physically over-shadowed them like judges in a courtroom looking down on the proceedings.

There were several closets in the committee room. When the hearing ended, I went through them and found a lectern. I took it out, dusted it off with my handkerchief, and moved it onto the floor, next to the witness chair.

Wilbur Mills, the chairman, smiled a little when he saw me standing up at the lectern the next morning. "Mr. Roth, wouldn't you be more comfortable if you were seated?" he asked.

"No, thank you, Mr. Chairman," I replied.

Standing, I could look those fellows in the eye.

I had a long statement—sixty pages long—that I offered in evidence. It was much too long to read. Besides, I knew that I could emphasize the key points in my spoken testimony.

The main part of my statement was the report by the special committee of the New York State Bankers Association. I had been a member of that committee of eight, which included men from the two largest banks in the state—First National City and Chase Manhattan.

The key finding in the report was "The existing tax discrimination between mutual institutions and commercial banks should be eliminated. . . .

"Considering the tremendous size of the [mutual] institutions, their economic power, and the fact that they can no longer be considered as primarily philanthropic, they should bear their fair share of the tax burden. . . ."

New York's commercial banks paid $862 million in federal income taxes in 1954—equal to 42.7 percent of their combined net income. The net operating income of New York State mutual savings banks had gone up from $463 million in 1954 to $584 million in 1956, but their total income tax had gone *down* from $2.9 million in 1954 to only $253 thousand in 1956—equal to only one-quarter of 1 percent.

Typically, the pro–savings bank forces on the committee attacked me—not my testimony, but me personally, and my bank.

First was Mr. Forand. He put into the record the fact that at Franklin our savings deposits had risen from $31 million in 1950 to $178 million in 1956. This was true; about half of it had come from consolidations with other banks.

FORAND: That is a growth of about 550 percent.
ROTH: Yes, that is right.
FORAND: I think you ought to be congratulated on that.

And he went on to read into the record a statement from our 1954 annual report:

. . . at the beginning of 1940, for example, the bank's stock, then having a par of $50, was quoted from the market at $40, the stock with a registered par at $10 was being traded at $95 per share. . . . The purchase of 100 shares on January 1, 1940, at the then market price of $40 would have represented an investment of $4,000. On December 31, 1954, that 100 shares would have, through stock split-ups and stock dividend, become 13,223 shares valued at $1,256,285.

FORAND: Personally, I don't think you have done very badly and I don't think you have too much ground for complaint. . . .

This was totally irrelevant, of course. I wasn't just representing my bank, but the state Bankers Association. And our bank's success was no rebuttal to the very detailed figures showing the enormous growth of mutual savings institutions practically free of taxes, at the expense of the commercial banks—which was the issue.

Franklin had had a tremendous decade, and was, in 1958, for the first time among the top fifty banks in the country as selected by *Fortune* magazine. We were fiftieth in assets, but *number one in earnings* in relation to capital. Our ratio was over 18 percent; the closest any other bank came was 15 percent. The average of all banks was only about 10 percent.

Naturally, we were proud of this record. But because it was atypical, it undercut the value of my testimony. Wilbur Mills told me privately that our success was a handicap when testifying against abuses that were hurting banks. After all, if they weren't hindering *our* bank, what right had we to complain?

After Forand, Representative Eugene Keogh of Brooklyn came in to pitch for the savings banks. He was, as he freely admitted, a member of the board of trustees of the East New York Savings Bank. He brought up all his guns. First he showed that savings banks had been exempted from income tax before 1951, and that knowing this I had freely chosen a career in commercial banking. Then he started in on Franklin— how successful we were, how few savings banks there were in Nassau (only one), and Suffolk (about four or five). He slid by the fact that the huge New York savings banks were advertising for deposits in all our local papers and in the big-city papers, which our residents read, too, since a great many were commuters.

> KEOGH: So you cannot contend that the growth of your institution in the last eighteen years has been adversely affected by the tax advantages of any mutual institution in Nassau or Suffolk County.
> ROTH: I would say it has been.
> KEOGH: How would that be?
> ROTH: By the very fact that they pay a higher rate of interest dividend than we are permitted to pay.

Keogh then asked how many times in the past forty years the rate of interest had been the same in both types of institutions.

> ROTH: We found that during the early Twenties the interest dividend paid by commercial banks was almost exactly equal to that of the savings banks. . . . The reason for that, sir, is the fact that taxes were more nearly equal then. . . . Our tax burden was very small. Today it is very big.

Keogh maneuvered all over the playing field to try to find a weak spot in our story.

> KEOGH: When did the Chase Manhattan announce its three-percent rate on savings deposits?
> ROTH: They announced that the day after the Federal Reserve Board allowed them to go to three percent, which was December 1956.
> KEOGH: Do you have any idea by how much the savings deposits in that institution increased during the year 1957?
> ROTH: I saw the figures. It seemed to be a couple of hundred million dollars. Of course, you must remember that in a commercial bank, whenever we raise the interest rate, people take money out of their checking accounts and they transfer it to their savings accounts.

KEOGH: Will you admit that the reverse process also follows?
ROTH: Would you explain that to me?
KEOGH: Withdrawals are made from mutual types of institutions to be put in the savings deposits of commercial banks when the interest rates in the latter are more attractive?

This was a red herring. It had been decades since any commercial bank could pay as much interest as a savings bank. Currently, savings banks were paying 3.25 percent; commercial banks were limited to paying 3 percent, by the Federal Reserve.

When I'd disposed of this question, Keogh immediately went on to other matters—spending some time, of course, on the size of Franklin National. Almost all of it was irrelevant to the issue at hand—tax equality. But when he got into that question, he enabled me to bring out the following:

ROTH: We [commercial banks] are permitted to set up a tax-free reserve and what is referred to as a reserve for bad debts . . . of about two and a half percent of their nongovernment loans . . . those loans that are not insured in any way by the United States government. Now, in our particular case, our noninsured loans are the equivalent of about forty percent of our deposits.

So 2.5 percent of forty percent is the equivalent of about one percent of our deposits . . . before we pay income taxes. Under the Curtis bill, the savings and loans and the mutual savings banks would be permitted to set aside five percent. We know it is not full equality, but we know that it will have the effect of virtually taxing all of them.

KEOGH: That is not my point, but I am not going to press it.

In the printed record many remarks by Mr. Keogh were edited out of the final record. Congressmen have the right to do that, to create any kind of impression they want. It is one of the many ways legislators lord it over witnesses. One may win an argument in front of a committee, but it may not seem that way in the record; and even if it does, this doesn't mean that you've changed the legislator's mind. Obviously, the fact that Mr. Keogh acknowledged himself to be a savings-bank trustee looked good on the record—he was being honest, forthright—but he was still talking like and acting like a savings-bank trustee. He wasn't being swayed by the merits of the commercial-bank argument.

When the public hearings ended for the day, he called me over and said, "As long as commercial bankers don't speak with a single voice, they're never going to get the legislation they want."

"What do you mean?" I asked.

"Well, you testified one way for the commercial banks. But the ABA says something different. And the Bankers Committee for Tax Equality speaks only for a small number of the banks. And the Independent Bankers Association [the organization of small banks] is another splinter group."

Keogh was telling me that the Curtis bill would never get out of committee.

I said, "Thank you, Mr. Congressman."

By then we had received well over 4,000 replies to our questionnaire, and the percentages were holding up—about 98 percent of replies were favorable to tax equality.

Yet the American Bankers Association was ignoring this nearly unanimous expression of opinion. They were not representing what this great majority of their members felt were their basic economic interests. It seemed that there would be only one way to make them responsive to this opinion and those interests. That was to follow through on the sentiments expressed by the commercial bankers of the country and institute formal proceedings to amend the ABA constitution so as to exclude mutual savings banks from membership.

12 • Campaign to Expel the Savings Banks

On July 10, I submitted our amendment to the ABA constitution to the executive manager of the ABA:

> Words underlined to be added to Section 1, Article ii of the Constitution:
> Sec. 1 Any National Bank, State *Commercial* Bank, *stockholder-owned* Savings Bank, Trust Company, Private Banker, Banking Firm, or Branch of any such institution, any chapter of the American Institute of Banking, and the secretary of any State Bankers Association . . . may become a member of this Association. . . .

This new wording would automatically exclude any mutual savings bank from joining the ABA, although it would admit those few savings institutions (mostly in California) that were stockholder-owned.

Welman and his vice-president Lee P. Miller (who would be the next ABA president) issued a statement saying that they were opposed to the amendment, but would leave the decision up to the membership.

William A. Lyon, president of the National Association of Mutual Savings Banks (and of New York's Dry Dock Savings Bank), reacted more harshly.

> It is not clear whether Mr. Roth is trying to unseat the President and Council of the ABA and take over its control or whether he is merely adding another sordid chapter to the tale of his defamation of savings banking.
> In any case, he is doing the cause of deposit banking a disservice by continually displaying his phobias and obsessions. I hope someday to see a really responsible statement by Mr. Roth.

The *American Banker* pointed out that "the savings banks can also count on the support of many large commercial banks known to be opposed to any discriminatory action against the savings banks and a host of smaller banks. That the latter group exists was evidenced recently when they voiced criticism of the ABA stand favoring passage of the Curtis bill [for tax equality]. . . . Another element in the savings banks' favor is the considerable amount of dues they pay into the Association."

The newspaper also said that the amendment would probably be supported by the Independent Bankers Association and the Bankers League for Tax Equality, as well as some midwestern state bankers' associations.

"Thus, the elements for a knock-down, drag-out fight at the forthcoming ABA convention in Chicago are in the making," it stated.

Until that point, I had been carrying on a one-man crusade against the savings banks and the ABA's do-nothing leadership from our bank on bank stationery. Now a real campaign was under way that required active votes; so I ordered letterheads that read, "Committee for an Effective ABA to Accomplish Tax Equality." There was no committee— just our bank officers and myself. The words *tax equality* were also printed in blue on white within a blue circle, also containing a red ℞ prescription symbol underneath. In the margin was a three-point program:

- ABA to adopt a policy advocating tax equality (accomplished February 6, 1958)
- Commercial banks to have their own national organization dedicated to the welfare of stockholder and privately owned banking, by adopting the resolution of the September ABA General Convention, eliminating mutual savings banks from membership
- ABA to coordinate efforts with other organizations striving for tax equality among financial institutions.

On the new stationery, I sent a four-page letter to 4,000 commercial banks that had responded affirmatively to our poll—including 1,500 commercial banks in a radius around Chicago where the ABA convention was to take place. Two forms were enclosed, one a straw vote on the amendment, and the second a report form on which they could list the results of contacting seven banks of their own selection (which we suggested they do) and asking these seven to go to Chicago and vote for the admendment, plus some detailed information on desirable voting procedures such as:

> Secret ballot. No proxies permitted. Voters must be registered at the convention to be eligible to vote. All members in good standing may vote. Banks with branches for which ABA membership dues have been paid are entitled to one vote for each branch, provided that an individual branch officer is present to vote.

These stipulations were extremely important. The last time there had been a floor fight at an ABA convention, 9,572 delegates were registered but only 1,847 were certified to vote.

There would be room for only about 2,300 people in the auditorium of the Conrad Hilton Hotel in Chicago, where the convention was to be held, so a voice vote could not possibly represent the thousands of delegates expected. But in a letter to member banks explaining voting procedures, Joseph Welman said, "Mr. Roth, in a circular letter dated August 11, stated that the voting will be by secret ballot. I have heretofore informed Mr. Roth and others that this method of voting will be recommended to the general convention, but that this, nevertheless, is a matter for determination by the general convention."

This was a signal that the leadership was going to do everything possible to see that its position—against the amendment—would prevail.

Ray Gidney, then U.S. comptroller of the currency, confirmed this to me. "Arthur, you have gone to the well once too often," he said. "You have taken on some difficult fights, and won. But this time you are going to be badly beaten." He said the predictions were that we would get only 5 to 7 percent of the vote for our amendment.

I couldn't believe this, with the tremendous straw poll supporting us. But Ray was a levelheaded, honest person—it would have been foolhardy to write his judgment off. And if he was right, and we were defeated so soundly, any future cause we undertook might be seriously handicapped.

So the officers of Franklin National immediately got busy. We laid out a schedule of letters and telegrams, and a strategy for the vote. And we set up in the basement of our bank a special telephone switchboard, the first one with direct dialing to every part of the country. We put our officers to work in shifts, phoning all the key banks, asking them to try to get to the convention and to be sure to pay their dues.

We would saturate an area. One day our officers called so many

Chicago banks that all trunk lines to Chicago were tied up. The phone company traced the traffic jam to our switchboard; they asked us please to spread our calls geographically so as not to impede other users—and we complied.

The other side reacted swiftly. The Savings Bank Association of New York mailed a letter to their members urging them to use every vote at their command against our amendment. The letter, signed by Kilgore MacFarlane, Jr., and George M. Penny, reported that the ABA Administrative and Legislative Committees had voted "unanimously" against supporting my amendment. They pointed out that members in good standing could vote—and this included every branch represented by an officer. A bank with 100 branches would have 100 votes. But no proxies could be used.

I responded in a letter to these two gentlemen, saying in part:

> Were any mutual savings bankers at the [committee] meeting? Did their presence embarrass and influence others?
>
> Surely, a unanimous decision must seem as strange to others as it does to me. Does our Supreme Court vote unanimously? Does the Federal Reserve Board? Are there not usually minority and dissenting opinions in almost every case?
>
> May I remind you that at the time the so-called "unanimous" decision was reached by the ABA joint committee, I had received 3,500 responses from ABA member banks favoring exclusion of mutual savings banks from the ABA. . . .

MacFarlane and Penny had termed "irrelevant" my contention that tax equality was the key issue. They said savings banks had been members of the ABA for eighty-two years.

"Times have changed," I wrote. I pointed out that "mutual savings banks had become members of ABA many years ago, when there was little difference in tax rates between commercial and savings banks," and gave a tabular summary of this:

FEDERAL TAX RATES ON INCOME 1909–1958

Year	Commercial Banks	Mutual Savings Banks
1909	1%	None
1925	13%	None
1940	37%	None
1950	42%	None
1951	52%	*
1958	52%	*

*No tax payable until surplus exceeds 12 percent of deposits.

"Now," I said, "the need for tax equality is one of the most pressing issues of the day and the underlying reason why ABA's constitution should be amended to give the nation's commercial banks their own national organization—*to fight for tax equality*, just as your national association of mutual savings banks is fighting against tax equality."

The ABA leadership pretended to be objective. This was exposed as a sham when John Adikes, president of the Jamaica (N.Y.) Savings Bank as well as president of the ABA's savings and mortgage division, told the *New York World Telegram & Sun* that the fight against the savings banks was "only a battle between one man and the entire ABA leadership. . . . The one man . . . is Arthur T. Roth . . . a longtime foe of savings banking in this state, whose tactics at Albany have been widely held to be a chief stumbling block to passage of legislation the mutuals have regarded as necessary for their healthy growth."

When the Executive Council of the Massachusetts Bankers Association voted to oppose the amendment to expel the savings banks from the ABA, I wrote to Hildreth Auer, association president:

> Captive banking has clanked its chains!
> What else could your Council do? You are controlled by mutual savings banks.
> All of the elected officers of the Massachusetts Bankers Association, or their respective superior officers, serve as trustees of mutual savings banks. Five of the directors of the Malden Trust Company, of which you are president, Mr. Auer, are also trustees of mutual savings banks. . . . Your commercial bank boards of directors are interlocked with trustees of mutual savings banks. Mutual savings banks wield the influence of their deposits with commercial banks.

And I reminded him of the fact that some of Massachusetts's major commercial banks were dominated by savings banks who owned their stock: The First National, fifteenth-largest bank in the country, was 24 percent owned by savings banks; the National Shawmut 31 percent owned; the Second Bank–State Street Trust 72 percent owned; the Merchants National 70 percent owned; and the Rockland 52 percent owned.

> These statistics illustrate the bondage which is being suffered by commercial banks in Massachusetts and New England. There ought to be a law against it! We herewith appeal to your Governor and State Legislature to initiate an investigation of this stifling of competition and free-will.
> The action by the Executive Council . . . in opposing the ABA amendment brings captive banking to light, shows how mutual savings banks can influence decisions to their own advantage, and proves that as long as mutual savings banks are in the ABA they will block ABA from becoming effective to accomplish tax-equality.

I suggested that the "captive banks" in Massachusetts examine their conscience and vote "yes" at Chicago, "even though their captors will instruct them how to vote. . . . You have nothing to lose but your chains!"

A technical change was made in the wording of the amendment so that it could not be interpreted ambiguously: "Renewal membership shall be limited to those that may qualify for membership."

Then Kilgore MacFarlane wrote me a three-page letter attacking my motives, and released it to the *American Banker* on September 12, 1958. The letter asked and answered a number of loaded questions—the main thrust of all the arguments was *ad hominem*: Was I claiming that the tax laws were hurting my banks when Franklin had more than $500 million in assets and had grown so fast in recent years? Was my attack on savings banks only a diversionary tactic, part of my giant design to "prevent any disturbance of [my] private banking domain in Nassau County?" Wasn't I also attacking commercial banks who wanted to intrude into Nassau? And what about a group of eight banks, of which Franklin was one, that had joined forces to seek national business—wasn't this a first step toward setting up a bank holding company, when the laws would permit?

As I told the *Journal-American* three days later (September 15, 1958) in response to their inquiry, these issues were local and extraneous—I had made no secret of my attitude toward large banks intruding into Nassau in the past. But this was diversionary to the main thrust of the ABA amendment, which was to get commercial bankers throughout the country united on an issue that concerned their welfare.

MacFarlane accused me—again by question—of having plans to throw other banks out of the ABA after the savings banks were expelled, and of making the organization over in my image. He claimed that I wanted to "run the ABA, choose its members and establish its policies."

The fact was, I had often been offered positions in the ABA and had consistently refused them, because I wanted to be free to cricitize the organization. And I never did accept any position in the ABA. The only connection I ever had with it was as a lecturer in an ABA-sponsored course on banking at Rutgers University.

My sole concern with the group was to have it represent the interests of commercial banks from coast to coast.

One paragraph in MacFarlane's open letter stated: "If the Comptroller of the Currency had not disapproved your recent attempt to merge with another large bank in Nassau County, the bank resulting from that merger would today hold about 64 percent of all the commercial banking resources of Nassau."

As John M. Greene, the financial columnist of the *World Telegram & Sun*, reported later, just before the convention, "This brought a reply from Ray M. Gidney, the Comptroller of the Currency, who notified MacFarlane that he was 'completely mistaken' and that he had 'not received or had occasion to consider any recent application of the Franklin National Bank to merge with another large bank in Nassau." MacFarlane apologized in a telegram to Gidney.

I had been getting a great deal of personal publicity as fallout from the campaign. This was inevitable since it was as had been said "a one-man fight." That is, while giving verbal support in private, other bankers were content to leave the public controversy to me.

A savings and loan officer wrote to the *American Banker* complaining, "For a long time now you have given a man named Roth a H – – – [sic] of a lot of free personal advertising. There must be some better subject for your headlines."

The publication noted that "six months ago, when the ouster project was beginning to take form, we repeatedly appealed to officials of the savings banks associations to give us an opportunity to tell their side of the matter. We wrote letters to the more than 500 mutual savings banks offering the freedom of our news columns to any banker who might care to answer or attack the Roth ideas. The response was uniformly that the Association headquarters wanted to do the speaking and, from it, the response was that it had nothing to say at the time.''

Business Week (September 20) summed up the struggle in a story that began, ''In Chicago next week, the usually decorous annual convention of the American Bankers Assn. promises to explode into a public row.'' They didn't give me much chance of succeeding, although the talk was now that the amendment wouldn't get more than 40 to 50 percent of the votes—a far cry from the 6 or 7 percent predicted a month before by Ray Gidney. So the campaign had made an impact. ''*Newsweek* said, whether we won or lost, the campaign was ''stirring up banking sentiment to get the bad-debt reserve for commercial banks boosted.'' Which was not really my intention; there were inequities in that situation, however, which we would explore and rectify later on.

On September 20 the *Chicago Sun-Times* reported that six state banking associations were in favor of keeping the mutuals in the ABA, but three were going to vote against them. ''A registration for the convention of more than 10,000, largest since 1922, is expected,'' they wrote. Howard F. Sammon of the Forest Park National Bank said, ''It is going to be a scrap and there's plenty of hot feeling for and against.''[10]

Many bankers felt it was uncouth, almost indecent, for their colleagues to squabble in public. But it seemed the only way to bring the issue to the attention of all. Too long had it been buried in logrolling committees by accommodating executives. Shut off from light and air, it had begun to fester; the only way to cure it was to expose it.

The weekend before the convention opened, leading newspapers from coast to coast were carrying stories about it; ordinarily it attracted little attention. The *New York Times* wrote, ''Mr. Roth has stirred up what has been billed as the biggest back-fence brawl in the history of American banking.''

On Monday, September 22, the day the convention opened, we ran a full-page advertisement in the *American Banker* in the form of an open letter to the ABA Executive Council, which was meeting that day. The letter urged them to vote for the amendment since they were representing thousands of banks that would not appear at the convention to vote for themselves, but who had voted for the amendment 3,500 strong in our straw poll, and who would have so voted by proxy at the convention if it were possible to do so.

The Franklin contingent had checked into a suite at the Conrad Hilton Hotel in Chicago, where the convention was being held, several days before it opened. We distributed numbers of paper stickers in the form of the blue and white circle calling for tax equality. If you peeled the back off, there was an adhesive that would stick to any surface. We had a good time slapping them on the backs of ABA executives, and savings bankers, such as Earl Schwulst, and on John Adikes—John got very mad at me for that. And we had huge signs all over the lobby and the auditorium, saying "Tax Equality."

We sent an urgent telegram to all ABA members within driving distance of Chicago:

> THIS IS PERSONAL PLEA . . . PASSAGE IS NIP AND TUCK. NEED TWO-THIRDS FAVORING TO WIN. BIG MUTUALS IN EAST WORKING TO DE-FEAT MEASURE. INDEPENDENT MIDWEST BANKS HOLD KEY TO PASSAGE. PLEASE MAKE SACRIFICE AND DRIVE TO CHICAGO TO VOTE YES ON AMENDMENT.

We were hoping that the small banks would heed our plea; for we were certainly being opposed by the big banks—mutuals as well as many commercials. Never before in the history of the ABA had so many branches paid their $25 dues and showed up to vote. Banks with multiple branches were bringing their officers in by the score. The atmosphere was feverish.

As the leader of the drive to oust savings banks, I was the target for press interviews. I told William Clark of the *Chicago Daily Tribune* that mutual savings banks were phoning commercial banks from whom they bought mortgages, and threatening to stop doing business with any banks that did not vote against my amendment. I had plenty of evidence that this was so, although the National Association of Mutual Savings Banks denied it.

I also told Clark that the mutuals were threatening to close out their deposits in banks not supporting them; likewise denied—but neverthe-less true. He had some fun with a mixed metaphor I made about the ABA's ineffectuality in Washington tax matters: "The ABA has no juice because it has been carrying water on both shoulders and straddling issues for years."

In the same story, I was amused to read that William A. Lyon, president of the Savings Bank Association, denied that his group had a

Washington lobby. He might get away with this in Chicago, but in Washington he would have been hooted out of the room. It was known that the savings banks had one of the most effective and active lobbies in town, which was why they had been able to set and maintain their tremendous tax advantage for so many years.

Lyon became increasingly shrill and angry as the vote drew near; it was plain he was worried. In a speech to savings bankers, he called the possibility that mutuals might be voted out of the ABA a "witches trial" and a "lynching bee" and said that the ABA without the mutuals would lose support in Congress, since it would no longer represent all banking.

"Booting savings banks out as members will not solve any tax questions," Lyon said, "but it might satisfy some desires to be disruptive, to commit an act of violence, and to shove and gouge one's way to a prominent position in the banking world." I wonder whom he was referring to.

Sunday we ran a full-page advertisement in the *American Banker* titled "SUNDAY MORNING Prelude to the Great Convention?" which quoted some of the strong support from bankers all over the country. (We deleted names, but all quotations came from personal letters, which I had in bound volumes.) It concluded by saying that "merit is on our side. There is deep comfort in knowing that stockholder banks throughout the United States have said '*We are for the amendment*' over nine thousand times since the program began last November."

The *American Banker* reported that it was "impossible to cross the lobby of the Conrad Hilton Hotel without being buttonholed a dozen times by banker acquaintances who ask what is going to be the outcome of the expulsion drive."

Many newspapers noted that President Welman, who would have liked to discuss larger economics subjects, was constantly forced to talk about the amendment. It may have gotten under his skin, because he opened the convention with what the *New York Herald Tribune* called "a highly unbankerish bang," saying that the debate over the amendment was "definitely detracting from the public image of banking. . . ." The issue wasn't tax equality, he said, but whether the savings banks had exerted "undue influence" in the ABA—which, he said, they hadn't. I was quoted as saying that after the savings banks were expelled, the next target would be their captive commercial banks, particularly in New England and in New York.

Lyon held a press conference, where he "took exception to Mr. Roth's use of the word 'captive' to describe 'relationship of commercial and savings banks working side by side.' "

The Executive Council considered the amendment before submitting it to the convention. They voted against it, 74–16. At least it wasn't unanimous.

There was considerable debate before the convention: Eleven delegates spoke, six against, five in favor. One of the former was Fred F. Florence of the Republic National Bank of Dallas, a former ABA president. Florence had written to me supporting the drive for tax equality. He had voted in the mail poll for the amendment. But he told me at the convention that he had voted against it in the Executive Committee because he felt that the issue was tearing the ABA apart. It was better to settle such things quietly within the organization, he said. And he made a strong plea for handling the matter that way, in front of the convention.

L. M. Schwartz, president of the Citizens State Bank of Paola, Kansas, who called himself "a little country boy," made a plea for "Grandma. By Grandma I mean the mutual savings banks. Grandma has lived with us a long time . . . has lots of friends and some friends that we need, in legislative halls and other places. [This seemed to undercut Mr. Lyon's contention that the savings bank had no Washington lobby.] Grandma has a lot of influence," and so on. But, he said, "a few of the boys in the family have said: 'Well, Grandma is getting too fat. Let's throw her out.' . . .

"If Grandma is getting too fat, let's put her on a diet. But let's leave her plate on the table. Let's not throw her out." (applause)

Another small-town banker, Harry E. Strand of the Cashton (Iowa) Bank, said, "A little while ago we heard from another small-town banker an awful lot about Grandma; that Grandma eats at our table and Grandma sleeps in our bed.

"There is another Aesop Fable about Little Red Riding Hood. I would like to recall that Little Red Riding Hood's Grandma wasn't what she seemed, was she?" (applause)

Mr. Strand went on to say that he had appeared before the Ways and Means Committee for the Curtis bill, and found very intensive opposition from the savings and loan associations working together with the mutual savings banks. "I feel the tax equality is a basic and the important element in the vote on this amendment and urge you to vote a yes." (applause)

Before the vote, I made a last appeal to expel the mutual banks and give commercial banks tax equality—not by decreasing our own taxes, as some wanted, but by making the mutuals pay a more equitable share.

"How long can we exist if the mutual banks continue to grow two, three, or four times as fast as we do?" I asked.

At last the balloting started. There were 3,000 voting delegates present, according to the *American Banker*. And the politicking and voting was heavy from 1:00 P.M., when the polls opened, until 6:00, when they closed. And then the counting and accounting started. It went on all night.

The next morning, Wednesday, September 24, 1958, dawned bright and clear. It was going to be warm; by 10:00 A.M., when the convention opened, it was 78 degrees outdoors.

"Was it [going to be] Roth Day–Expulsion Day," the *Savings Banker* questioned in reporting the drama later, "or was it ABA Day–Mutual Day?"

As the clock ticked off seconds that seemed like minutes, a senior partner of the accounting firm, which had worked through the night and into the morning hours to check and recheck ballots, to calculate and recapitulate the totals, stepped to the lectern and handed Joseph C. Welman, the untiring president of the American Bankers Association, a sealed envelope in the Waldorf Room of the Conrad Hilton Hotel.

Commercial bankers and savings bankers, national bankers and state bankers, association officials, and even the working press edged forward on their chairs as the president of the American Bankers Association slit open the heavy envelope. To us, sitting directly beneath the stage, the rending noise sounded as if a window shade had been torn in an empty room. The atmosphere was galvanic.

In clear and unwavering voice, Joseph Welman read: "The total number of votes cast in the Tuesday balloting was 2,965 . . . the total numbers needed for a two-third majority, 1,977. . . . Voting for the Amendment, 1,445 . . . voting against the amendment, 1,520. The proposal to amend the constitution of the American Bankers Association to exclude mutual savings banks from membership is defeated. . . ."

Almost as one man the press corps rose and hastily sought exits through the backstage wings. Wire services quickly flashed the election figures. . . .

The *Savings Banks Journal* wrote:

Three paramount problems were brought constantly to the fore: (1) Will the mutuals agree to "tax equality"? (2) Will the mutuals stay in the ABA? (3) Do the mutuals think they are well known and well liked? . . .

Though the Roth regiments went down to defeat in the Battle of the Ballots in Chicago . . . neither the voice nor the passion of the General of the Army was hushed or diminished. No one, save Arthur Roth himself, knows what next he will do . . . only an alert and aggressive opponent can match stride and strategy with the temporarily deflated Brigadier of Banking. . . .

By William Lyon's own calculations, savings bankers, who numbered only 522 out of the nearly 14,000 members of the ABA, had contributed 400 votes in their own cause. If you subtracted these from the total vote against the amendment, they had received only 1,100 votes from commercial bankers; while more than 1,400 opposed them.

They had won a "victory" by some calculation, but in the *Savings Bank Journal* of October 1958, Lyon said:

Some are tempted to define it as a "stay of execution." It may be that, if mutual savings banking does not act swiftly to meet the implications of Chicago. We have our work cut out for us. . . . First, we must have complete unity within the savings bank industry. . . . And we have an education job to do that is almost staggering.

If we do not get our story across during the next year, we may again find Mr. Roth, or someone like him, capitalizing on the animus against savings banks that he has so sedulously been trying to build.

Lyon urged that savings banks stay in the ABA, reporting that their board of directors had recommended strongly that they remain.

The *Chicago American* reported:

Commenting on results of the balloting, Roth said he felt the ABA had been given a year's reprieve in which to seek a solution to the tax controversy between the commercial bankers and the mutual savings bankers which precipitated the proposed amendment. . . .

He served notice that if a tax equality program were not affected [sic] within a year he would again raise the question of ousting the mutual savings bankers at next year's convention in Miami Beach, Fla.

Franklin National's vice-president, Harold V. Gleason, issued a press release from our suite 1724 in the hotel, based on quotations from me, which read in part:

We were assured time and time again that such an accord could be reached "within the framework of ABA." Those assurances were the basis of the amendment's failure to pass. Now it is up to those who made the promise to redeem it.

Joseph Welman told the convention after the vote that "the basic problems underlying this controversy and which found their way into this controversy remain unsolved. It is my earnest hope that we will close ranks and solve them."

Although the vote had gone closely against us, I felt that we had won—we had made our point. One evidence of that was that the ABA convention unanimously passed a strong resolution calling for tax equality; it is almost certain that this would not have happened if we had not campaigned for the amendment. A reporter from the *American Banker* asked the "spokesman" for the savings banks whether they might now voluntarily withdraw from the ABA. The spokesman (unidentified) said that the matter would be on their agenda when they met in New York within a few days, although he felt they would not do so.

William A. Lyon said that his organization's directors had authorized him to set up a committee to discuss tax equality with a committee to be selected by the ABA.

All this indicated that we had made enormous progress, and that those in banking who deplored the open fight were missing the point. The fact that the ABA had gone so strongly on record for "the elimination of inequity in the taxation of financial institutions" showed that the commercial banks had forced their organization off dead center.

On October 1, George A. Mooney, the New York State superintendent of banks, "questioned how much of a victory the savings banks had really won in the fight over the Roth amendment."

As my statement after the balloting had reminded the bankers, the vote to retain savings banks as members had been based on assurances that the problem of tax equality would be ironed out within the structure of the ABA. The means for doing this had been spelled out. Savings banks and commercial banks would set up committees to negotiate the problem.

Now the savings bankers had to make good on this promise.

But the gulf between the two positions was so sharp and so deep that "negotiation" could only postpone the inevitable. As Ralph Cox, editor of the *Mid-West Banker*, wrote:

They have no intention of "bargaining" at these meetings. And why should they? They are now in firm possession of preferential tax treatment and what person—in his right mind—would give up such a favored position?

It is apparent that they are using these meetings (1) to show that they were willing to sit down and discuss the subject, and then (2) to go away from these meetings protesting for public notice that commercial bankers are out to destroy them. . . . Their minds have been made up that they won't "give an inch" on . . . tax equality.

In 1959, after months of the fruitless bargaining—during which I resolved to remain silent so as not to be accused of influencing the decision—the prestigous Dime Savings Bank of Brooklyn, whose previous president had been president of the ABA, resigned from that organization with a bitter attack on it as being a "tool for a certain greedy element in commercial banking."

This was the first step. Soon, most savings banks had resigned from the ABA. More important, the sophistry of their position had been fully exposed. Whether they stayed in or left the ABA, their influence had been eroded within the organization. As their spokesmen had predicted, their "victory" was really only a reprieve—and they ultimately had to face the inevitable consequences of their untenable position.

At Easter time, the Executive Committee of the ABA was meeting at Greenbrier in West Virginia—and I was vacationing with my wife at the Homestead in Virginia. It was only an hour's drive from one to the other. On a rainy Sunday, I got to thinking about that committee meeting, and sent off a long telegram to the ABA. The gist of it was that I was only an hour away over the mountains, and that I supposed they were discussing tax equality, and that perhaps we ought to get together about it.

John Remington of the committee telephoned me and asked me to come over. The committee had worked out a complicated formula on tax equality, which they wanted to introduce as a bill in Congress. I didn't think it was very sound, but I told them I'd accept it as a basis for compromise if they would promise to sit down with the Independent Bankers Association, the Bankers Committee for Tax Equality, and the Roth Committee and work out one unified approach to the problem, so that commercial banking could never again be accused of coming before Congress with conflicting proposals. They agreed, so I went along with their formula.

When I told R. E. Gormley, president of the Independent Bankers Association, about the understanding, he said, "Arthur, you've sold us out. You're a traitor."

I said, "Not at all. All we've done is to agree to sit down together so that we can work out a unified approach to Congress. If we can't do that, all our individual efforts will be useless."

Shirley Tark and Vernon Scott of the Bankers Committee for Tax Equality went along with the idea, and then we had to pressure the ABA to make good on the promise of their Executive Committee. But they did send representatives, and all four groups had a series of meetings in Washington where we finally hammered out a joint legislative approach—which was not the same as the bill the ABA had proposed at Greenbrier. It was a simpler and more workable measure, which got consideration from the House Ways and Means Committee.

I remember testifying for it, along with the others, and we all said similar things. And after the hearings, I went up to Congressman Eugene Keogh and said, "Well, I want to thank you."

And he said, "What for?" Since we were always adversaries.

I said, "For making me understand that banking had to testify with one voice if they ever hoped to get tax equality. Did you notice at these hearings, all the factions in commercial banking testified with a single voice? And we owe it all to you, Mr. Congressman."

Gene doesn't remember this any more, but I have the picture very clear in my mind of how rueful he looked.

13 • Conflict with the Rockefellers

I'd had several clashes with David Rockefeller over branch banking. Starting in 1958, I came into direct personal conflict not only with David but with his brother Nelson; and this went on over several years.

It first came into the open during hearings on the new omnibus banking bill in Albany in February 1958. A good part of the legislature was present, because we'd sent telegrams to each assemblyman and senator the night before, saying that if he wanted to learn the answer to the bank controversy, to come to the legislative chamber the following day.

I pointed out that there were two important issues behind this bill. One was that the First National City Bank had applied for permission to use the holding-company provisions of federal law so that they could absorb the largest bank in Westchester, the County Trust Company. But also Chase Manhattan, "the other contestant in this race to be New York's biggest bank, already controls, through its own major stockholder, the second-largest bank in Westchester."

When I finished my statement, Senator McCullough said, "Mr. Roth, you made a statement in which I am very much interested. You said that Chase Manhattan has control of Westchester's second-largest bank. What did you mean by 'control'?"

MR. ROTH: Well, I should qualify that a bit. The Rockefeller family, I believe, owns twenty-eight percent of the second-largest bank. Is that right, David?

[The hearing was held in the semicircular legislative chamber, and I remember David Rockefeller coming down the steps toward the hearing area waving his finger at me.]

MR. DAVID ROCKEFELLER: No, it isn't right. I would like an opportunity, if I may, to deny categorically the statement that Mr. Roth made. In fact, I am surprised that he made it, because I believe that he made it last year and Mr. McCloy denied it for the record last year and I think I am in a good position to deny it categorically today because the Chase Manhattan Bank does not control, directly or indirectly, any bank in Westchester County.

MR. ROTH: May I ask whether you and your family corporations control about twenty-eight percent of the stock of that bank?

MR. ROCKEFELLER: My family-owned corporations own about twenty percent of the [Westchester] bank, but the Chase Manhattan Bank does not control the investments of my family.

MR. ROTH: Naturally.

THE CHAIRMAN: Let us not get into domestic matters.

From this time on, David Rockefeller no longer took an active part in pushing for new banking laws; he let his chairman, John J. McCloy, represent the bank.

Actually, he had no need to appear in public for another reason. His brother, Nelson A. Rockefeller, took office as governor of New York in January 1959. Governor Rockefeller appointed a new superintendent of banking, G. Russell Clark, who immediately began lobbying for the "omnibus bill."

Governor Nelson Rockefeller owned personally at this time 18,000 shares of Chase Manhattan stock, worth about $1,800,000. And as governor, he began putting all the weight of his office behind the omnibus banking bill.

He called in Walter Mahoney, the Republican majority leader of the New York State Senate, and told him he wanted the bill passed. Mahoney replied that he didn't have the votes, but Rockefeller insisted. He could be a very unpleasant individual when he didn't get his way.

I was in the visitors' gallery when the bill came up for a vote in March 1959. And Mahoney got up and pointed at me and said, "There's a man here today who has bragged that he has the vote of the legislature in his pocket, and that this bill will not pass."

As it happens, the Democratic minority in the State Senate was firmly against the bill: U.S. Congressman Emmanuel Celler had forcibly reminded them that they were the party of the little man. And enough small-town Republicans were against the bill so that it didn't pass.

Some time later, I asked Mahoney why he had said something so outrageously untrue about me. And he said, "Because the governor was putting so much pressure on me. I didn't have the votes, and I thought I could get some that way. Actually, I lost as many as I gained, so the net was zero."

Rockefeller didn't accept defeat. The omnibus bill was slightly amended, reintroduced, and more hearings were held. At one, in the Garden City Hotel on September 10, 1959, I said that David Rockefeller was the bill's chief proponent.

"It is the top bank that wants what the omnibus bill contains," I testified. "That apparently is what you want also," I said to Russell Clark, state superintendent of banks, at the hearing.

Walter E. Van der Waag, head of the Meadow Brook National Bank, the other large commercial bank in our area, testified that the New York City banks, "led and supported by the Rockefellers," were fostering monopoly. Mr. Clark "displayed obvious anger. He said this was the first time, in meeting with more than 1,000 bankers across the state, that his integrity had been questioned."

Now Governor Rockefeller made the omnibus banking bill a top priority.

The issue had somehow to be dramatized to the public, as well as to the legislature, in personal terms, to make people see the connection between banking and their daily lives.

I sent three Franklin officers to California to investigate at first hand where the billions of dollars of "flight money" from New York savings banks were going, and how they were being used. They went around to housing developments in Los Angeles and found that most of the mortgage money came from New York. Californians could get a 100-percent mortgage—no money down on a house—and sometimes even more than 100 percent.

This was illegal. It worked like this: A builder would apply for a mortgage for $15,000, but only $13,000 went to pay for the house; the other $2,000 was cash to the purchaser to buy furniture or pay moving expenses. But it was all bank money, and the entire loan was guaranteed by the U.S. government.

The reason the banks were lending in California was because they could get a higher return with very large discounts. On a $10,000 mortgage, they would advance only $9,200 and keep $800 as a fee. This was much more than they could get in New York.

While New York dollars were raining on California, we hired a firm of professional women interviewers to ask New York savings banks about getting an FHA loan or a GI loan to buy a house on Long Island.

The record in New York was even worse than I had anticipated. These giant savings banks held deposits equal to 50 percent of all commercial banks in the state—and remember, New York State is the pivot of big business; all the major corporations, starting with General Motors, have deposits there in commercial banks; it is the hub of nationwide and international banking as well. When the women interviewers asked for mortgage loans at the enormous New York savings banks, they were told time after time that these banks made no FHA loans and no GI loans, or, if they did, that these were only partial mortgages (no 100 percent here!) with large down payments necessary.

We published the results of this survey in a "blot sheet" with a large ink blob on the cover, and identified each bank by name. They included the Dime, the Dry Dock, the Bowery—all the savings banks. Here is the summary:

	Number of Savings Banks
Savings banks making no GI or FHA mortgages under any conditions	26
Savings banks making only GI and FHA mortgages to long-time depositors with substantial accounts	19
Savings banks making FHA and GI loans with high down payments (however, they purchase GI mortgages outside of New York State with no down payment requirement)	6
Savings banks not making GI mortgages: only consider FHA on a very selective basis	1

Along with this, we published the report of our own state superintendent of banks, which showed that our savings banks were lending from 60 to 100 percent more money out of the state than inside it, adding up to a total of just under $7 billion in flight money.

A graph illustrated that while new housing starts had been rising sharply in number and percentage in the rest of the country, in New York State they had dropped sharply since 1955—down more than 36 percent. This was not only frustrating people who wanted to build homes but was throttling the building industry in the state.

Governor Rockefeller, although only in his first year in office, had already begn to try to launch himself into the presidency of the United

States; he wanted to become the 1960 Republican candidate. As part of his campaign, he had hired a large private airplane and invited about thirty reporters to go with him on a visit to the key state of California in November 1959 to see what political support he could cultivate for himself at the 1960 Republican National Convention.

As he and the reporters boarded the plane, we handed each of them our "blot sheet" and some supplementary information, including a copy of a letter I had written to Superintendent Clark about the horrible lending record of the New York savings banks.

A letter to Nelson Rockefeller, dated November 10, was part of the package:

> Dear Governor Rockefeller:
> On the eve of your departure, I am sure you are too conscientious a first-term governor of New York to forget our problems here at home while you are surveying the scene in other strategic states.
> In your penetrating diagnosis of the ailments of New York before the Economic Club this week, you said:
> "Industries of certain types are fleeing the state at an accelerating rate.
> "The growth rate of the state has dropped way behind the national average."
> In California you and the excellent staff of analysts on your research team will have a unique opportunity to examine at first hand a "flight from New York" that veterans in New York State understand from painful personal experience.
> This difference in treatment of veterans and other home buyers is the primary reason why housing in New York State has declined so fast in contrast to the favorable showing for the rest of the country.
> I know you would find it impossible to believe that New York savings banks are largely responsible for the bright showing in California and the poor showing in New York State.

I referred him to the "blot sheet" and quoted Alexander Paulsen, president of the Long Island Home Builders Institute: "Savings Institutions have a *moral obligation* to satisfy the mortgage and other financial needs of their own communities *before any other consideration*."

The letter ended: "To the extent to which savings banks are draining funds out of New York State—which should be used for housing, school bonds and other New York needs—they are harming the economy of New York State." And I referred him to the team of Franklin officers investigating New York State mortgages in California, who were stopping at a Los Angeles hotel.

Rockefeller was locked into his airplane for hours with thirty reporters asking him questions about the blot sheet. When he got to California the local radio and television people were alerted to question him, too. We invited him to visit California developments and see at first hand where New York savings were going, but of course he never did.

A good personal friend of mine, who was in a position to know, told me that at a subsequent directors' meeting of a Rockefeller enterprise, the conversation was largely about our blot sheet and the effect it had had on the governor. "He is hopping mad at you," my friend told me. "He was so upset during the trip that he couldn't conduct himself properly in California. The visit was a bust."

Instead of being convinced by facts, Rockefeller bulled ahead with his omnibus banking bill. In 1960 it came up before the legislature again, and this time we were assured by Joseph Zaretzki, the Democratic minority leader in the Senate, that it had no chance of passage. The Democrats were holding firm against it; and, as before, many Republicans from small towns were opposed because of the threat to local interests.

In fact, as late as Thursday, March 16, 1960, Carmine de Sapio, the New York county Democratic leader, assured a lawyer whom I know that the bill hadn't a chance.

"The first tip-off that a switch was in the works came shortly after noon on Monday when bank stocks, long depressed, started to zoom," wrote Harold H. Harris in the *New York Journal-American* two days later.

That same day, Senate Minority (Democratic) Leader Zaretzki changed his mind; he said he wanted the omnibus bill to pass.

We were told that Rockefeller called Zaretzki in and told him that he had had a commission looking into the affairs of New York City, where the Democrats were in power (Robert Wagner was mayor), and that they had uncovered the fact that certain legislators had taken money in connection with contracts let by the city. Rockefeller threatened an investigation. But there would be no investigation if the Democrats supported his bill. It was the last day of the session; Zaretzki had his back to the wall. He changed his vote and got other Democrats to go along.

The press reported it this way:

Newsmen who observed the incredible steamroller activity in the Legislature Monday [March 21] said it was the result of the tremendous pressures exerted by the New York City banking giants.

Others attributed the switch to a trade between Governor Rockefeller and New York City's Mayor Robert Wagner. The governor had proposed a relief bill for $70 million to the city, and Mayor Wagner wanted $85 million.

Before the bill was jammed through the legislature, there were innumerable telephone calls between Rockefeller and Wagner. The New York Democrats held a special meeting, called by de Sapio, at which New York City senators and assemblymen were told they must vote for the bill. One man, who refused to go along, "described the bill as 'the biggest haul since the great bank robbery.' " The *Independent Banker* wrote:

The first clue came when the Senate began at 8:30 P.M. with S. 3503 (the omnibus bill) as its first item of business. It sailed through 34–20 (14 affirmative votes came from Democrats who had been opposed until the day before). Joseph Zaretzki actually cried.

The bill then went over to the Assembly, where it was debated until 1 A.M. A fourth amendment to the bill was brought up so hurriedly it was mimeographed rather than printed. The amendment allowed savings banks from New York City to branch into counties of 700,000 and over. This amendment referred to was the price of the support of James Buckley, Bronx Republican leader. It would permit Bronx banks to branch into rich Westchester.

When an amendment is offered, it is required that at least three days pass before the legislature can vote on it.

But Governor Rockefeller, waiting in his office below the Assembly Chamber, sent a "message of necessity" upstairs waiving the three-day cooling-off period.

The bill was passed at 1:05 A.M. on Tuesday, March 22, by a vote of 91–56; 47 Democrats and 44 Republicans were for the bill. Only twenty-seven minutes later, at 1:32 A.M., Governor Rockefeller, who had stayed close by, signed the bill into law.

I suggested publicly that there might be a conflict of interest involved, considering his ownership of so much Chase Manhattan Bank stock and his family's control of the Bank of Westchester.

The following day (March 24) the *New York Times* reported that "the Governor told reporters that there was 'no conflict of interest.' " He had sold his 18,000 shares of Chase Manhattan stock just two months previously. But David Rockefeller still held 135,746 shares of Chase stock; and the "Rockefeller brothers as a group are reputed to hold about 20 percent of the shares of the National Bank of Westchester."

I had been expecting that the holding-company bill would pass eventually, but not so soon (and I did not think that savings-bank branches would be permitted). State law had had to be brought into line with national law, now permitted bank holding companies. We had been fighting a rear guard action; the reason was that we wanted to grow big enough and strong enough to repel boarders and mount a counterattack. Now we could only submit to being raided or we could use the new law to expand our own bank.

Immediately I wrote a letter to stockholders telling them that

- Franklin would now try to acquire more banks through merger;
- we would set up more branches, anticipating that these would now be permitted;
- we would pursue our entry into New York City, which had to be permitted under the new law;
- we were prepared to form our own holding company.

None of the changes could take place overnight under the new law; it did not go into effect until July. Nor could the New York banks move faster than the authorities allowed.

There was still time—and we intended to play for as much time as possible. We had one more trump card.

On May 5, I wrote a letter to ninety-two New York banks, warning them that any invasion of Nassau County would be resisted in the courts. We published an advertisement in metropolitan newspapers entitled "Notice of Intention to Sue." Meanwhile, we invited them to join with us in seeking a declaratory judgment by a court on the constitutionality of the omnibus bill. We hired Howard H. Spellman, a constitutional lawyer, to represent us in any legal contest. Mr. Spellman said that there were "forty valid grounds" for declaring that the law was illegal and unconstitutional.

On May 6, the *New York Herald Tribune* reported, "There was no official reaction to Mr. Roth's letter from most major banks yesterday, but few seemed inclined to take his charges lightly. Mr. Roth is noted in banking circles for the fights he has waged in the past—and often won."

On May 13, Laurence S. Rockefeller announced that he and his brothers Nelson and David were selling their $4,750,000 interest in the National Bank of Westchester. Reported in the *Herald Tribune* on May 14, 1960, by Don Ross, Mr. Rockefeller said, "Since one of my brothers is Governor of the state and, therefore, responsible for the State Banking Department, and another of my brothers is vice-chairman of the Chase Manhattan Bank, it seemed to us that . . . if we continue to hold these shares there might result constraints or misunderstandings which would be in nobody's interest."

To say the least. It was mighty late in the day for the Rockefellers, with all the legal talent at their command, to realize that they had a serious conflict of interest. The same day the *Tribune* also announced a tentative merger between two local Westchester banks, the Bank of Westchester and the Rye National Bank. This could only result in better banking services for the people of that county.

The new banking law went into effect on July 1, and by July 17 applications were filed by eleven New York banks for twenty-eight branches in Westchester and Nassau counties. We had prepared a brief to be presented as soon as any action was taken; now was the time. We filed suit in the state supreme court against the superintendent of banks and the banks who were asking for branches in Nassau County.

Our case rested on five main points, one of which was that Governor Rockefeller was acting in conflict of interest when he signed the law. There were also several strong constitutional points. The law was held up for eight months, waiting for the judge's decision.

On March 14, 1961, Justice Irving H. Saypol declared the law unconstitutional on narrow, technical grounds, having to do with the fact that it had not rested in final form on the legislators' desks. But he ruled that the courts were in no position to judge the governor's motives, nor did he consider the other important constitutional questions.

When his decision was announced on March 15, the *New York Post* headlined:

BANKS IN TURMOIL
OVER COURT RULING

Other papers carried similar stories, discussing the problems faced by the banks that had gone ahead and opened branches that were now illegal. Many people were withdrawing money from these branches. There was absolutely no market for bank shares for two days—no market at all.

However, the legislature was in session, and Governor Rockefeller issued another Letter of Necessity. This time the occasion was that the original bill hadn't been constitutionally passed. Which was, of course, his fault. The leaders of the Senate rallied all their forces, appealing to many on the specious grounds that they had to resist the court's meddling in legislative affairs.

A slightly changed version of the omnibus bill was passed on Thursday, March 16, 1961, only two days after Judge Saypol had overturned the old law.

The constitutional questions remained unanswered, and I said that I might bring suit again.

Actually, I had no intention of doing so. It was evident that, as the *White Plains Reporter Dispatch* wrote on March 17, 1961, we were being ruled by "harsh political pressure by the Republican bosses of the Legislature, and the Governor, responding more to the anguished howls of bankers than to any demonstrated public need."

I met the governor a number of times afterward—once he refused to appear on a platform with me—and each time he asked, "What are you suing me for now?"

We had gained some time, and now it was up to us to move quickly and take advantage of the opportunity that the omnibus law opened to us as well as to our giant New York competitors.

14 • In the Public Interest

In 1958, the year after we reached fiftieth position among the nation's banks, we jumped six notches to number forty-four; and our assets rose by more than $100 million to reach a total of more than $626 million.

Profits were high, although we had to put a large investment into construction of new buildings, additions to buildings, and refurnishing parts of a dozen of our now thirty-two bank branches—the thirty-second being the former Central Islip National Bank with which we consolidated in 1958.

As usual, in 1959 we declared both a stock and cash dividend. But one shareholder was unhappy about our activities for tax equality. I asked that his letter be read aloud at our annual shareholders' meeting in January 1959.

Dear Mr. Roth:

It is my understanding that a full page advertisement in the New York Times costs approximately $4,500. To have reprints made and widely circulated is an additional expense. As a stockholder in your bank, I believe it is my privilege to ask the following questions:

1. Are the earnings of the bank being utilized for this purpose?
2. Are you personally bearing the expense of anti-savings bank propaganda?
3. Is there a group of "silent partners" who are financing this ridiculous tirade?

I shall look forward to hearing from you—

Cordially,
Charles W. Carson.

I answered at the meeting: "During the past few months, I have received one other letter, somewhat along the same lines. I might say that Mr. Carson is the president of a savings bank. [The other was not.]

"The cost of the ad in the *New York Times* is not $4,500 but $6,000. . . .

"In regard to the three questions: Yes [the earnings of the bank are being utilized] . . . it is part of the expenses of the bank.

"Are you personally bearing the expense? . . . No, I am not . . . the bank is paying for it."

I also said that there are no silent partners.

Then I explained that I felt it was necessary, and good business, for us to carry on the campaign against a practically tax-free competitor and why we had to bring this to the attention "of the governor, the legislature and the Congress . . . [and] the American Bankers Association. . . .

"The cost of these campaigns . . . has been approximately $60,000 [for] advertising, legal fees, train expense and hotel expense. . . ."

I did not go into other benefits of our outside activities. One was that they brought the bank a good deal of good, clean publicity. The name of Franklin became nationally known as a result of the campaigns, and this brought us business. It also gave us stature in our dealings with the comptroller's office, and with the Congress and the Senate. And there was another benefit generated by a fight for principle. Our officers willingly pitched in and worked extra hours and days and had a good time doing it. I think it is a fair assessment to say that never was morale at a higher pitch than during those years of controversy. This is not just my own opinion; I have checked this with others, including those outside the bank.

Thus, although our campaigns cost the bank some money and took a good deal of our time, the work of the bank never suffered, nor did its profits—on the contrary, our business momentum only increased.

Our shareholders generally recognized and approved. At that 1959 meeting, shareholder Nicklas got up and offered a resolution of support, which was adopted with almost no dissenting votes.

Shareholder Schlagel, noting that we were bearing the burden of the campaign for tax equality, asked, "Wouldn't it be possible to go [to the other banks in Nassau and Suffolk] to form a pool to help us . . . ?

I explained that we had thought of that, but felt it would hamper our efforts if we had to work through a committee; it would slow down our reaction to current opportunities, and it might vitiate our message, since other bankers tended to be less outspoken.

About $16,000 had been contributed to our work by other banks to aid in the ABA campaign. Some months before, our board of directors had discussed tax equality and passed a resolution strongly supporting our work: "Arthur T. Roth . . . in opposing the program [of the mutual savings institutions] for wider banking powers and additional branch offices, and sponsoring income tax reforms . . . has advanced the interest of this bank and enhanced the position and influence of the bank, both locally and nationally." The resolution not only supported what had been done but asked that it be continued, and ratified in advance the spending of "reasonable amounts" of money to that end. Miss Ruth Fischell, representing the United Shareholders of America, read a special citation from their board of directors commending our work.

At the end of 1959, our assets neared the $700-million mark. More important, we were again number one among the top fifty banks in the percentage of earnings in ratio to capital funds. Ours was 20.3. The nearest competitor was just about the thirteenth percentile.

We were still a long way from the goal of tax equality. One key step forward came when Aubrey E. Austin, Jr., of the Santa Monica (California) Bank appeared before the Resolutions Committee of the Democratic National Convention in July 1960. Mr. Austin's presentation was so persuasive that the Democrats included as a plank "We shall close the loopholes in the tax laws by which certain privileged groups legally escape their fair share of taxation" in their 1960 platform— the first time either of our major political parties had taken a stand on the issue.

After President John F. Kennedy's election, all of us who were engaged in the fight for tax equality did what we could to persuade him to make good on the platform. William Battle, a lawyer retained by the Tax Equality Association (of which the Bankers Committee for Tax Equality was a part), was a friend and adviser to Kennedy. He discussed the subject with the president. He knew that the president's father, former ambassador to England Joseph P. Kennedy, had been a commercial banker in Boston, and might be receptive to some accurate information on how the government might equalize bank taxes.

The savings and loan people had already contacted the Democrats, who were always in a financial hole after elections, and promised to take up half the party's deficit, which was about $7 or $8 million. The unspoken price was that the president not advocate tax equality in his tax message scheduled to be given to Congress in April 1961.

A customer of our bank—a good friend of our then vice-president, Pat Clifford—was Carroll Rosenbloom, who at that time owned the Baltimore Colts football team. Mr. Rosenbloom, a close friend of Joseph P. Kennedy, the father of the president, knew about our fight for tax equality and offered to deliver a message on the subject to him. Rosenbloom was going to Florida during Easter, and said he would see Mr. Kennedy there. He asked me to put the whole story on paper, clearly and concisely, in the form of a letter.

It was Holy Thursday, but I went to the bank and worked all day on the letter. Mr. Rosenbloom delivered it to Kennedy in Florida. Then Kennedy gave it to his son the president, saying, "I believe that this matter is worth your attention."

Now, it was President Kennedy's method of working that when he was presented with a problem or a suggestion he might want to consider, he would appoint a task force to look into it before making a decision. He chose a three-man group to study tax equality, consisting of his aide, Theodore Sorensen; Mortimer Caplin, the commissioner of Internal Revenue; and another lawyer. They reported back to him, and their report must have been favorable, because in his April 21, 1961, tax message to Congress, President Kennedy said:

> . . . special provisions have developed into an increasing source of preferential treatment to various groups. Whenever one taxpayer is permitted to pay less, someone else must be asked to pay more. . . . Of course, some departures from uniformity are needed to promote desirable social or economic objectives. . . . But many of the preferences . . . do not meet such a test.

He went on to discuss a number of categories in which tax reform was necessary and desirable. One of these was cooperative enterprises: many had developed into huge businesses, free of taxation because of court decisions. And among these institutions were the mutual savings banks and savings and loan associations.

> Some of the most important types of private savings and lending institutions in the country are accorded tax-deductible reserve provisions which substantially reduce or eliminate their Federal income tax liability.

These provisions should be reviewed with the aim of assuring non-discriminatory treatment. Remedial legislation in these fields would enlarge the revenues and contribute to a fair and sound tax structure.

I thought that statement showed great political and moral courage in the face of the $4 million or so that Kennedy could have garnered for his party from the savings and loan people merely by keeping his mouth shut. On our side there had been no offer or hint of any offer of *quid pro quo*.

Later that year, Stephen Smith, President Kennedy's brother-in-law, told me that there was going to be a private luncheon at the White House. The purpose was to try to raise some money to pay off the deficit of the Democratic party; it was hoped that each person who came would be able to raise about $50,000. I was being invited to represent the banking community.

I had been a Nixon supporter; my wife and I had, in fact, given his campaign $10,000. But President Kennedy's display of principle could not be ignored. I said I would be present. And I induced six members of my family to contribute the legal limit of $5,000 each; together, our contribution totaled $35,000.

This was most emphatically not a payoff, but an honest attempt to give some support to the party of a president who had placed principle far above gain. Remember, he could have had some $4 million for the party if he'd just kept his mouth shut.

There was no talk about contributions at the luncheon, at which I was seated between Vice President Lyndon B. Johnson and Bobby Kennedy. President Truman was also present, as was Henry Ford. It was a lively and informal group, about twenty or twenty-five people, and the president made a light and amusing speech. but I remember that many of his remarks were quite pointed, directed at Johnson. LBJ was always a butt of the Kennedys. In their presence he seemed awkward and crude. It seemed to me that the president was too rough on him; that the vice president was made to feel like two cents.

Just before the luncheon, I was able to exchange a few sentences with the president. I asked him what he thought might be done to expedite the bill to tax the savings banks and savings and loans. He said, "I saw Wilbur Mills [the chairman of the House Ways and Means Committee] the other day, and he thinks that he may be able to move it along."

I said, "Mr. Mills certainly understands the problem, but the dog in his manger is Eugene Keogh of his committee, who is a savings banker, as you know." I knew that Kennedy was very close to Gene Keogh. "What are we going to do about him?" I asked.

"Well," said the president, "we'll just have to find out who his friends are. Come on, we're going to have lunch now."

Before the tax message, I had seen Stan Surrey, undersecretary of the Treasury. The Bankers Committee for Tax Equality had noted, "Although the Treasury had recommended the full taxation of mutual financial institutions, it did not favor including provisions for such taxation in the Revenue Act that was being considered in 1961." It was so difficult to get such legislation through Congress, the Treasury preferred to avoid the issue. I did not tell him about my letter to Joseph Kennedy.

I saw him after the president's tax message to Congress, and he was truly astonished. "I can't understand it," he kept saying. "He went so much further than we asked him to."

The *American Banker* had forecast a month before the president's message that he might call for tax equality; but they were "virtually certain" that he would recommend withholding tax on interest and dividends. This was another Democratic party platform plank: said the *American Banker*, "A group in Congress has long advocated it, as has organized labor."

And indeed, a substantial portion of the president's special tax message had been devoted to a proposed withholding tax on interest and dividends at the source, the way we did with salaries and wages. Some $3 billion of taxable income in these categories was escaping taxation because it was not being reported by taxpayers under the existing voluntary system. The president proposed a 20-percent withholding rate on dividends and interest, including interest earned by savings accounts in banks. This was calculated to bring an additional $600 million a year into the U.S. Treasury.

Now this was not going to be popular. But the president's figures showed that interest and dividends made up only about 1 percent of the income received by people who earned up to $5,000 a year; it was a major part of the incomes of those in the $100,000 to $150,000 bracket. So closing this enormous loophole would not hurt little people; but it was going to cost the well-to-do a lot more income tax—which they should have been paying anyway.

Congress adjourned too early in 1961 to pass a new tax bill, but the bill was presented for discussion at the next session.

Treasury tax officials had been questioning the American Bankers Association officials, as well as the savings banks and savings and loan institutions, about how to go about withholding tax on interest. All these people were negative; they said that the mechanics of the transaction would cost banks too much money. This was a real problem. And some concern was voiced about the small investor, whose interest or dividend withholding might be larger than his tax; he'd be deprived of the difference until the Treasury refunded the money, which might take considerable time. It might not amount to much money in an individual case; but to people with small incomes, small sums are obviously very important. So this difficulty had to be overcome.

The ABA was circulating a questionnaire that, by emphasizing the high cost of collecting tax revenues at the source, seemed designed to elicit nothing but negative views from bankers. And, of course, the savings bankers, and savings and loan bankers, were not at all interested in collecting their depositors' taxes—it made them appear like government watchdogs and was bound to create some resentment among those who were dodging their legal tax liabilities.

In fact, about 99.9 percent of the bankers in the country were looking for excuses to avoid a withholding tax on interest and dividends.

But their attitude seemed to me directly contrary to principle, and to the national interest. Bankers ought to have been trying to find a way to circumvent difficulties in collecting legitimate tax, rather than creating more obstacles.

Since systems have always been one of my personal interests, I studied the problem with Franklin National's comptroller, John Sadlik, and came up with a simple and inexpensive proposal. On savings deposits, banks could pay the depositors 20 percent less—2.4 percent instead of the full 3 percent then paid by commercial banks—and we could forward a single check, quarterly, covering the difference for all depositors to the Treasury. Our bank had, at the time, 212,000 savings accounts with total deposits of $241 million. We figured that the mechanics of the plan would cost us $20,000 the first year and $5,000 a year thereafter. And we worked out a similar system covering dividends, coupons on bonds, and interest on government savings bonds. Altogether, withholding the taxes and paying them direct to the government the first year would cost the bank $28,000, or $35 per $1 million of our assets; and from then on only $8,000 per year, or $10 per $1 million of assets.

To take care of the small depositors who might not be subject to federal income taxes, we devised a simple form so that they could get their money back immediately. It was a claim, drawn on the Treasury of the United States, which the depositor signed, saying that he was not subject to income tax and requesting that the amount withheld from his savings interest be returned. All he had to do was put down the amount of money, his Social Security number, and his signature. The form could then be deposited or cashed in the bank that had withheld his money—he got paid on the spot.

John Sadlik put the plan into a memorandum, which we mailed to 15,000 banks throughout the country. And he testified in favor of withholding income tax at the source in banks before the House Ways and Means Committee, and before the Senate Finance Committee. Sadlik, Howard Stoddard, Chairman of the Michigan National Bank, Shirley Tark, and I were the only bankers in the United States who testified for withholding taxes on interest and dividends. Our position was so diametrically opposed to what senators and congressmen heard in weeks of testimony that Senator Paul Douglas of Illinois was moved to make some comments during Sadlik's testimony in April 1962.

MR. SADLIK: My name is John Sadlik. I am vice-president and comptroller of the Franklin National Bank of Long Island. I appear on behalf of the bank in support of withholding of income tax at the source of interest, dividends, and patronage dividends.
SENATOR DOUGLAS: Just excuse me. Did I hear this aright?
MR. SADLIK: You heard me right.
SENATOR DOUGLAS: Would you repeat it again? [laughter]
MR. SADLIK: I appear on behalf of the bank in support of withholding of income tax at the source of interest, dividends, and patronage dividends.
SENATOR DOUGLAS: Would someone please get me a pill to avert a heart attack. [laughter] My heart is fluttering.

The Senate Finance Committee seemed ready to accept our simplified tax-withholding plan, but for one reason or another—perhaps because they didn't understand how simple it was—the ABA took a position against it, and the savings and loan associations began a letter-writing and advertising campaign against it. Congressmen were deluged with negative mail.

The fight got so intense that President Kennedy said at his news conference on May 9, 1962, that rejection of his proposal would be a several-hundred-million-dollar victory for tax evaders. He said that the bankers opposing withholding had created "four misconceptions": that the withholding proposal involves a new tax or tax increase, and that it would take money unjustly from honest taxpayers, would create red tape, and would hurt the elderly, widows, and orphans.

"Not a single one of these charges is true," Mr. Kennedy said.

Really, a good deal of the opposition seemed caused by lack of understanding on the part of bankers. Wherever the members of the Roth Committee spoke to groups of bankers, questions would be asked; and when our simplified withholding plan was explained, the bankers were usually satisfied to go along. At a meeting of our own bank's officers who would have to deal with the mechanics of withholding, and with the supposedly bad public relations attendant to it, three out of four endorsed the idea.

The new 1962 revenue bill did not contain a withholding provision. It was too much of a hot potato for the politicians. But the bill as approved by the Ways and Means Committee did go some short distance toward making up for tax inequality. The Senate Finance Committee agreed with the bill—which proposed that mutual institutions be permitted to transfer 60 percent of their annual income to a bad-debt loss reserve, until that reserve reached 6 percent of qualified loans on property. Then Senator Kerr of Oklahoma attached a special amendment, which penalized *stock* savings and loan associations (as opposed to the mutuals) by permitting them to transfer only 50 percent of their income to the reserve. The effect would have been to increase the stock associations' taxes by 5 percent over that of the mutual savings and loans. This amendment was eliminated in the Conference Committee, and the Revenue Act of 1962 was passed by both Houses of Congress.

The reason I mention this is that there is an interesting sidelight on this amendment, the only one that would have raised taxes for one category of taxpayer above the level set by the House. Five days after the bill passed *without* the penalizing Kerr provision, a representative of the Great Western Finance Corporation, the Home Savings and Loan Association, and the First Charter Financial Corporation—all stock building and loan associations—came to Washington with a bundle of cash, in $100 bills, for Mr. Robert G. ("Bobby") Baker, the secretary of the Senate. It was the first payment in what was eventually to total

$99,600. According to Baker's lawyer, Edward Bennett Williams, the money was to be paid to Senator Kerr if he succeeded in eliminating his stock savings and loan penalty in conference. This he did. But whether Kerr was actually supposed to receive the money, or was aware of Baker's dealings, will never be known. For Senator Kerr died before Bobby Baker was indicted and convicted several years later of income-tax evasion, theft of the $99,600, and conspiracy to defraud the United States government.

Tax withholding on dividends and interest was still unresolved when I testified on the Revenue Act of 1963—at which I also pointed out that tax equality had been far from achieved in the 1962 law. Savings and loan associations were now paying roughly half the rate of commercial banks; but savings banks were paying only about 12 percent as much as commercial banks.

When I finished testifying, Senator Douglas said, "Mr. Roth, I don't know that I agree with you in all your proposals on taxation of mutual building and loan associations and mutual savings banks because of the element of mutuality which these organizations still have, and which could be, in my opinion, and should be further developed. But I do want to pay tribute to you for two things that I know about:

"First, you with your associates, including my friend Mr. Tark of Chicago, and Mr. Stoddard of Michigan, were the only bankers in the country, so far as I know, last year to endorse and advocate the imposition of withholding the basic individual income tax on dividends and interest just as this is withheld on wages and salaries, and I want to say you set a great example of public spirit in doing this.

"You were of tremendous help not only by your example but in the concrete suggestions you offered. . . . Now, unfortunately, we lost that battle and it will be some years or some time before we can return to it, but I want to tell you how grateful I personally am for this."

MR. ROTH: Thank you, Senator. Since you bring it up, I might say I don't think we really lost the battle. . . . I still firmly believe and many bankers now recognize that this system of reporting that we have today is far more costly than withholding would have been . . . Someday we may have withholding . . . [it] may have been delayed for a few years but a lot of good may have come out of all the discussion."
SENATOR DOUGLAS: In other words, that was a sacrifice fly which brought the run in from third base. [laughter]
There is a second reason why I admire you, and that is the fact you

started with a very small bank [and] your assets are now over a billion dollars. . . . What is your relative size [among banks]?

MR. ROTH: Twenty-fifth in size.

SENATOR DOUGLAS: I noticed you have also been . . . largely successful in fighting off the efforts of the gigantic New York banks to move onto Long Island, and to take over the business in that area. . . .

MR. ROTH: To a large extent we have. The years we fought them we grew in size and now we are of the size where we can effectively compete with them. . . .

SENATOR DOUGLAS: I want to congratulate you because I happen to believe in a broad distribution of economic power and . . . I don't think it is a healthy thing to have a relatively small number of huge institutions dominating the lending and the investment field. . . .

I want to say that I take a great deal of pride in seeing you successfully carry out what some of us believe the essence of the American system is, namely, ethical and competitive capitalism rather than monopoly capitalism.

We then went into tax inequality. Senator Douglas asked me if real-estate lending, the mainstay of building and loan associations and savings banks, was not more risky, therefore requiring a higher reserve.

I said ordinarily this kind of loan wasn't more risky. The way such loans were being handled by building and loans in California, and his home state of Illinois, created more risk, but this was unnecessary. They were making poor loans. "We are starting at the wrong point when we say give them a higher reserve to compensate for poorly made loans. . . . Say [rather] that they should be properly supervised." My suggestion was that the Federal Home Loan Bank Board should be given more authority over building and loan associations, to see that they conformed to good banking practices.

It was now clear that the essential reason for tax inequality was the difference in treatment of different banks on reserves for bad loans. There was even a considerable spread—from 0 to 17 percent—on such treatment among commercial banks, too; so it behooved us commercial bankers to work out a uniform bad-debt provision for our banks. Then we could try to get Congress to make this universal for all banks, or to permit the Treasury to do so; and by this means we'd arrive at tax equality.

I testified to this for the Bankers Committee on Tax Equality before the Senate Finance Committee on October 23, 1963. But my own ideas went somewhat beyond those of the committee. So, when I had finished my testimony for them, I added my own proposal. To show that this was a matter of principle, not self-interest, I made it clear that this was "a reform which will cost my own institution, Franklin National Bank, $4 million in additional taxes, in the interest of tax equality.

"Franklin National Bank has an unfair advantage over the average commercial bank. We are permitted a tax-free reserve for bad debts which is 25 percent higher than the average commercial bank. This reserve formula is based on the experience of our bank in the Thirties when we were a half-million-dollar bank, and today we are a billion-dollar bank. . . . We don't need this kind of reserve. And, more important, the average bad-debt reserve is, in my opinion, also too high."

What I proposed was a reserve for 4 percent on the first $5 million of eligible loans and 2 percent on loans over $5 million. Thus, all banks under $10 million of assets would have the 4-percent reserve, and there would be a sliding scale down to 2 percent for those over $500 million. Under my formula, 92 percent of the country's banks would have a better bad-debt reserve than they then had. Many small banks had been denied a bad-debt reserve because they didn't have the records required by the Treasury for calculating their reserve. These represented approximately 40 percent of all banks—our smallest banks. Under our plan, they would have the benefit of the reserve. The net effect of the entire plan would be to collect more taxes for the Treasury—because the big banks, which could afford it, would have their reserve reduced below the then 3 percent. They didn't need this any more than we did, but of course it would have cost them money, so naturally they did not like it.

This formula was not adopted; but eventually a sound plan, involving bad-debt reserves based on a bank's actual experience with long carry-forward and carry-back privileges was adopted. And it was applied equitably to the mutual institutions, although with some variation. So long as a mutual savings bank keeps 73 percent of its assets invested in home mortgages, it receives favored tax treatment; and the same is true of building and loan associations so long as they are 82 percent invested in mortgages. Thus, if they fulfill their basic function of financing home building and buying, mutual savings banks pay only 15 percent effective income tax; savings and loan associations pay 22 percent; and commercial banks pay 26 percent.

What we have achieved through a fight that lasted more than a decade was a good measure of tax equity—not full tax equality. But so long as the mutual savings institutions fulfilled their basic purpose, and didn't intrude into commercial banking, it seemed reasonable for them to retain this much tax advantage over commercial banks.

15 • Abilities, Inc.

Not long after the war, a young girl named Marie Schmidt came to Franklin from West Hempstead looking for a job. By the standards of those days, she was completely unemployable. A tiny slip of a thing, she weighed only about eighty pounds. Her right arm was half the length of the left, and on her right hand she had only two fingers. She was wearing an iron brace on one leg, which was shorter than the other. My first reaction was: How could we employ a girl who looked like this, in an exposed position where the public would see her? It might have been embarrassing for her or for customers.

I asked if she had tried other employers, and she had, but no one would give her a job. And she wanted to work. She had graduated from Sewanhaka High School with honors. And she could type very well, handicapped as she was.

The memory of my retarded sister flashed through my mind; she could never have held a job. But this girl was much less handicapped; she deserved a chance. I said, "We'll give you a typewriter to take home, and we'll arrange for work that you can do there."

For a while she would pick up work and deliver it. But it soon became obvious that it was an imposition to have her travel back and forth between West Hempstead and Franklin Square a couple of times a day. So to save her that trouble, we fixed up an office for her in a file room in the basement next to the lunchroom. But she had to come upstairs from time to time, and many customers saw her. And their reaction was wonderful—they complimented us for employing a handi-capped person in our bank, something that they had never seen in any other bank. We moved Marie to the main floor. She was so dedicated, and so intelligent, that she rose to become our first public-relations specialist.

Marie Schmidt did not live long; she had an enlarged heart and died when she was in her middle twenties. But she never missed a day's work; she was never late; and her job performance was always excellent.

Then I hired a young war veteran who had lost an arm—again, considered unemployable. And I gave instructions to personnel to hire handicapped people whenever possible. But our personnel people didn't think it proper; the many handicapped people employed by the Franklin National Bank during the early years were all hired personally, by me.

These experiences had certainly prepared me to be receptive when in 1948 I got a telephone call from Preston Bassett, the president of the Sperry Gyroscope Corporation, who asked me to lunch with him and a young man at the Garden City Hotel. The young man was named Henry Viscardi, Jr. He had been born practically without legs. As a child he couldn't wear artificial legs, and the other children called him a monkey. But when he grew up a German doctor constructed a pair of artificial legs for him, and he was able to get a job in the Personnel Department of Burlington Mills. Because of his own history, and out of gratitude for the help he had received, he decided to devote his life to helping others who were handicapped. He wanted to start a subcontracting business employing only handicapped people. To do this, he needed capital. He had been going around making speeches to civic groups and had received a warm welcome but no cash.

My recollection is that he was looking for only about $4,000. I told him it wasn't nearly enough; that the amount ought to be at least double that. I would raise half if he could raise the other half; and I gave him some direction as to whom to see and arranged visits for him. We raised the money in a very short time.

He incorporated as Abilities, Inc., and rented an old garage in West Hempstead. Sperry gave him contracts, as Bassett had promised. I made a point with Viscardi that he wasn't starting a charitable enterprise, but a business. Handicapped people had proved to me that they could work as well as, even better, than others. They should not be coddled; they didn't want that. They wanted the self-respect that came from earning their own way. And so I insisted that Viscardi pay back his loans, with proper interest, and counseled him never to accept any gifts. And that has always been the policy of Abilities, Inc. As a nonprofit company, hence it need not pay taxes. But it is most emphatically not a charity.

The organization grew until it had several hundred employees—all handicapped. And they were a great labor resource for the electronics industry on Long Island.

They made abilities of their disabilities or overcame them—one man with a metal hand was able to handle hot metal for soldering purposes. A boy with no legs or arms came all the way from Brooklyn. Someone brought him in a car, but at Abilities he was able to sweep the floor; somehow he could manage a broom with the tiny stumps of arms. And a special rig was built so he could collect small items and put them in envelopes. He even managed to get a license to drive a car. He has always earned his own way; today he is married and has three children.

But only about one out of three who applied for work could be hired at Abilities, Inc. Not because they could not be useful—but because their families had instilled in them the idea that they would never be able to be "like other people." So many lives were wasted because those people had been given a "cripple" attitude.

Abilities, Inc., got into serious financial trouble during a recession in the electronics business in the early 1950s. By this time they had about 200 employees. Even then, they did not seek handouts. They needed to borrow about $165,000; and by that time in my life, I was able to arrange a business loan on the basis of my own collateral. Of course, they repaid it when business got better.

Viscardi's firm had been largely a defense subcontractor. At one of their directors' meetings, I suggested that perhaps we could give them some bank work. We had a school savings program, in which children in about seventy county schools in Nassau and Suffolk saved coins and deposited them in savings accounts. About eighteen of our bank people handled this work.

I suggested to Viscardi that this operation could be transferred to Abilities, Inc. I told him, "We expect that you can do it for ten percent less than we are spending; and we expect you to make about a ten-percent profit even at this rate." We would send our eighteen employees to Abilities, Inc., to do the work and to explain it to their people. Then we would gradually phase in the handicapped workers. We would reassign our people to other bank duties; nobody would lose a job.

It fitted with Viscardi's approach—he always used to sell other businesses on giving him the tasks that were difficult or impossible or just plain boring. He would take them over.

Eugene J. Taylor, adjunct professor of physical medicine and reha-
bilitation at New York University, referred to our department of handicapped workers in his testimony on manpower before a Senate
subcommittee in 1963. Said Professor Taylor:

> The project started with Abilities, Inc., assuming the entire operations of
> the Franklin National Bank junior savings program. . . . The project [now]
> handles a junior savings program for 129 elementary and junior high schools
> for Nassau and Suffolk counties with approximately 80,000 individual ac-
> counts, with an aggregate balance of $3,500,000. Abilities' personnel handle
> some 450,000 individual transactions a year.
>
> This project was so effective that Mr. Arthur T. Roth suggested to Mr.
> Henry Viscardi that it should be expanded to include employment of the
> handicapped in other phases of banking. . . . A budget was established for
> this training program and Franklin National Bank purchased a uniquely
> designed bus, with a lift platform in the rear, for persons who use wheelchairs.
>
> Mr. Roth has stated that he expects the contract with Abilities, Inc., for
> the junior savings program will save Franklin National Bank ten percent of
> its previous operational costs after . . . a full year.

Actually, it never worked out to a 10-percent savings for the bank;
but then again, it didn't cost us any more than we had been spending.

About this time Viscardi became involved with the Kennedy Foundation for the mentally retarded and set up a foundation to train mentally
retarded workers. Strangely, when the retarded people with IQs of 50 or
60 were introduced into the same places where physically handicapped
people were working, the handicapped resented it very much. Later,
however, they came to accept the retarded for their childlike qualities.

We found that the mentally retarded enjoyed repetitive, monotonous
operations, such as separating and counting nickels, dimes, and quarters, and posting them into passbooks. They were extremely accurate
and were never bored by the work.

Even though there was now ample proof that the physically handicapped and mentally retarded could do many tasks better and more
cheaply than our regular employees, I was still unable to persuade our
officers to hire such people. The only way was to let our bank officials
see for themselves how well Abilities, Inc., could perform; so we began
holding weekly officers' meetings at Viscardi's plant. There would be
perhaps 100 officers there, and they could actually see the variety of
work being done. Then they began hiring the handicapped.

16 • No Smoking

I have never smoked, and have always thought it a dangerous and costly habit—costly not only to the smoker but to the employer.

At Franklin, starting about 1958—which was some four years after the important studies on the relationship of smoking and disease began coming out—I issued a rule that there would be no smoking at work. To enforce it, I had all ashtrays removed from our bank buildings. But the rule didn't stick; the chief excuse was that customers wanted to smoke and that we had to go along with the wishes of our customers. Gradually, the ashtrays began to reappear.

I tried the same tactic a couple of years later, and again it didn't work.

Then several things happened. A young man in charge of our computer department, William Nagel, died of lung cancer. He had been smoking about three packs of cigarettes a day. And it occurred to me that as chief executive officer of the bank, I was responsible for the bank's investment in its people. Loss of a key executive like Nagel was not only a human loss to us who knew him and to his family, but an economic loss to the bank.

This put smoking into a new frame of reference. If I couldn't convince people that smoking was bad for their health, perhaps it could be demonstrated that smoking was costly to the bank. So I had a study made.

At that time Franklin had about fifty branches and 1,200 employees. Half of these smoked. Now it was known that smoking caused illness and absenteeism. This was a cost. And then the smoker had to stop work to light up, and interrupt his work to smoke. And there were burns on furniture and rugs. And there was extra cleanup of butts and ashes. It averaged out, in dollars, at least $7 per smoking empoloyee per month, we figured, or $100,000 per year.

Soon thereafter I was driving to a directors' meeting in Mineola at 8 A.M. one humid, drizzly day. I had a sinus headache and the pain was especially fierce. I thought of having to sit in a smoke-filled room for a few hours, and how I'd feel afterward.

At the beginning of this meeting I told the directors of the high cost of smoking to the bank. I also said: "I feel it's discourteous to blow smoke in a customer's face; and many of our customers do not smoke. And, in my own case, I know I'm going to leave here this morning in real pain, much worse than I'm feeling now, just because of the smoke. I feel it's time we enforced the no-smoking rule at the bank. But we can't do that unless we set the example."

And I asked them to back me on this, and went around the table polling each man. I started at my left, where I knew I'd be supported by Herbert Mirschel and Philip Weisberg. And after their two yeses, when it got to John Gibson he was reluctant but he said he'd go along to see how it worked out. And then no one said no—it was unanimous.

Two days later there was a meeting of top administrative officers of the bank, perhaps twelve people, and I told them what had happened at the directors' meeting and asked them if they'd go along. They agreed to give it a try.

The next step was a larger one: the bank's officers, about 100 people. We met that same week. This time I presented the problem a bit differently. I mentioned Nagel, who had died at about age forty. I said that if they all continued to smoke, we could expect to lose one or two more young, valuable men in the same manner. I said, "Truly, this isn't a concern of mine. But I was given the responsibility to see that the bank operates as profitably as possible, and the fifty percent of employees who smoke are costing us a hundred thousand dollars a year. It's inequitable, unfair, and wrong, and so we'll follow the example of our directors and our administrative officers, and from now on there will no longer be any smoking at any time in the bank, except in the washrooms and lunchroom. And this means even if someone comes in to work on the weekend. And it includes monthly officers' meetings at hotels— even during the cocktail or dinner hour."

Well, the silence was deafening. And later you could hear them talking in the hallway about the new edict. I told them I wanted to tell all employees the next day, without delay. When I did, it was obviously not a popular announcement. People never like to be told what to do; and it would certainly be better if no one had to tell them. But executives are paid to make judgments and to put their decisions into practice. If we're wrong, we're responsible.

At first it seemed that the no-smoking rule had lit more fires than it put out. The bank's washrooms were crowded and blue with smoke. The lunchroom was much smokier than before. But the working areas of the bank were blessedly free of the rich, ripe aromas of tobacco smoke. This was true not only in the headquarters branch but in all the branches. I made a point of stepping up my visits to branches to see that the rule was enforced.

It took about a month for things to settle back to normal—I mean that the no-smoking practice continued, but no longer were the smoking areas so crowded or smoky.

Once or twice at officers' meetings someone would light up to demonstrate his independence. But it would always be a lone smoker, and his cigarette would stand out like a smoke signal in the desert.

The rule helped many smokers who had wanted to quit or cut down. Our company doctors' reports indicated that about a third of our officers had reduced their total smoking by about one-third. Several quit altogether: One was Jimmy Smith, who became president (he started smoking again), and another was Jim Boshart.

We had an enormous number of letters from customers; those in the vending-machine business took their borrowing elsewhere. But we received more than enough compensatory new business from people who commended our action. On balance, the publicity was enormously favorable to the bank. At the next shareholders' meeting, Lewis D. Gilbert, the corporate critic who had often supported Franklin's policies, got up to attack us for limiting employees' liberties to smoke on the job. He was smoking a cigarette while he talked. When he got through, I explained our reasons, and the reactions; and then called for a vote from those present. It went 250 to 1 against Mr. Gilbert.

I was on the board of Mercy Hospital in Rockville Centre and I spoke to Sister Mary Jean, the superintendent, about the fact that the waiting rooms were thick with smoke. This seemed to me a violation of all that a hospital stood for. Sick people came there to be cured of disease, and they might have their symptoms exacerbated by having to breathe in other people's smoke. Sister Mary Jean said, "What can I do about it?" And I said, "Just put up a no-smoking sign. If people must smoke, they can go outside." I also suggested having cigarette machines barred from the hospital. Why sell poison in a health institution?

A friend of mine had to go into Mercy for a serious operation. He was a three- to four-pack-a-day smoker. After his surgery he asked the nurse for his cigarettes. She said they'd been removed from his clothes. "Well," he said, "then buy me some cigarettes." She said she would, but the next day there were no cigarettes. He repeated his request. And she agreed again. The third day the man demanded his smokes. And the nurse said, "You know, you're here for a serious operation. The hospital is trying to cure you. We don't think you should try to damage your health while we're doing our best to get you well."

Well, the upshot was that he never did get his cigarettes. And being forced to do without them for several weeks made it easier for him to quit altogether. He told me later he was everlastingly grateful to the hospital for helping him to get rid of his habit.

In 1968 I used the economic approach to smoking in testimony before the U.S. House of Representatives when they were considering the Cigarette Labeling Act—the one that strengthened the "Caution" to a "Warning" and dropped the "may be hazardous" for the more definite "The Surgeon General Has Determined that Cigarette Smoking Is Dangerous to Your Health."

At that hearing I projected the bank's figures into the United States as a whole. Smoking causes a very high percentage of building fires; this raised fire-insurance rates for everybody by about $200 million a year, considerably more today. Smoking-caused forest fires cost another $100 million or so. I calculated that smoking cost about $4 per week per smoking worker in increased absenteeism and illness. In England, about ten to twelve times as many man-days are lost to chronic bronchitis and emphysema, largely caused by smoking—as well as about 30,000 deaths each year from these diseases—as are wasted in *all the industrial disputes in that country*. Passing the cost of smoking workers on to the consumer added about $8 billion a year.

Life-insurance premiums cost more, too, since the nonsmoker paid the same rate in most companies as the smoker. A few companies give nonsmokers discounts; it should be the other way around—they ought to charge smokers a higher premium since they are at a greater risk from a whole list of diseases, mainly heart attacks, strokes, and various forms of cancer. I calculated the extra cost of life insurance attributable to smoking as $600 million a year; another $500 million had to be spent on health insurance for the same reason.

Cost in higher auto insurance hasn't been figured; but one company gave large discounts to nonsmokers because they had so many fewer accidents; another company gives really substantial discounts to non-smokers for their homeowners' policies because they are so much better fire risks.

Add all these things in, plus the expense in public buildings, cleanup of cigarette butts, etc., and you were well over $9 billion a year in costs. Then, add to that what people spend on cigarettes—it's now more than $30 billion a year. And the cost of smoking-caused disease and death is up around $32 billion or more. Now you've achieved a total cost to the country as a whole of more than $60 billion. Deduct the "benefits" in the form of cigarette taxes, which mount to about $6 billion a year, and you come out with a net social cost of cigarette smoking of around $55 billion a year.

Leaving out the cost of cigarettes (and the taxes), the net cost is still about $20 billion. This is what smoking costs all of us, mostly the nonsmokers since we are the great majority.

In 1973 I testified before the House Ways and Means Committee on revisions of the tax law and suggested that we could help make the smokers pay their share of this national burden, and at the same time help many reduce their smoking if not eliminate it, by raising the federal tax on a pack of cigarettes steeply, at the rate of 25¢ a year for about three or four years.

It is a proven fact that when the price of cigarettes outruns the general rise in prices of all commodities, the amount of smoking tends to drop. A tax commissioner in California once stated that smoking had tailed off in his state only twice: once after the famous 1964 *Surgeon General's Committee Report on Smoking and Health*, and then in 1969, when the state tax went up from 3¢ to 10¢ per pack.

I testified: "You are never going to stop people from smoking. But I hope that such a tax will first of all cover the costs of cigarette smoking, and secondly I hope it will cut in half the amount of smoking that is being done at the present time." The Nordic governments have taken a step along these lines; cigarettes there cost several dollars a pack, and the main purpose isn't tax revenue but deterrent. Some people will do more to save a dollar than they will to save their health or their lives, and young people just can't afford to start smoking.

Of course this has to be done nationally, since it was well known that there was smuggling of cigarettes from states like North Carolina, where the tax was only about 1¢ a pack, to New York, where the state and local taxes added up to about 20¢ or more. If the tax is national, then the only smuggling that makes economic sense would be from abroad— and it would hardly be worthwhile to run the risks for the amount of money involved.

17 • Franklin 1960 to 1966

1960

In 1960 we earned nearly $9 million, showing an increase of 19 percent over the previous year. *Fortune* magazine rated Franklin first among the fifty largest commercial banks in earnings, with a ratio of 21.1 percent of capital funds. The median return for all fifty banks was 10.1 percent. Total assets of the bank had increased to $801,674,585.

This was the year that the omnibus banking bill passed the New York State Legislature, and was declared unconstitutional through legal procedures instituted by Franklin National Bank. It won us a year to plan our actions under the new act which would inevitably become law.

1961

An important year in American banking. The New York State Omnibus Bank Act became law, and the U.S. Justice Department brought several suits against bank mergers under the Federal Bank Merger Act of 1961. The federal act was designed to prevent mergers or acquisitions if these had the effect of lessening competition or creating monopolies.

The proposed merger between First National City Bank and the National Bank of Westchester was denied by Comptroller James J. Saxon. The Federal Reserve Board also held public hearings on important applications for the creation of holding companies, and on mergers affecting two Long Island banks.

Franklin announced its forthcoming expansion into New York City.

We opened our forty-second, forty-third, and forty-fourth branches in Manhasset, North Valley Stream, and Merrick. Total resources were up to $904,817,991. Earnings of more than $9 million after taxes equaled 17.3 percent of capital funds, still first in the country among the fifty largest banks. Franklin had moved up to the thirty-second position, from thirty-fifth the year before.

1962

We jumped seven places, to number twenty-five among U.S. banks in 1962. Total resources were now well in excess of $1 billion and we were still number one in profitability. We added three branch banks— now up to forty-seven.

Preparing for our entry into New York City, we decided to increase our total capital funds to $100 million. To achieve this without substantially diluting our shareholders' equity, we decided to do something that few banks had done for many years: issue preferred stock. Our shareholders approved this on October 15, 1962. We marketed $20 million of 4.6-percent $100 par value preferred through Eastman Dillon, Union Securities and Company. The dilution was only 7¢ a share of common, as against an estimated 34¢ dilution had we sold additional common stock. To further augment our capital, we transferred seventeen of our banking properties to an affiliated corporation, which mortgaged them with institutional investors for $15,861,000. The bank then leased back the properties for twenty-five years at annual rents equal to amortization and interest. We could renew the options at reduced rentals, or repurchase the properties.

Meanwhile, the $15 million cash was invested in long-term municipals yielding 7.5 percent pretax, which equaled the amortization and interest on the money. Thus, in twenty-five years, the bank would own the properties at no cost, and meanwhile had the use of an extra $5,837,264 in surplus and undivided profits. These transactions were cleared with the Internal Revenue Service. The rules have since been changed—such leaseback arrangements must now exclude repurchase to qualify for tax benefits.

My salary as chairman and chief executive officer stood at $75,000 a year, $5,000 more than the then president's, Paul E. Prosswimmer.

We took a suite in the Hotel Chatham in east midtown Manhattan and installed Patrick J. Clifford, the most brilliant business-getter in

New York banking. We could start creating the connections with prime-rate borrowers in the city preparatory to the bank's entry. Pat Clifford did a magnificent job bringing in New York City customers whom we would need when we actually opened offices in Manhattan.

1963

We opened our fiftieth branch. Still number one in profitability, we slipped back one notch to twenty-sixth place in size; although our total resources had risen to $1,272,839,777. A tabulation showed that if someone had owned four shares of Franklin stock in 1940, at a total original price of $200, by 1963 he would have 1,695 shares through stock dividends and splits. Market value of the shares: $79,665. Cash dividends would have amounted to $12,000 during those twenty-three years.

We were building branch offices at Hanover Square and at Madison Avenue and Forty-eighth Street in New York City. Signs at the construction sites read: "A Country Bank Coming to New York." A third office, at 189 Montague Street in Brooklyn, was also planned to open at the same time as the Manhattan branches.

At our November 1963 examination by the office of the comptroller of the currency, two large loans were criticized. In 1963 we were forced to charge off $5,612,144 against our reserve of $18 million.

1964

We entered New York City after several years of planning and preparation, opening three offices the same day—May 18. By the end of the year, we had opened two more branches in New York, for a total of five. Our resources for these new offices on December 31 totaled $479,303,084, including $331 million of deposits.

Our expenses to achieve this quantity of business—including occupancy, advertising and promotion, personnel in training, stationery supplies, and the increased Federal Reserve requirements—amounted to 43¢ per share in 1964 and would cost another 32¢ in 1965. Through 1967 it was projected to cost $1.07 per share after taxes; much less than the price of merging with any available New York City bank.

The bank's total resources were now above $1.5 billion, and we had moved up to twenty-first position among the nation's banks. Our profitability was still high, but because of the extra expenses of expansion we were, for the first time in many years, only second in profit as a percentage of capital funds, .3 percent behind the most profitable bank which was considerably smaller than we were. My own salary was $85,000; Prosswimmer's was $80,000 that year.

1965

The bank's total resources rose to $1,707,953,060 to make it the twentieth largest bank in the country. Fifteen years before, we had been number 1,231. The ratio of profit to capital equity rose to 13.4 percent, putting us again in the leading position among the nation's twenty-five largest banks.

In June 1965, Franklin became the first New York bank to inaugurate a savings-bond program—what we call today "certificates of deposit." We sold bonds with face values of from $25 to $500,000 with five-year maturities at a rate of 4.80 percent. This brought in a great deal of liquid funds in a tight money market. We were able to increase our loans to $921 million because we had the money available more than 20 percent above the 1964 total. Almost all were commercial loans; our real-estate loans actually dropped by $5 million that year. Personal installment loans rose by some $15 million.

However, our charge-offs for bad loans were unusually high in 1965, at $7,438,746, up nearly $5 million from the previous year. In our report to shareholders we wrote:

All bank loans contain some risk, and some loss experience is inevitable because economic conditions and the affairs of the borrower can change quite drastically in a fairly short period of time. Our high loss experience this year is primarily attributable to the sharp decline in real estate values which took place in 1962 and from which that market has never fully recovered. Franklin owes much of its rapid growth to an aggressive lending philosophy and has been especially active in financing building. In the perspective of time these policies have been both successful and profitable since the bank has sought to be compensated by charging higher rates on loans which contain more than the average risk. Over the past 10 years our earnings on loans have averaged 6.28 percent before average losses of .33 percent. The net of 5.93 percent compares favorably with the net 4.45 percent earned on loans in the same period by other New York City banks with deposits of over $1 billion and a net of 4.88 percent for New York City banks with deposits of over $100 million but under $1 billion. . . . All losses estimated by the National Examiners in their latest report of July 1965 have been charged off.

1966

Franklin National came close to the $2-billion mark in resources: $1,928,896,000, an increase of more than 14 percent over the previous year. The bank now had sixty-seven branches, including two unique New York offices: Le Banque Continentale and the Bank in a Park.

One significant event of 1966 was the charge-off of $12.9 million loan losses; the bank had more than $1 billion loaned out at the time. The Annual Report explained:

As we noted last year, most of the possible losses developed in loans to builders and real estate investors as the result of the depressed state of the real estate market since 1962. This was further aggravated in 1966 by the scarcity of funds for real estate financing. With easier credit and improvement in the real estate market, recoveries are anticipated.

Our lending policies have undoubtedly contributed to Franklin's rapid growth. But in the light of the unusual loan losses, we have strengthened our lending procedures and policies, and have continued to diversify our loan portfolio. We have also expanded our internal loan review system by the establishment of an enlarged Loan Review Department. A Special Loan Department has also been created to recover as much as possible from our previously charged-off loans.

Franklin had been negotiating for a merger with the Federation Bank and Trust Company, a New York–based bank with $246 million in deposits. Federation had thirteen branches in parts of the city where Franklin did not. We agreed on the terms in December 1966, and proposed the merger to our shareholders at our annual meeting, March 14, 1967. (The proxy statement had been sent out a month earlier.) The merger would result in an expanded bank of seventy-nine branches and $1,884 million in deposits. It was to be accomplished by an exchange of stock. Franklin issued slightly more than $20 million of a new voting convertible preferred stock to pay for the Federation shares.

Too, the resulting bank, still known as Franklin National, would expand its board of directors. Franklin had had only eleven directors. These would be retained; and to them would be added six of Federation's officers and directors, to form a board of seventeen members. The new members from Federation would be John P. De Santis, 47, president and chief executive officer of Federation; Vincent P. DiNapoli, 67, president and chairman of the board, Tully & DiNapoli, Inc., General Contractors; Sol Kittay, 56, president and chairman of the board, the B.V.D. Company, Inc., Manufacturers of Apparel; Michael J. Merkin, 74, senior vice-president of Federation; William J. Tracy, 69, president, M. & J. Tracy, Inc., Towing; Harold A. Webster, 63, chairman of the board, T. T. Frederick Jackson, Inc., Electrical Contractors.

The new board would therefore have seventeen directors, one of whom (Merkin) was already over the age limit for directors according to Franklin's regulations.

18 • "A Country Bank Comes to New York"

We had been forced to move into the New York market by the logic of events. Once the omnibus banking bill became law, the New York banks were free to invade Long Island. We had participated, and would continue to participate, in the growth of Long Island. To my way of thinking, that was our home base. But now, with the big commercial and savings banks free to move into what had been excluded territory, we knew that our possibilities of expansion on Long Island would become limited. There were only so many people, so many businesses, and so much real estate—and with the giants moving in, much of our area of expansion would be crowded, much business would be sponged up.

We were being forced to compete with the big city banks—it was that or eventually be absorbed by them. When Knute Rockne was coaching the Notre Dame football teams that beat everything in sight, his favorite expression was "The best defense is a good offense." Before the giants got into our backfield, we had to break through into theirs. And that meant, inevitably, that we had to move to New York.

We had been thinking about moving into the big town for some time—we hadn't wanted to be hasty about it. We were only the second Long Island bank to make the move—the first had been the Meadow Brook. We wanted to come in with plenty of business, plenty of cash to lend, and with a dramatic move that would not only be substantial but *look* substantial. That was why we decided to build our own distinctive buildings. This kind of debut had much more impact and would therefore be worth much more money to the bank in the long run.

As the *American Banker* said later, quoting an unnamed competitor:

He had really come out swinging, and that's the only way to crack this market. His personal touch is already obvious in the bank's bid to get a toehold in New York City. Slow to start (his rival Meadow Brook National Bank took the plunge in 1960), Mr. Roth subsequently has moved with dispatch and in his own distinctive style.

Not content to open one branch at a time, he will open three for a starter; promises six by the end of the year, has scheduled 25 by 1970. . . .

We had made plans for this much earlier, as soon as we realized that our fight against the omnibus bill was only a delaying action. In the 1961 *Annual Report* (published in the spring of 1962), the chairman's letter stated that we were going to open two branches in Manhattan in the fall of 1963 (Hanover Square and Madison Avenue).

"I have been asked about the possibility of your bank purchasing established New York City banks instead of starting from scratch. The answer is that we have not found a situation that has appealed sufficiently to us in terms of location, personnel, economical operations, and price."

At the public hearing on the proposed merger of the First National City Bank with the National Bank of Westchester. I had testified (in part) that this was only the first in a series of projected mergers that threatened the structure of banking in New York State; multibillion-dollar banks like the Chase Manhattan, the Chemical New York Trust, and Morgan Guaranty were planning to take over banks with a total of 587 branches throughout the state: Of these, 275 were regional banks. Franklin National was not threatened; we were almost unique among regional banks in our ability to fight on even terms against even such powerful competition. But if the mergers were permitted, it would just about destroy the system of regional banking in the state—a system that had not only permitted but encouraged the establishment and growth of small businesses. Once the big banks took over the regional banks, they would institute the kind of lending practices they had with their big-city customers.

The large banks are used to dealing with large customers—"prime-rate customers," they're called, because they pay the lowest rate of interest—and think in terms of profit and loss. The local banker, the regional banker, is in a different kind of world. His customers are his neighbors, who are usually small businessmen. They live in and work in the same towns. They have relationships with many dimensions beyond the narrow range of profit and loss.

To prove the difference between how Franklin and big-city banks made their loans, we asked twenty-one of our leading officers who had previously worked in large city banks to analyze at random 1,400 business loans made by Franklin. How many of these loans would have been made by their previous big-city affiliations? The average was only 33 percent—that is, 66 percent of the local loans that we at Franklin found meritorious would have been turned down by big city banks.

As part of our testimony, we appended an earlier statement made by Joseph M. Landow, a certified public accountant for a great many Long Island business firms. Mr. Landow had said, in part:

> Financing for the small businessman by large city banks has not been adequately developed.
>
> This had not been malicious or intentional, but is due to a basic failure to understand the problems of the small businessman. . . . The local banker is our last remaining link of any consequence with the small businessman, and especially to the fellow who needs $10,000 or less.
>
> If local banking, as we now know it, is replaced by large city banks; if credit approval is taken out of the hands of the very bank officers who know the businessmen; if the personal relationship between the bank president, vice presidents, directors and the borrower, especially the small borrower, is lost; if the small businessman is frustrated in borrowing, then loan sharks, high interest rate factors and check-cashing companies will become as prevalent here as they are in the large cities . . . where financial wolves prey upon the desperate needs of small businessmen and their inability to obtain much-needed and merited loans from reputable financial institutions.

As previously noted, the comptroller of the currency rejected the merger between First National City and the Bank of Westchester. Later, one of our own applications—for a branch in the Village of the Branch— was rejected, and I complimented Jim Saxon publicly for this, not because our application didn't have merit but because I felt that there had been far too many new branches, far too much bank expansion: We had been forced to set up new branches in order to keep up with the trend, but it would be much better for banking if this kind of runaway expansion could be curbed.

Not that Franklin was suffering in any way. When I addressed that New York Society of Security Analysts on November 9, 1962, I recalled that back in 1947 I had been introduced to Governor Thomas E. Dewey of

New York as head of a bank that earned 20 percent on its common equity.

Governor Dewey had asked, "How big is your bank?"

We then had only $30 million in assets. The governor said, "Well, the trick is to have those kind of earnings when you have $300 million."

The fact is, Franklin continued to earn the same kind of percentage; the lowest was in 1956, when the profit was only 14 percent of equity; highest in 1947, 29.2 percent. Now that we were over a billion dollars, earnings were still above 16 percent. One reason our profits were slightly lower was that we were paying out a great deal more in interest for savings accounts.

I predicted that for the next eight years we would be earning around 20 percent on equity; that we would become eighteenth in size among U.S. banks; and that we would not have to sell any new common stock except to meet stock options.

The reason I selected an eight-year period was that the analysts often asked where we were going over the long range—and because in eight years, in 1970, I expected to reach the retirement age of sixty-five.

A number of their questions dealt with the coming entry of Franklin into New York. One was why we had chosen to open our own branches, instead of buying another bank. Buying an available bank would have cost a premium of about 25 percent over book value. We expected to go into New York with committed assets of $200 million—at a cost of about 3 percent.

Asked how soon we expected our New York branches to be in the black, I replied, "Immediately," and explained that we had been planning this move for some time, and had been putting a great deal of New York business on our books.

We also discussed our new buildings. We were constructing two, both in the Georgian colonial style that had become the bank's trademark. Not only were they distinctively our own, but they were actually cheaper to erect then the banal curtain-wall skyscrapers that were going up all over town like so many cereal boxes. At Madison Avenue and Forty-eighth street, we'd have a seven-story building with about 60,000 feet of floor space. I knew this wouldn't be large enough for very long, so had made an effort to buy the adjoining property. This was owned by two sisters who refused to sell. However, they might one day change their minds, so our building had a curtain wall at the rear. If the adjacent property became available, as one day seemed likely, we could always knock out that wall and join the two buildings. Our elevator would be able to serve both—it was designed with that in view.

Hanover Square was our flagship building—a thirteen-story structure with 110,000 feet of space. When I began buying the land, the area was very run-down—mostly old warehouses, a saloon, a printing plant. It was a kind of slum. The land was cheap—only $100 a square foot. I bought three or four adjoining plots. There was one more I wanted, but it was occupied by a bar and grill that was doing well, and the owner refused to sell.

This was the only adjacent area into which Wall Street could expand. Yet because of the physical appearance of the place at the time, I was considered almost a little out of my mind for buying it and for putting up such a large building for a bank that was just coming into the city. I was told that the building would remain largely vacant; but it was designed only for the bank, it wasn't space that could be rented out. The entire project was called "Roth's folly." Who would be so stupid as to put up a brand-new building in a run-down area like that? Today, of course, Hanover Square is surrounded by huge glass-fronted skyscrapers that dwarf Franklin's rather elegant brick building. Which only makes it the more distinctive.

We planned the move like a military campaign. There were the buildings, plus another in Brooklyn. There was the personnel, not only the officers but all the people who would work in our branches. I wanted the public to have an impression of something new, fresh, really our style—a country bank in the big city. We hired guides from some of the big agencies in the city, people who were trained to deal with tourists, and we asked them to train our young ladies in grooming, walking and dress, to give the same kind of welcome.

But all this was the facade—important, but still only the surface. It was what was underneath that counted. A bank's merchandise is money, and I wanted to be sure that we had plenty. We planned the move into New York during a period of easy money. But I was certain that this would not last.

The bank held many mortgages with interest rates of 4.25 and 4.5 percent. Such mortgages sold at a large discount, for about 85¢ on the dollar. These were twenty-year mortgages; the average life of our holdings was about ten years.

We devised a program to sell these mortgages that would give the purchaser a 5-percent return—the bank would guarantee to make up the difference. In this way we were able to sell about $35 million worth at par. We sold the mortgages to savings banks, which, at that time, were looking for such investments; the transactions were approved by the IRS and the comptroller of the currency.

This looked, on the surface, like a money-losing proposition. But we had all our money in cash—and we had it at a time when money became tight. So we actually were able to lend out this money at favorable rates of interest, and to earn more that way, even though we would have been content to break even just to have the money to lend to new customers in New York City.

The country had been in a boom, which was accelerating. It seemed almost certain that the Federal Reserve would have to slow things down by reducing the supply of money to force banks to raise interest rates. I wanted to have plenty of cash on hand when this happened, so that Franklin could make loans.

Another way of raising cash was certificates of deposit or CD's. We had tried to use this legal device a dozen years earlier and had, as so often, been forbidden to do so by the comptroller of the currency. He said it was "borrowing money" which we had no right to do.

But we learned that some commercial banks in Georgia were selling CD's in the early 1960s and apparently weren't being stopped by the comptroller. So I sent several officers down to see how they were doing it; they bought some and brought back application forms.

CD's were attractive to investors for the long term; they carried a high rate of interest and they were like bonds, redeemable after a fixed period from one month to twelve years, in our case.

I held a meeting of our senior officers and told them about the plan: that we were going to offer 4.8 percent interest—one-half of one percent above the going rate.

I was supported by several of the top men, but about 90 percent of the officers opposed the idea. And they found leadership in the man whom I had always trusted, who had been my right arm in a number of controversies. I hadn't known how deep or broad this opposition was. But I said we would go ahead and gave the necessary orders to buy the forms and the certificates, whatever was needed to put the plan into effect and to set up procedures within the bank to handle the business.

This was in May when we were going into vacation time and things were slow. But it seemed to me that things were slower than they should be in regard to our certificates of deposit. There was one excuse after another—the printer was busy, the paper wasn't available, and so forth. And then I really looked into it and found that the plan was being deliberately delayed. My orders were actually countermanded by this subordinate, a man in whom I'd had fullest confidence until that time. He was going around and saying that my certificates-of-deposit plan was crazy, that I was going off the deep end, and he was giving instructions to delay and just not follow my orders. It was outright sabotage: The forms just were not printed.

This man who sabotaged the plan for four months was not really a commercial banker by training—he had worked in savings banks and I had hired him as a public-relations officer, to help in the fight against savings banks. When I learned of his insubordination, his sabotage, I reprimanded him very sharply, and took over the plan myself. Made sure that the forms were printed, wrote the advertisements for the newspapers and saw that they were inserted. We ran them in the largest newspapers in major cities all over the country, and the response was terrific. We raised $400 million via certificates of deposit; we did so well, in fact, that the savings banks began screaming to the Federal Reserve—they were paying less than we—and the Feds again stopped us from continuing the sale. If the plan hadn't been sabotaged, we would have had an additional four months of selling time, and I estimate we would easily have raised another $200 million for a total of $600 million.

As it was, we were the only bank in New York with money to lend when the money supply tightened. But with the additional $200 million, we might have had from CD's, we would have been able to take on some big customers who would have helped to guarantee Franklin's future in the competitive New York market. The delay was to cost Franklin very dearly.

Another way we raised cash was to buy federal funds from banks all over the country. The background is: Banks required to carry a certain amount of credit reserves sometimes have more money than they need in the Federal Reserve, and they sell that money. It's called "federal funds sold." And sometimes they're short of federal funds and they have to buy. Small banks around the country are rarely fully invested, so they usually have more federal funds than they need.

Federal funds were bought and sold daily. But we sought out the small banks with surpluses and bought these weekly. To get this money, we paid them a bit higher return than they had been getting. In this way we built up sizable amounts of funds which were available to our customers as the credit market tightened.

All of these methods of raising cash were legal and honorable. But we were one of a very few banks who undertook them—and perhaps the only one to exploit every possible means of raising money. The reason was that I foresaw a return to tight money, and was particularly concerned since we were opening new branches in a new market and wanted to be able to operate freely in that market.

Each of our schemes was expensive—we attracted funds because we paid more than others were willing to do. If my forecast had been wrong, we would have lost money. But my forecast was correct and because I had confidence in my judgment and took the prudent risks to back it, we not only made money, we were able to establish our bank in New York—the most competitive market in banking.

We opened our three New York branches on May 9, 1964, and had a week of festivities—a Ben Franklin ball; and in the banks, women dressed in gowns of the period to go with our architecture. But the important thing was that while the biggest banks were short of cash, Franklin was overflowing with money to lend. And as a result, we got started with a rush of business.

19 • La Banque and the Bank

In 1966 Franklin opened two unique branches, La Banque Continentale at the elegant corner of Sixtieth Street and Fifth Avenue, and the Bank in a Park, at Broadway and Howard Streets in the heart of the then very inelegant loft and warehouse district.

La Banque originated this way. About 1965, my wife and I went to the opera one night. We had four tickets but no guests. We decided to give the two extra tickets to anyone waiting to buy seats. As it happened there was no line at the box office, but we saw a man wearing formal attire who seemed quite perturbed. I asked him if he was looking for tickets, and he replied in a foreign accent that he had expected to meet someone—I think he called her Princess Doria—who had tickets. I offered him the extra pair and he thanked us.

No one sat in those seats during the first act but during the intermission the man came down and returned the tickets. He said that his hostess had shown up, and asked us to join them for a drink. He said he was a physician and asked me what my profession was. I said I was a banker. He said, "I wish that American banks would offer the kinds of personal service we get in Europe. They take care of your mail and your jewelry and perform many services that banks do not do here."

That stuck in my mind. I decided to look into the operations of private European banks. I went to Europe with one of our directors, a real-estate man, Norman K. Winston, and visited a number of private banks in London and Paris.

Most were in converted palaces or private houses. Very little space was devoted to paying and receiving tellers; most of the bank's business was transacted on an upper floor, in private offices. There was no feeling of hustle and bustle; they weren't like business establishments. You felt you were visiting someone at home when you visited the head of the bank.

In starting our special branch, we decided to give it a French name, La Banque Continentale, which doesn't require a knowledge of French to be understood. The architectural theme and decor were to be late Louis XVI, about 1780, a refinement of French rococo.

I wanted a bank where important depositors could come and feel at home, where they could receive personal services such as buying tickets for the theater, or having servants hired to open a country house, or finding a school for a child—things that few American banks were equipped to do. Obviously such services would be too costly for the average branch. This one would require depositors to maintain a large minimum balance to provide these services without charging for them.

Minimum balance for a personal checking account was set at $25,000, very high in 1966. The bank would also take savings accounts for checking-account customers; the minimun in savings was $5,000. For a business concern wishing to use La Banque, the minimum balance would have to be at least $50,000.

When I presented the idea to our board of directors, they didn't like it. They thought it wouldn't pay—that there weren't enough depositors of this type. I was sure there were; I had taken some private soundings. Of course the start-up cost would be fairly large; we would have to spend a considerable amount on decorating the bank to give it the private-house atmosphere. And we would have to find some highly trained, highly educated people to staff it. I thought it might take seven years before the branch became profitable, as against about three years for an ordinary branch, but that the prestige and the type of business it would bring would be worth the extra cost.

The directors reluctantly agreed and I began looking for space on the Upper East Side of Manhattan. I had been told of a location at Sixtieth and Fifth Avenue some time previously but hadn't taken it seriously. Now I went inside and looked and saw how beautiful it was, with a view of Central Park across the street. Hanover Bank had financed the building, which was an apartment house, with the idea of using the ground floor as a branch. Then they merged with Manufacturers Trust Company, which had a branch at Fifty-seventh and Fifth, and they had no need for the space at Sixtieth. They held a thirty-year lease on the ground floor, which was vacant, at a tremendous bargain because of their financing the building: They were paying only $6 a square foot, with a small increase due after thirty years.

I spoke to Fisher Brothers, the people who built the building, and I said I was willing to buy the lease. That would be advantageous for Manufacturers Hanover since they were obligated to pay for the next thirty years. After some negotiating, I assumed the lease but caused Manufacturers Hanover to pay Franklin $150,000.

We wanted the bank to be run like a private club. We set a limit of 800 depositors. It would take more than just money to get in. We created a board of overseers to decide who could become depositors; on this board were a number of people who were quite well known and knowledgeable about New Yorkers with money. They included: Admiral John J. Bergen, Enos Curtin, Miss Mildred Custin, Vincent Draddy, Hon. Leonard W. Hall, Howard K. Stoddard, Ed Sullivan, and Mr. and Mrs. Norman K. Winston.

We were quite serious about the standards. One man who actually lived in the same building where La Banque had its offices, and was a large business depositor in one of our other branches, was refused "membership" because he had some unsavory connections in horse racing. There were other such cases.

The exclusivity, as well as the personal services offered by this beautiful bank, attracted a great number of the kind of depositor we wanted. One woman walked in and opened a checking account with $750,000. A safe-deposit box was given without charge to each depositor. For people like this, the ordinary tin boxes didn't seem very accommodating; so I designed a safe-deposit box made of wood, with special compartments inside for securities and jewelry and an inventory form that depositors could take home and so keep track of what was in the bank vault. The form also had information about securities—what they had been bought at and when; what dividends were due and the dates; and so on. I had thought of this as just another service for our customers, but our lawyer suggested that it was unique and therefore patentable. We took out a design patent, Number 205,641, August 30, 1966, made out to Arthur T. Roth of Rockville Centre, New York, and assigned to the Franklin National Bank.

We designed every aspect of the bank to reflect taste and personal attention. Eugenia Sheppard, the fashion authority, wrote in the *New York Herald Tribune* on opening day, April 20, 1966:

You can't help feeling sorry for all the banks that have been luring lady depositors with pastel checks and checkbooks. . . . The whole pastel check bit was completely upstaged yesterday by a simple, snobbish, snow-white check. Simple, but how elegant can you be? This check is not printed at all. It is engraved in the old, upstanding style that passes the finger test. The vacant lines for sum of money and signature aren't black, but thick, raised strokes of gold. It's the Mainbocher of the check world.

None of those plastic button-over covers, either. A lady who signs engraved 14-karat-gold decorated checks carries eight of them folded into a flat little gold box that drops into her handbag. Her signature is engraved on the inside of the lid.

The check-beautiful arrangement is all part of an overall mood engendered by La Banque.

Miss Sheppard went on to describe some of the bank's antique furniture and pointed out that the guard, whom we called "host," was born Baron Henry von Tuyl. The baron kept a pistol discreetly in the back pocket of his striped pants. "A kind of Claridge's of the banking world," she concluded. "Nothing is too much trouble, even to making a hair appointment, or paying for anything sent collect."

An AP wire story was widely published. In the *Cleveland Plain Dealer* of April 24 it read, in part:

"Personnel who speak as many as six languages, some of the finest art in the world, an 18th century French residential atmosphere, a butler, maids to serve tea as you undergo the arduous task of withdrawing money, six-days-a-week banking service, 14-carat-gold membership cards that cost la Banque an average of $150 each, but cost you nothing, personal accounting and bookkeeping, evening vault and safe deposit hours [there was a Savonnerie carpet on the floor of the vault] and delivery of cash to residences in Manhattan."[2] *Business Week* gave the opening two full pages, with pictures; *Time* headlined their story "The Swank Bank."

Of course some large New York banks had special departments to serve their rich customers; they had kept this from the general public. One banker sniffed that we would attract only the nouveau riche. This did not prove to be the case; our own policies of reserving membership in our branch to those recommended and passed on by the overseers saw to that. But La Banque was an attention-getter; it brought Franklin a great deal of unusual and valuable publicity.

But it was only one new aspect of our variegated institution. Eight months after the elegant uptown branch opened, we built a new little branch in a run-down neighborhood in the Lower West Side, at Howard Street and Broadway.

We bought the property on the corner, which had been a 75′ × 100′ parking lot in the heart of the machinery and textile district. With the very creative help of Eggers & Higgins, architects, we constructed a compact hexagonal building, in the bank's traditional Georgian style, which took up only the rear portion of the land. The rest was left open, landscaped with twenty-one linden trees and large flowerpots. The sidewalk was repaved and the property bordered by hedges set in a low brick wall. There were benches to attract neighborhood folk who wanted to rest for a moment in our small park.

It was an immediate hit with the neighborhood. One woman who refused to disclose her identity in her letter to the *New York Times* called it "the most beautiful thing that has ever happened in this neighborhood." The opening on December 12 was attended by, among others, Thomas P. F. Hoving, then administrator of recreation and cultural affairs for the city of New York, who said he hoped that other businesses would emulate Franklin in establishing neighborhood parks.

We offered the same sort of help in sprucing up the area we had given to our old neighbors in Franklin Square so many years before— special long-term loans to finance face-lifting their properties. To give the bank a proper setting, we covered the decaying walls of adjacent buildings with huge squares of white marble, and set a cluster of old-fashioned lantern-style lamps into the corner.

It was altogether a charming and unexpected oasis that attracted not only attention but business as well. We gave away Scotch pine seedlings to all on opening day, and more than 2,000 had been handed out by 3 P.M. We opened 200 accounts the first day alone. No fewer than 7,000 of the businessmen in the area came to visit during the opening week. It was a sure thing that the new branch would be in the black far sooner than the conventional three years.

20 • A Country Bank Acquires Big City Problems

Opening new branches means hiring new officers, and these of necessity come from other banks. The fact that they are available may have meant that they are dissatisfied with their previous employment. Perhaps they weren't promoted when they felt they deserved to be; and perhaps their employers had good reason to believe that they weren't really qualified for promotion.

In other words, not all of the new officers we hired were the pick of the litter.

We brought key people with us, of course—some of our best. Our president, Paul Prosswimmer, was our chief lending officer. He had done very, very well for the bank on Long Island, which had been in a perpetual building boom. When you lend money to builders, and the market continues to rise, you never have any problems.

But the real estate market fluctuates, especially in New York City. When there are periods of overbuilding, there are times when the real-estate market goes flat or drops. And if you lend money to New York builders and the market turns down, you may have some shaky loans on your hands.

Things began to come unstuck in 1965, when New York City was overbuilt in apartments and office buildings. We had some very substantial loans with New York builders. Such loans are usually uncovered by bank examiners. But outside examiners, no matter how shrewd or careful they may be, are limited in what they can find out. If they locate a problem loan, they discuss it with the officer in charge, and if he can reassure them, they don't report it.

This is what was happening with Franklin. We had problem loans that we didn't know about. It took about a year or more for them to surface. One day a bank examiner came to me with a small loan, about $8,000 or $9,000, and said that it looked as though it had problems. I looked it over and said, "That's a bad loan. It should be charged off, no question about it." The examiner was shocked. That was what brought the situation to my attention. I looked into more loans and found that if we could collect 10 percent of some of them we'd be doing well. And I realized that this had been going on for a long while without my knowing it.

What made the situation even more urgent was the fact that we were negotiating a merger with the Federation Bank of New York. The comptroller's office in Washington asked me to come down and discuss the merger; they were reluctant to approve it. They said, "Your bank isn't in very good condition. You have criticized loans totaling more than $50 million."

I said, "I'm shocked to hear what you say. I'll make myself personally responsible to clean up those criticized loans. And I'll see that they are reduced by at least seventy percent within a year."

When I returned to New York, I called a meeting of our top lending officers and told them what I had learned. "We have a disproportionate number of criticized loans in this bank. We're permitting questionable loans to be renewed when we should be asking for substantial liquidation." I asked them to put on paper what they felt should be done in the way of corrective action so that these loans would be paid off in a reasonable time.

As promised, I took personal control of the loans: set up a committee of four officers—Prosswimmer, Lewis, Clifford, and myself; told them we would have to reduce criticized loans by 7 percent each month. They said it couldn't be done, it was too much.

I hadn't been involved in lending for some time but said I would prove it could be done—that I would personally take over the five biggest and most troublesome loans and wanted each of them to do the same. We would be personally responsible for seeing that those loans were cleaned up.

As an example, our biggest and worst loan was All State Properties. We had loaned them about $5.6 million and the bank examiner wanted to charge it off—all of it. I talked it over with him and convinced him that we ought to delay on the write-off. He insisted that we charge off at least $1 million; but I held out for the other $4.6 million.

All State owned a lot of land, about 50 or 100 acres near Montauk

Point at the tip of Long Island, and other such holdings, including parcels of property near Fort Lauderdale, Florida. They would buy up underdeveloped land and build on it. Each purchase was made in the name of a wholly owned subsidiary, but the loans were in the name of All State.

I separated the loans into individual transactions, identified by the name of the subsidiary, and worked with each one to try to put it in bankable condition. The bank accepted some All State stock, and we had to advance some additional money. But that nearly disastrous loan has since paid off. The bank lost nothing, not even the $1-million write-off.

Another large loan, around $800,000 or so, was to a large builder who had done a lot of the construction at O'Hare Airport in Chicago and also around the New York City area. He had run into some cost overruns and was in trouble. But we worked it all out—that $800,000 was all collected.

In the first year we reduced our criticized loans from $48 million to $24 million.

Paul Prosswimmer felt the brunt of the pressure, as chief lending officer. The loans which he personally handled were quite sound. But there was general laxity in the administration of loans, and the resulting problems had a poor effect on Prosswimmer's health. He got stomach ulcers and had to spend time in the hospital. This forced him to lighten his burden, to dispose of much of his work.

While Paul Prosswimmer was out of action, his work was taken over by William Lewis, the bank's executive vice-president. Bill Lewis criticized many of Prosswimmer's loans. This was the first time in more than twenty years—since Prosswimmer had joined the bank in 1946—that his loans had been criticized. He resented it very much. So we asked for another expert opinion. Howard Crosse, who was in charge of our bank's examinations by the Federal Reserve, was asked to step in and look over these loans. And he agreed with Bill Lewis. Lewis was a very sound lending officer, but extremely conservative. He and Prosswimmer never hit it off. And their lending policies were exactly opposite. Where Prosswimmer knew real estate well and concentrated in that field, Bill Lewis refused to make any builders loans.

I said that builders' loans could be sound and profitable if administered properly. We set up a special real-estate-loan department and we transferred all real-estate loans from all branches to that department. We increased the charges all along the line. It became one of the most profitable departments in the bank.

Many of the loans had been administered by new personnel. But Paul Prosswimmer, perhaps because of his illness, hadn't stayed on top of that business. When you administer loans you're supposed to get proper financial statements from the borrowers. We hadn't been getting them. Then, a certain amount of a loan is allocated for operating buildings. The builder has to know his costs, and the lending officer must know the builder's costs, and if these go up the officer must know about it. In those days costs were running up the flagpole—and this wouldn't have been so bad if renting had kept pace. But it hadn't. Vacancies increased, which meant that the builders didn't have the cash income to meet their loans.

In lending, you must plan beyond the initial investment to the source of repayment. Suppose a building goes sour? You must have knowledge of the builder's other resources in the form of land that the builder owns, or other properties, or other collateral. These may have to be tapped for money to repay the loans.

These considerations are elementary in lending—but these fundamentals were being ignored. However, it wasn't merely a question of dealing with the poor loans, or with the people who made them or administered them. What we needed, obviously, were clearer guidelines, better methods, materials and documents that would make lending as foolproof as possible.

Systems training taught me to begin at the beginning in analyzing a problem. You start with the mail in the morning; you open it and read it. You work alongside the clerks and the messengers. Gradually, you work your way up the pyramid so that when you reach the top you know what has been happening.

I looked at the liability cards—there is one for each borrower—and the loan journals; I examined the notes to see how they were drawn, to learn whether they covered the items that should be covered. Many, many changes had to be made in the notes. For example, if the borrower didn't keep a sufficient supporting balance in his account—a problem more common today than it used to be—he would be liable for additional charges.

In a large bank you need some internal control. You can't depend on the lending officers to evaluate their own loans. And you certainly don't want to wait for the bank examiners to come along and tell you that certain loans are problem loans. The bank's own auditors should be competent to find that out. At Franklin, our auditors were examining loans and criticizing them; the lending officers would say, ''We don't know what they mean—these loans are just fine.'' They put the auditors on the defensive.

I wrote a memo to Bill Lewis on June 20, 1966, about the procedure of having criticized loans reviewed by our Loan Review Section:

> Effective immediately loans classified [questioned] by our Loan Review Section are to be reported to Harry D. Loester in the same manner as loans criticized by the National Bank Examiners. This applies in those cases where the National Bank Examiners have not criticized a loan as substandard, doubtful or loss and it is criticized by the Loan Review Section. Also, if a loan is more severely criticized by the Loan Review Section than the National Bank Examiners, then the Loan Review Section criticism is to be accepted. In other words, the more severe criticism is to be considered.
>
> This memorandum places the Loan Review Section's criticisms on an equal basis with that of the National Bank Examiners.

Another thing we instituted at that time was a penalty for all past-due loans. There was a great deal of slackness in administration; when a loan was overdue, the officer might call the borrower and ask him to come in. Now I wrote into every loan that effective immediately all past-due loans would be charged an extra 3 percent interest. If a customer neglected to pay his obligation when due, or didn't take the trouble to renew his loan, he would immediately be charged an extra 3 percent. That perked up the administration of loans considerably, and, of course, the only people who were bothered by it were those who neglected to pay or at least take care of the problem when it came due. These weren't our good customers, they were our problem borrowers, the ones we didn't need or want.

I insisted on charging a rate of interest commensurate with the risk of the loan—the riskier the loan, the higher the interest rate. I did this not only to protect the bank but to discourage marginal borrowers.

In those days it was unheard of to charge more than 6 percent interest. But we charged 8, 10, 12, 15 percent. Charging a high rate gave us leverage in forcing problem borrowers to reduce their loans. Borrowers would propose that if they paid off part of their borrowings, we ought to reduce the amount of interest. Which, of course, we were glad to do.

I remember Bill Lewis coming to me and saying, ''We're getting a terrible reputation as a high-rate bank.''

I pointed out that we were doing it only on those loans that had been criticized. "Those loans weren't bankable loans. Let's force them out with high interest rates. We don't want their business now or ever; let's get some good customers."

I recall one loan in particular where I set an interest rate of 12 percent. The man had put up an art collection as collateral. But he had kept custody of his paintings; the bank had no protection—he could have sold them. I asked for custody of that collection and the appraisals. If you don't have custody of collateral, you don't have collateral. Furthermore, I instructed the officers to ask that the collection be insured in the bank's name. And wanted a contract calling for repayment of a fixed portion of the loan every quarter.

The man came to see me to complain about having to pay such a high rate of interest. I said, "You've been borrowing well over a million dollars from our bank, and you're keeping only 5 percent of that amount in supporting balances. You should maintain a balance of at least twenty percent."

He wasn't the worst, by any means. We charged some of the less desirable borrowers as much as 18 percent. I believe they got the message; so did the officers who had been so lax in dealing with them.

We set up a rating system of all the loans made by each officer to see how many were fine loans, good loans, fair loans, problem loans. Nobody liked the idea of that kind of analysis; it made their performance too visible for comfort. But it put them on their toes.

We insituted a new system on maturity dates of loans. The way it had been working was this: A customer would borrow money, usually for ninety days. Then he'd come in ten days later and say, "I need a little more cash," and take out another loan due ninety days later. Within the period of the first loan, he might come in as many as twelve times, taking twelve different loans, each with a different maturity date. That way it was impossible to know how much the customer had borrowed, or how well he was doing at repayment. It was almost total confusion.

Under the new system, let's say a man took a loan due on February 1. Then he came in a few days later and took another loan—that, too, would fall due on February 1. All his subsequent borrowings would be lumped together and would fall due on the same date. Under the old system we had had three times as many maturities as we should have had. We reduced them by this simple device.

Furthermore, when a man borrows in sums of $100,000, he can do so six times and you've got a total of $600,000. Well, an officer looks much more carefully at a $600,000 loan than at a $100,000 loan. Merging the maturities merged the amounts and tended to make officers much more careful. But we had to enforce the system; it wasn't automatic. We had to look over the liability cards, and when officers ignored our maturities rule we had to call them down and lecture them.

All this was done in a series of intrabank memoranda and forms in 1966. It was, of course, impossible to cover all contingencies in advance, but the general rule was that there should be as few exceptions as possible—and each exception had to be justified as beneficial to the bank.

Lending had never been so codified; we learned that our memoranda and lending forms and policies were widely circulated and adopted by other commercial banks.

21 • 1968: Year of the Knife

Nineteen sixty-eight was a year of great financial turmoil in the world. The United States was at the center of the storm, and the dollar was under great pressure. For the first time, U.S. tourists in Europe found their dollars being refused. The U.S. balance of payments became more and more unfavorable. Our gold stocks had dropped from a high of $24.6 billion in 1949 to a low of only $10.7 billion. American companies, using Eurodollars, had bought heavily into European industry—we owed some $34 billion overseas. And with the international gold standard still in effect, it was no wonder that the world became jittery at our economic irresponsibility.

It was an election year in the United States and President Johnson had committed himself to increased federal spending. This would have led to more inflation, and further worsening of our position in international trade. According to the Federal Reserve in its April 1968 bulletin, "A considerable range of U.S. goods may have become somewhat less competitive since 1965. Average wholesale prices in this country have risen faster than similar prices in other countries." This should not be thought of as a "temporary aberration, but as a new trend that can be changed only slowly and with difficulty." The Fed recommended a program of slowing the inflation of costs and prices in the United States. It also recommended the resumption of economic expansion in Europe.

The problem was twofold: We had to put our own economic house in order, and we needed our allies to work with us to prevent worldwide economic collapse.

A number of European bankers sent strong signals to Congress, via interviews in the U.S. business press, to do two things—raise taxes and cut spending. Both of these were thought to be necessary, but in a presidential election year there were few politicians who were willing to follow Wilbur Mills, our House fiscal expert, and come out and say so.

And many people's minds weren't focused on finance during the spring of 1968. There had been the shocking assassinations of the Reverend Martin Luther King, Jr., on March 4, followed by massive riots in many cities and much unrest. Later came the assassination of Senator Robert Kennedy, on June 5. It seemed that the fabric of our society was being ripped to shreds.

The economy was also in real danger. Something had to be done. A joint House-Senate Conference Committee agreed early in May on the Tax-Adjustment bill of 1968, which provided for a 10 percent tax surcharge, a $6-billion reduction in government spending for fiscal 1969, a $10-billion reduction in new obligational and loan authority for the same year, and a recision of $8 billion of past appropriations. The bill had a fair chance of enactment until organized labor announced its opposition. However well intentioned that opposition might have been, it seemed fiscally irresponsible to me and other people in finance. Because of labor opposition, the vote on the bill was delayed until after Memorial Day.

At the American Bankers Association Monetary Conference in Puerto Rico on May 21 to 24, the threatening international crisis was the key subject. Leading international bankers from many countries were there.

Secretary of the Treasury H. H. Fowler came to the conference on the last day, a Friday. He divided the 100 U.S. bankers into groups of about fifteen and met with them separately. To each he described the impending crisis, and asked for help. To the meeting which I attended he said, "We're in the worst condition this country has ever been in. If we don't put our affairs in order, we're in serious trouble. We have to get the tax legislation through, but this is an election year and we just can't get a nose count on how congressmen will vote." President Johnson had been elected on the strength of his Great Society program, and the men who had been elected with him were afraid they might lose if they came out for cuts in government spending.

Secretary Fowler said: "This is a financial problem. You are the experts. I'm asking you to contact your congressmen and senators and tell them about this critical problem, and ask them to vote for the bill."

The bankers reacted negatively: They said they had no contact with

Congress; perhaps they could work through some of their clients or friends who did have contacts.

I said, "Gentlemen, all your congressmen know *you*. This is our responsibility. If the country goes down the drain, it will be banking's fault if we don't take direct action. We don't have to know our congressmen, all we have to do is call them and visit their offices and tell them the whole story. If this is so critical, we all ought to take two weeks off from business and do nothing but this."

As we left, Secretary Fowler stopped me and said he had been told he could count on my support. I said that when I got back to New York I would write to every bank in the country asking for this kind of help. And I would call up the Bankers Committee for Tax Equality, representing about 5,000 small banks, which had done such important work on the tax structure of banking, and get their help as well.

When I spoke about my plans at the bank, I found that our new president, Harold Gleason, was opposed to the idea of getting involved in a controversial piece of tax legislation. We might make enemies; we might lose business.

Such considerations had never deterred us from standing up for principle, I pointed out; and here the entire country was facing a desperate crisis and most people knew nothing about it. They would suffer if corrective measures weren't taken—we would all suffer.

Gleason said that two of our directors were opposed to this kind of activity. I had called a meeting of Franklin's senior officers to discuss this national financial emergency and to explain what we were going to do. I invited the two critical directors: Sidney J. Hein, a sixty-year-old lawyer; and Michael J. Merkin, the seventy-five-year-old former senior vice-president of the Federation Bank, now vice-chairman of our board. They were both knowledgeable in politics. They said that I was wrong; that the bank would lose deposits by taking a position in controversial legislation; that we had no right to do it; that other banks weren't doing it. They said that I ought to have board approval before acting.

I replied that what I was doing was in the best interests of the nation—and that Franklin's interests were not opposite to that. I had never asked for board approval of any of the many controversies we had engaged in, and none had damaged—but had only enhanced—the bank's reputation. I said I was going ahead on my own judgment.

They didn't like this at all. They lost face before the officers; and they got together with the man I had made president, Harold Gleason, and began organizing opposition against me and my policies, although I did not know it at the time.

My letter to bankers went out on Franklin stationery, printed in the middle with a solid red ball, "to signify the grave DANGER facing you and our nation if we do not start placing our house in financial order by passing the bill to increase taxes and reduce expenditures.

"The House is now ready to vote on this bill. If the bill does not pass, then we can expect chaos and calamity. And, we bankers must assume most of the blame, for our profession makes us experts on finance."

The letter pointed out the serious changes that had taken place—high mortgage rates heading for 10 percent; the U.S. government paying over 6 percent on borrowings; the rise in cost of manufactured goods; the accelerated increase in the cost of living; and the loss of confidence in the dollar. I pointed out that the huge overseas credits could lead to a run on the American dollar.

"Many Congressmen do not want to vote for this bill. However, the grave seriousness of what will happen if this bill is not passed overrides all objections.

"Defeat is unthinkable. Passage by a slim margin is likewise unthinkable. *Responsibility to our country calls for 100 percent approval.*"

The letter concluded by asking them to contact their congressmen and to fill out a card indicating the Representative's response.

The Bankers Committee for Tax Equality got busy, too. A report from Vernon Scott in Washington told about organizing votes to defeat an amendment by Congressman Burke of Massachusetts to H.R. 15414 (formerly the Tax Adjustments Act of 1968). The Burke amendment would have instructed the House committee to bargain with the Senate for a reduction in spending of less than the $6 billion in the bill. The amendment was defeated. Now we had to have some help from the president. I told Fowler we couldn't really organize support for the bill until Lyndon Johnson came out unequivocally for it.

On May 31, Secretary Fowler sent me excerpts of the president's news conference on May 30 in which LBJ did state very strongly the need for a tax increase and an expenditure reduction. "Without [the bill]," President Johnson told reporters, "the gates of economic chaos, I think, could open. And I think this country would face . . . an inflation tax of at least four cents on every dollar; second, interest rates could go up as high as ten percent; third, a severe housing depression . . . ; fourth, the disappearance of our world trade surplus;

fifth, the end of our unprecedented eighty-seven months of prosperity. . . .'' He urged Congress ''to adopt the conference report at as early a date as possible and give me the opportunity to sign the measure.''

Secretary Fowler wrote, ''I thought you would want to have this handy during the crucial twelve days that are ahead.''

We continued the campaign, with the encouragement of the House Ways and Means Committee, using every means of communication— letters, telegrams, telephone calls, personal visits. Replies began coming from bankers all over the country, indicating that we were building a positive vote on H.R. 15414. We ourselves contacted all twenty New York State congressmen and found sixteen surely in favor, one who would vote *aye* if needed, and another who would be favorable if fifty other Democrats approved. There were only two negative votes: Representatives Tenzer and Wolf.

We informed Representative Wilbur Mills. On June 7 the *Wall Street Journal* reported his saying, ''I'm not worried about the vote. I feel confident this bill will pass.''

But on June 10 Vernon Scott wrote me, ''The Revenue Bill is in serious danger.'' He pointed out that a great majority of the 186 Republicans would be for it if we could persuade about 125 Democrats to vote for it. The Republicans would not support it as a party although we would get some Republican votes—unless we had at least that majority of the 247 Democrats in favor. It was a matter of politics because labor and liberal sentiment were opposed.

On June 12 Vernon Scott tabulated votes as he saw them:

	Republicans	*Democrats*
For	75	117
Leaning for	37	29
Undecided	37	41
Leaning against	18	23
Against	20	37

That day the *New York Times* came out strongly for the bill, pointing out that narrow self-interest on the part of politicians was blocking a law that would ''keep things from falling apart and give the nation time to consider a sounder and more comprehensive fiscal program.''

On June 20, the bill passed the House of Representatives by a vote of 268 (154 Democrats, 114 Republicans) to 150 (77 Democrats, 73 Republicans).

The next day, Charles E. Kendall, Franklin's vice-president in charge of metropolitan sales and development, who had handled a good deal of the detail and follow-up of our campaign for the bill, reported in a memorandum: "The overall reaction is excellent. The senior bank officers contacted [in other banks] were very expressive about the unusualness of a banker taking the initiative on a countrywide basis. . . . Judging from the telephone response, we believe that the National Division [of Franklin] will receive many side benefits from the program."

Thank-you letters came from Wilbur Mills and Henry Fowler, the latter writing, "Without your assistance, and without the concern and dedication of other financial leaders like yourself, I am confident that the Congress would not have acted on this important legislation."

I mention these things because it became a matter of criticism against me at Franklin by several of the directors, and by our president, Harold Gleason, that I had taken part in a "political" activity, and had involved the bank's name in a fight over controversial legislation.

At our annual meeting on March 12, 1968, I had told shareholders that I was unhappy about the low (29¾) price of Franklin shares, down eleven points from the previous year, while other bank stocks were up. I explained that we had suffered too many loan charge-offs and had had to invest heavily in opening our twenty-four New York City branches. I also said that we expected earnings to increase to $3.75 in 1969.

I reported that we would raise additional capital either by selling shares in a holding company, the Franklin New York Corporation we were planning to form, or by selling more shares in the Franklin Bank, with shareholders getting an option to buy. The reason our board had decided not to recommend a stock dividend in 1968 was because it would unreasonably complicate exchanges of stock between the proposed bank holding company and its constituent bank.

There were questions from the floor about officers' salaries—"Why aren't they in the Annual Report?" professional stockholder John Gilbert wanted to know. It was "a serious omission," he said. I agreed that it was a serious omission, but it hadn't been intentional. We were ready to disclose all salaries—my own was $130,000, representing an increase of $5,000. President Harold V. Gleason had been raised to $75,000, commensurate with his new responsibilities—but this was still lower than the $88,000 that retiring president Paul Prosswimmer had been getting. I explained that we had a salary committee on the board of directors which measured Franklin's salaries against those of comparable banks. We had to pay competitive salaries in executive jobs.

The meeting was unusually rancorous, probably because of the poor market record of Franklin shares during the year. Yet we had had a good year in 1967, and were doing better. As predicted, year-end profits were up in 1968 to $3.60 and we were able to increase the cash dividend to $1.15 a share. The bank had more than $1 billion in demand deposits (the first time above the billion mark), a 21-percent increase over 1967. Total deposits were up to $2.3 billion; loans to $1.3 billion. We were eighteenth in size among all U.S. commercial banks. The bad loans were receding; we charged off $2 million less then the year before and our collections on previously charged-off loans were up over 1967. Franklin was still growing, and healthier.

Yet next day Franklin received its first critical headline. *Newsday* captioned its article about the meeting "All Not Rosy at Franklin National."

With Franklin stock selling well below its real value, at a price/ earnings ratio of only 11, as against 14.7 for other banks, the situation was ripe for an outsider to step in and buy control. I don't know when it started, but some then unknown investor began buying up Franklin stock quietly that spring. By June he had bought enough to provoke media interest.

"Who would have thought that a rumor of possible takeover of the Franklin National Bank could possibly get started?" wrote Robert Metz in the *New York Times* of Saturday, June 22. ". . . [T]wo leading bank-stock traders scoffed at the idea," he went on, but "What gave life to the idea was the fact that someone has been picking up substantial blocks of the bank's stock, according to one specialist. He was asked if the buying involved tens of thousands of shares . . . and he said, 'yes.'

"One other trader commented that there had been heavy buying from the West Coast during Franklin National's recent rights offering. . . . The stock was very weak at the time. Then the price snapped up, indicating that somebody had moved in and bought some."

Another specialist said that Franklin was a "natural takeover choice. There is a huge floating supply of stock and the trust departments of New York City banks haven't been buying the stock for investment . . . because of bitterness when Franklin opened branches in Manhattan . . .

Some rapacious investor was shaking the underbrush while trying to conceal his identity. But it was a fairly common piece of information that the beast in the forest was Loew's, Inc., a conglomerate controlled by the Tisch family, which had been buying into such companies as P. Lorillard.

At that time it was rather easy for outside interests to take over a bank. I felt that we should warn our shareholders that this could happen—that in fact it seemed to be happening. I decided to write them a letter about the rumor, and asking our good depositors and loan customers to buy up our stock to keep the bank independent, with ownership primarily in the hands of Long Island residents.

I wrote the letter and had about 50,000 copies printed to go to shareholders, customers, and friends of the bank. Harold Gleason, our new president, made it no secret that he was opposed to this letter. "Do you think we should do this?" he asked.

"In view of what the *Times* wrote, do you think we should ignore the situation?" I said.

"It may be illegal to mail this letter."

"Stan Waxberg [our lawyer] says it's legal," I told him.

"Do you think you should dignify a rumor?" Gleason asked.

"My checking indicates much more than a rumor," I said. "My information is that Lawrence Tisch has been buying our stock for months and intends to own a large interest in this bank, a controlling interest."

As it happened, my information was correct. Tisch bought up 20.5 percent of Franklin's stock, about 1 million shares, which gave him a controlling interest.

"Don't you care what happens to Franklin?" I asked Gleason. "You tried to sabotage our certificates of deposit; now you want to sabotage this warning to stockholders. What are you up to?"

What he was up to, I found out later, was meeting with a group of dissident directors. We had taken in the seven Federation directors, of whom their elderly Michael Merkin was most active. He was over the seventy-year age limit for directors, but an exception had been made because of the merger. I felt he was much too old to have so much authority; he should be retired. Our own Sidney Hein was also friendly with Gleason and Merkin. All they needed was to add a couple of Franklin votes to their cadre and they would have a majority of the board.

Gleason asked me if I wasn't going to call a special board meeting before sending out the letter to shareholders, and I said of course I would. The meeting was held on June 26 at the Madison Avenue branch; I cut short a vacation to head it as chairman.

At the meeting, Hein opined that my proposed letter was illegal. Stanley Waxberg's opinion was that it was entirely legal.

Sol Kitay, formerly of Federation, a large shareholder in Franklin and the head of the B.V.D. Company, said he had spoken to Lawrence Tisch about this rumor and Tisch had said he had no intention of taking over Franklin; he was buying our shares for investment purposes, just as he had been buying other stocks.

My proposed letter was put to a vote; the directors turned it down. It was now obvious that a majority of the board was going to oppose me.

After that, I was under a great deal of pressure. My wife and I were spending time at our house on Shelter Island, and Sidney Hein called me there and asked if he could come out to see me. He flew out by helicopter. He told my wife that several people who had a great deal of money invested in Franklin stock were worried about me. They thought that I had gone too far with my "red ball" letter and the campaign to support tax legislation.

And now there was my letter to shareholders, proposing to warn them of a "nonexistent" threat. I was unreliable, these moneyed interests felt, according to Hein. They didn't know what I might do next.

When Gleason was made president in 1967, I had told him that as the new broom he should sweep in some new ideas and new ways of doing things. I suggested that he look for a firm of management consultants to survey our operations, as a first step; when he had found a suitable firm, we would hire them.

We retained A. T. Kearney & Company, Inc.; they reported their findings and recommendations on June 28, 1968, to the board of directors. They found that all of the key officers of the bank reported directly to the chairman, which limited the effectiveness of the president and other senior officers.

But they said that "the strengths of Franklin National Bank are well known by the consultants and the financial community. . . . The bank has a record of leadership in banking innovation, a continued high rate of return on capital employed, and progressive growth in deposits and earnings."

In other words, they thought management control too centralized; but if this was so, it was not reflected in the innovative and moneymaking record of Franklin.

Still, these experts were willing to recommend a shift from a management that had created the "record of leadership" and all the rest "by transferring the responsibilities of the Chief Executive Officer from the Chairman to the President." No criticism of our past record—only the consultants felt they knew better than management how to continue doing what we'd already done; "To manage successfully in the future period of rapid change, Franklin must be capable of planning for the future, have capable trained personnel to perform a variety of tasks requiring high degrees of management and technical skills, and have the information and controls necessary properly to evaluate and to manage the institution." As fine a collection of platitudes and empty phrases as one could buy. And I might add that such surveys cost a great deal of money.

The recommendations were a handy excuse to carry out certain designs —something for the record, on an engraved letterhead, a facade behind which those who wanted to take control of Franklin could operate. They would come before the board at their next regular meeting, July 18, 1968.

Another of our directors, Harold Webster, told me that there were enough votes against me to do anything the opposition wanted. What they wanted was to change the bank's bylaws, so that the chairman would no longer be the chief executive officer. The chief executive officer would be the president; in other words, as Kearney recommended, Harold Gleason was going to take over the leadership of the bank.

"You can go along with it," I was told, "or you can oppose it. The result will be the same. But if you go along, it will obviously be less damaging to Franklin's image."

I felt there was no choice but to go along—or be responsible for making internal disputes public, with consequent injury to the bank's reputation. Since I did not have the votes to oppose, I said I would go along.

I had been planning to step down at the following annual shareholders' meeting; it was a matter of moving it up by about ten months. So I proposed it at the meeting. Several of my friends were shocked at the idea. But because I had proposed it, they voted for it. Herbert Mirschel, who had been a good friend for more than thirty years, became quite angry with me; he felt I had abdicated my responsibility.

The *New York Times* story on Friday, June 19 was headlined "Roth Steps Down at the Franklin—Directors Disclaim Pressure—Gleason Given Chief Post." Noting that I was sixty-three, the paper quoted my statement that "this change was made now rather than waiting until I became sixty-five [the bank's mandatory retirement age for active officers] in the interest of long-recognized good management practices. . . ." Gleason had been with Franklin since 1956, the *Times* noted, following a twenty-year career in a Brooklyn savings bank. He was forty-nine in 1968. Wrote the *Times:*

> One prominent Wall Street figure said there was "probably quite a bit of pressure from the directors." . . . Opposition to Mr. Roth, it was said, had centered in a group of directors on the Franklin board who had joined the bank last year when it merged with the Federation Bank and Trust Company.
>
> "It was a real power play," said a source close to this group.

Of course the key members of the group that had engineered the power play denied it. The *Times* story also contained the statement that I was "a bit too controversial for a bank with close to $2.5 billion in assets."

Finance magazine wrote in October 1968 that bank stocks had been in disfavor for a long time, and that "one starting result" was the shift at Franklin.

> It was abruptly disclosed that Arthur T. Roth, who built Franklin National Bank, was no longer chief executive officer. The designation had gone to Harold V. Gleason, Franklin's president, who joined the bank a dozen years ago as a kind of press agent.
>
> What happened was that the former owners of Federation Bank & Trust Co., which was merged into Franklin at the price of 800,000 shares of stock, had bought another 380,000 shares when the price was in the trough and Franklin's problems—of which it has a complete set at the moment—look larger with every qaurter-point lost in the market. With that added muscle, the Federation people had gone to the old Franklin directors and convinced them it was time for a change.

As might be expected, I received a great many letters from bankers and government officials about this sudden change. One was from Upton E. Liptrott, president of banking's daily newspaper, the *American Banker*. Mr. Liptrott wrote that when he read the news on July 19, "I said to my wife, 'No one can tell me that Arthur Roth really intends to put aside his mantle,' and I still have to be convinced.

"At any rate, if I was in Harold Gleason's shoes I would have my fingers crossed as long as you are with the bank, notwithstanding his great talents, as he will be facing up to a man who is surely one of the greatest bankers in the history of the industry, as well as a leader who could say 'yes' time after time and make it stick, while *all* others were saying 'no.' ''

I replied, ''Yes, it is true that I am going to slide out of some of my responsibilities at Franklin. Harold Gleason has been closer to me by far than anyone else at Franklin. He knows how I think and act. And, of course, I will be at his side for many years to come.''

I had made many forecasts for the bank and for business in general, with a fair record of accuracy. But this was one prediction that wouldn't work out.

22 • Resignation

On January 8, 1969, we had a bankwide officers' meeting at which I summed up the remarkable turnaround of Franklin during 1968. Our stock had risen from $31.50 to $46.50 a share during the year—a rise of 48 percent. I attributed half of the increase to the general improvement in all bank earnings; but one-half was certainly the result of the many improvements at Franklin.

- We had cleaned house of problem loans and their heavy losses.
- Those responsible for bad loans were no longer with the bank.
- Marginal accounts had been weeded out.
- Franklin had at last been accepted by the big New York City banks as a member of the "club."
- Our money-market operations were impressive.
- We had successfully sold 15 million shares of common stock at an attractive price.
- We were doing business with a growing number of prime national accounts.

Furthermore I could have added:

- Our net operating earnings reached an all-time high of $18,433,000—an increase of 23 percent over 1967.
- We held no loans classified as losses.
- Our substandard loans declined to only 16.2 percent of gross capital funds, proving the success of our loan-administration program.

- Our $20-million reserve for loan losses was more than ample to cover sub-standard loans of about $24 million.
- Our 5.9-percent capital loan ratio was good.
- Our liquidity was good.
- We had weathered the recession in better condition than many of the twenty-five largest banks (as shown by the year-end statement of condition reproduced on page 240–241).

One would have thought, with that kind of record, our directors would be a happy group. But such was not the case. The old spirit had been eroded. There was a new attitude I did not like. It used to be all shoulders to the wheel for the common good. Now it was all hands out for the brass ring. Too many were looking for a free ride.

The organization chart the Kearney group had prepared to go with their report showed both the chairman and the president, who was now chief executive officer, as reporting to the board. But the chairman had no operating responsibilities. The chart showed a dotted line between the chairman and the president, indicative, I suppose, of voluntary cooperation between the two. Many of Franklin's directors thought that this was being implemented; they had not visualized Harold Gleason's taking over and running the bank without consulting me. But this was, in fact, what he was doing.

I was not invited to committee meetings. I was not kept informed of current problems. The new group was determined to make me into a figurehead; they wanted only my name and presence.

There were two choices: to stay and to play along, or to leave. I chose the first course as a temporary option for several reasons. One was that an open rupture might have precipitated a stockholder brawl that could have done real damage to the bank. Also, I knew that Harold Gleason was not a strong person. His chief stock in trade was his personality, his desire to get along with others, to be liked. This had made him a pleasant companion. But there was a good chance that sooner or later he would need help and advice in areas where he did not have experience or expertise. It had been understood that I would be there to help out if needed.

But there was another aspect. Gleason's malleability left him vulnerable to others on the board who had selfish interests in building their power, in getting loans from the bank, and in other things.

This was reflected in the board meeting of December 18, 1969. At that meeting the Senior Officers Salary Committee of the board was scheduled to report on a revised salary schedule, which included a raise for Harold Gleason, who had already been given a substantial increase to $75,000 the year before. Gleason had told the Salary Committee that he would be satisfied with the proposed modest raise. And Director Sidney Hein had indicated his willingness to go along with the recommendations. But when John Tuohy, the committee chairman, attempted to give his report, Hein verbally shouldered him aside. He said that he had been mistaken when he agreed to go along with the committee. That since Gleason was now chief executive officer, his salary should be equal to mine—that is, $130,000. This represented an increase of $55,000 for Gleason, far beyond what the committee had contemplated. He also had $20,000 of deferred compensation coming in the future, for a total of $150,000.

Hein's action had the effect of precipitating what one director later referred to as a "donnybrook." There was shouting, there were personal insults, and so much confusion that no vote was taken and some people had the notion that the committee's report had prevailed.

Two weeks later I received a letter marked PERSONAL AND CONFIDENTIAL from Herbert Mirschel, who had been on Franklin's board for forty-three years. He was one of the bank's original founders. As he was going to be seventy-two, he had decided not to continue on the board after the next annual meeting, in March 1970. But following this bitter fight, he wrote me, "a 'small voice within me'—usually silent— came through to me in full volume saying, 'Herb, you don't have to take this. You are getting off the Board anyway—do it now! And in doing so—in present-day vernacular—tell it like it is.' I have heeded my 'small, usually still voice.' Gleason knows why I sent in my resignation."

It was a very, very bitter letter. He "could not fathom why [I] did not insist on order, decorum and proper procedure.

"You must know that what was done, and the way it was done, was to humiliate you in the greatest degree. You even allowed Hein to openly insult you. I do not suggest that you should have traded insults with Hein. Perhaps your lack of reaction was an exhibition of admirable self-control but to me it looked like you were a zombie."

He wound up by saying, "This letter is intended to be an attempt by shock therapy to recapture your noble spirit. . . . Favorable prognosis will depend on how deeply Gleason's personal press-agent-ism has contaminated your system—mental and physical."

He also spoke of his "surviving and continuing friendship." I felt that way about him, too. It shocked and wounded me deeply to

FRANKLIN NATIONAL BANK STATEMENT OF CONDITION—YEAR END (FIGURES ARE IN THOUSANDS OF DOLLARS) 1968

Resources	Year End December 31,			
	1968	Percent	1967	Percent
Cash and Due From Banks	$304,790	10.6	$317,860	12.1
U.S. Government Obligations	421,769	14.7	361,654	13.8
Municipal Obligations	482,778	16.8	485,005	18.5
Federal Agency Obligations	40,240	1.4	51,662	1.9
Other Securities	22,620	.8	20,182	.8
Total Securities	967,407	33.7	918,503	35.0
Federal Funds Sold	163,100	5.7	71,810	2.7
Loans	1,340,283	46.8	1,245,097	47.5
Less—Reserve For Loans	20,000	.7	20,000	.8
Net Loans	1,320,283	46.1	1,225,907	46.7
Bank Premises and Equipment	42,891	1.5	44,999	1.7
Customers' Liability on Acceptances	20,929	.7	20,456	.8
Accrued Interest Receivable	20,609	.7	17,344	.7
Other Resources	28,268	1.0	9,002	.3
Bank Premises and Other Resources	112,697	3.9	91,801	3.5
TOTAL RESOURCES	$2,868,277	100.0	$2,625,881	100.0

LIABILITIES

Deposits:				
Demand	$1,032,125	36.0	$ 849,669	32.4
Time	1,269,038	44.2	1,321,786	50.3
Total Deposits	2,301,163	80.2	2,171,455	82.7
Securities Sold Under Agreements to Repurchase	77,107	2.7	54,502	2.1
Federal Funds Purchased	231,841	8.1	161,090	6.1
Mortgages Payable	25,450	.9	26,105	1.0
Acceptances Outstanding	21,455	.7	20,752	.8
Unearned Income	17,685	.6	15,813	.6
Dividends Payable	2,325	.1	—	—
Accrued Interest, Taxes and Other Liabilities	21,496	.8	27,920	1.1
Total Other Liabilities	62,961	2.2	64,485	2.5
TOTAL LIABILITIES	2,698,522	94.1	2,477,637	94.4

CAPITAL FUNDS

Capital Debentures (4¾%—Due 1988)	30,000	1.0	30,000	1.1
Equity Capital:				
Preferred Stock ($4.60—$100 par)	20,000	.7	20,000	.8
Convertible Preferred Stock ($2.45—$25 par)	20,524	.7	20,524	.8
Common Stock ($5 par)	22,762	.8	19,907	.7
Surplus	65,000	2.3	50,000	1.9
Undivided Profits	11,469	.4	7,813	.3
Total Capital Funds	169,755	5.9	148,244	5.6
TOTAL LIABILITIES AND CAPITAL FUNDS	$2,868,277	100.00	$2,625,881	100.0

know that my actions appeared so ineffectual to someone with whom I had had mutual respect for so many years.

I determined to speak out at the next board meeting. I wanted Hein to be there to hear what I had to say. He didn't come in on time and I delayed for about three-quarters of an hour before starting the meeting. When he still hadn't arrived, I opened the meeting without him. I said that a fine director had resigned in disgust because of the disgraceful conduct of another director. He had wanted to give up his place on the board to a younger man in the due course of time; but after what happened on December 18, he had abruptly quit.

"This director, who had caused the disruption, had openly insulted me," I said. "He is a bad and disturbing influence in this bank. He creates disorder. He disrupts decorum and proper procedure. And for me to say that I could not expect proper decorum from him in the future would be futile."

My meaning could not be plainer. I felt that Hein should get off the board in the best interests of the bank.

Hein came in after I had finished my criticism, His opportunity for revenge was created early in February, 1970. I was in Florida playing golf. When I came back to the hotel, the message light was lit on my room telephone. My secretary, Marie Ballin, had been calling—she had left four messages. I called back. She said that *Newsday,* the Long Island newspaper, had been after her. They wanted to interview me about some real estate I was supposed to have bought in Suffolk County. It was all unspecific and vague; I didn't know what it was about—I had no papers with me. I said I didn't want to be interviewed.

Abut a week later, when I returned home, I found myself in the midst of a press blizzard. Headlines all over the place. Reporters calling up and demanding interviews. Because on February 5, *Newsday* had devoted the entire first page of the paper, plus three full pages of the first five, to me, and to a "land syndicate" to which I was supposed to belong.

The first page carried a large picture of me above the caption "Roth: A Question of Conflict."

The huge headline read: LAND SYNDICATE HAD A PARTNER IN THE PLANNING.

The gist of the sensational charges was that I was one of six members of the Nassau-Suffolk Planning Board and that I was a member of a "real estate syndicate" that had been buying up $2 million worth of land near the Grumman airport in Calverton.

The paper said that in March 1968 I had "obtained access to a confidental board proposal for a major airport and highway network" in Calverton. A few months later I had joined the "syndicate" to buy up this land.

It sounded terrible, and the way the paper presented it, it seemed much worse. Under the front-page headline, they had statements from several local government people who opined that it seemed there might be a conflict of interest between my public position on the Planning Board and my private activities with the "syndicate." In very large, bold type, also on the front page, was the statement "Roth's secretary, Mrs. Marie Ballin, after being telephoned four times yesterday with requests for an interview with her boss, said: 'No, on Mr. Roth's authority.' " The implication was clear that I was dodging an interview, that I must have something to hide.

The land "syndicate" included my son Donald; my son-in-law, John Madigan; my son-in-law's father; and our dentist; as well as former New York State Assembly Speaker Joseph F. Carlino, "a Rockefeller confidant" and therefore a *Newsday* target; Hempstead Town Councilman James D. Bennett, "son of GOP power John J. Bennett," the Nassau County surrogate; and several other well-known people in politics and business. Among them were William N. Robertson, Jr., and his son William Robertson III, both of Grumman Aircraft, who had openly and bitterly opposed any proposals to turn their Calverton airport into a jetport.

Actually, the "syndicate" was a group of forty-one people who were investing in Suffolk County real estate. When a piece of property was located, the members were polled, and those who wished to buy in would form a limited partnership, usually of about twenty-five people, who would make up that particular purchase.

Newsday spoke darkly of a "confidential map" that had been drawn up by the board's planners, which had marked out the Calverton airport as a possible jetport and had proposed the north-south Wading River Expressway as a potential link between the airport and a proposed bridge across Long Island Sound. That bridge had been discussed for years in the press; it was not a new idea.

Newsday said that the syndicate was formed after I had seen the map and began buying up properties near the airport.

Those of the forty-one members of the syndicate interviewed by *Newsday* were unanimous in stating "that Roth had provided no inside information. They said that they had joined the land syndicate because the expressway was going through and land values on Long Island were skyrocketing. They denied knowledge of the airport or racetrack proposals.''

Robertson of Grumman was quoted as saying:

> You can't go bad with an investment on eastern Long Island; the expressway is going there. It's the type of thing to hold on to for five or ten years and then sell for yourself or your kids. The jetport was not my consideration. We at Grumman are fighting it. The jetport, I think, will never happen; yet it might. If the jetport goes in despite Grumman, then [the land] is a windfall, but that's not my cup of tea. I've been with Grumman for 37 years and it's not my idea to sell them short. The fact is that Long Island is a good [real-estate buy] and it's a small island.

Along with the sensational inferences in the news stories was an editorial about the Planning Board as an untarnished institution, but condemning me by implication:

> The pattern of the syndicate's land purchases reflects knowledge of confidential planning information available to Mr. Roth as a member of the board. The syndicate spent $2,115,870 on 378.16 acres of land strategically sited in an area in which the planners envisioned major aviation and recreation facilities. If the recommendations of the plan were followed, independent real estate experts believe the syndicate's land would be worth as much as ten times the purchase price. . . . Mr. Roth should never have been involved in land speculation in an area in which his knowledge of confidential information offered such a clear-cut opportunity to enrich himself.

Along with the mud came a pat on the head in a story about me as a person and as a banker, which said only kind things about how much I had done for Long Island and banking.

This was, obviously, to avoid libel suits.

The facts were:

Each time a limited partnership was formed, the members' names and investments had been published in a newspaper.

The syndicate had bought a total of 245.16 acres and was under contract to buy another 133 acres, most of it bordering on the Long Island Expressway and more or less near the Grumman airfield. I had participated in four of the six purchases. My investment was about 2 percent of the $2 million—just under $40,000.

And there was no secret map, no inside information not available to everyone.

The way *Newsday* presented it, it seemed as though I had been violating public trust to line my pockets in a huge land grab based on secret, inside information. None of this was true. But after *Newsday* printed their stories and editorial, other papers picked up the same set of "facts" and built it up into a major issue.

Before the thing got any more grotesque, I thought I would go and talk to Bill Moyers, *Newsday*'s publisher.

I called Moyers and said I would like to meet him to discuss the matter. We met at his office, with a reporter named Green present. I did not put the meeting off the record, but *Newsday* never published what I said, or the fact that I had been there; instead they kept harping on the fact that I had consistently refused them interviews. It was all part of the pattern of slanting news to achieve a certain effect.

I told Moyers the background of the land purchase. My son Donald had been talking to me about buying Suffolk land for development. He and others I respected, like Edgar Senne, were starting to buy property near the expressway for possible development. It was obvious that Long Island had to expand eastward, and this seemed like a good long-term investment.

I had advised them that if they wanted to bring in industry, they would have to make provision for residential areas, homes, stores, schools.

We of the Planning Board were charged with the responsibility of trying to influence development in an orderly way; we had no enforcement powers, but used what persuasive powers we possessed to try to get builders to plan properly.

My son had said, "You believe in planning. Here's a chance to help create a real planned community out of vacant land. You can participate in the group."

I met with the group and could see that they needed direction in that area. I invited them to my office at the bank and offered the help of the Planning Board, as we did with other developers.

But I declined participation. I was too busy at the bank. However, when Gleason took over executive leadership, I had more time on my hands. And when my son asked again, I thought it over and decided to put in a token investment as evidence of my involvement, so that my advice would have my commitment behind it. Since we published our names every time we formed a partnership to buy land, there was obviously no attempt at concealment. I said to Moyers, "If I had wanted to conceal my interest, I could have put it in someone else's name—my son's, or my wife's."

Then we talked about the "confidential" map. I said, "I don't have any such map. I don't remember ever seeing it."

He said the minutes showed it had been presented at a meeting at which I had been present. I said, "Probably it was one of the maps put on the bulletin board. But I don't recall it." And I pointed out that we never kept our deliberations secret; that we always released them to the press afterward.

"Well, the press never knew about the map," Moyers said.

They could have. The map they made so much of probably had been presented to the board. But it was not secret, and never had been. Anyone—literally—could buy one for $1.50. It was public property.

I said that the *Newsday* stories had ruined the possibility of putting together parcels for a planned community at Calverton. Moyers said, "I leave these things up to my people. They're the ones who developed the stories." A man named Arthur Perfall was night editor; he was getting a reputation as an investigative reporter.

Moyers said, "I've always had a high regard for you. I do feel you should resign from the planning board. And we can be of some help when you do it. The stories will not be damaging."

I said, "I'm not sure that is the thing to do, since I've done nothing wrong."

"But," Moyers said, "the evidence is all against you."

I said I would think it over.

It would certainly have been the expedient thing to do, but in all my battles I had always stood up for principle and not for expediency. It seemed to me that if I quit the board, it would be knuckling under to the appearance of things, and not the reality. It was not my nature.

I spoke with many friends and advisers, and they all said pretty much the same thing: You can't fight a big newspaper. You can't win. If they want to make you look bad, they can do it and get away with it. It isn't a matter of law, and it isn't a matter of ethics—everybody knows you weren't out to enrich yourself in an unethical way. It's a matter of public relations: It's how it looks that counts, not the substance behind the headlines. The best thing to do is to resign from the Planning Board or sell out your shares of the syndicate.

But, I said, this will make it seem as though I did something wrong.

It already looks that way, they said. You have to deal with appearances.

I went through my files and ransacked my memory for any wrongdoing—any real conflict of interest. I found none. In response to a request by Eugene Nickerson, the Nassau County executive who had appointed me to the Planning Board, I wrote the facts and released the letter to the press.

Dear Mr. Nickerson:
You have requested that I write and give you the facts regarding my investment in property located in the vicinity of Calverton. Copies of this statement will be made available to the press.
I immediately want to say:

- I did not make the investment because of my knowledge of any Nassau-Suffolk Planning Board (bicounty commission) confidential information.
- I did not make the investment because of any expectation of a jetport, transportation center or new major roads.
- I never discussed with any of the investors, or with anyone else, any confidential information of the bicounty commission.
- I never suggested that any particular parcel of property be purchased or that properties be purchased in any particular locations.
- No purchases of property were made because of anticipated favorable rezoning beyond what would be fair and proper in the public interest.

Now why did I invest in Calverton?
You will recall that at the meetings of the bicounty commission I often asked the question whenever new reports were submitted by the staff, "What is being done to carry out the recommendations?" And, I was quite unhappy with the answers, which to me showed small progress. Of course, the commission is a study group and is only empowered to recommend.
One of the recommendations in which I was keenly interested was that the bicounty commission would do the planning for a large parcel of property if it was of sufficient size to create a complete planned community such as we have in Garden City and Stony Brook, which the bicounty committee was advocating.
When I was asked by the investors to join their group—about 50 in number—they had the financial means to acquire all the land needed for a colonial village of 1,000 to 2,000 acres. I recommended assembling land for this purpose. The management then had the colonial village program approved at a meeting of the investors.
I suggested that after we had assembled the required land we should

turn it over to the bicounty commission for planning. There was no secrecy about my participation.

The people in Nassau and Suffolk have been good to me. The bank I headed for so many years grew from a small country bank to a major bank in the United States. As it prospered, so did I prosper. The citizens of the area have showered many honors upon me. Whatever profit I may make in the Calverton venture will be paid to a foundation for the beautification of our counties.

In recent weeks there has been criticism of the unfair stories that sometimes appear in the news media. This is a case history that supports this criticism.

Since most of the expenses of the bicounty commission are paid by the federal government, should not the federal government investigate and take whatever action it deems proper?

I shall continue to offer my services to the people of Nassau and Suffolk counties by remaining on the bicounty commission.

I MUST NOT, I SHALL NOT RESIGN.

With respect for your fairness,

> Sincerely,
> Arthur T. Roth

After I submitted my statement, Eugene Nickerson said that the matter would have to be decided by the Nassau Ethics Board.

Newsday criticized the Ethics Board because three of the five members knew me well. The paper editorialized on February 10 that "Arthur T. Roth has decided to brazen it out."

On February 12, I received a letter from Richard Herstone of Glenndale Associates, who had helped assemble the properties for the group of investors. Mr. Herstone rebutted *Newsday*'s contention that all the land purchased has been zoned industrially; actually, only one of the pieces was industrial, the other five were residential. But these facts were ignored or buried in the controversy that the newspaper had created.

On Friday, February 13, *Newsday* attacked Eugene Nickerson for turning the problem of conflict of interest over to the Ethics Board. They said Nickerson should have asked for my resignation—i.e., prejudged the case in line with *Newsday*'s own prejudgment.

My enemies within Franklin National were attempting to use this controversy against me.

On February 16, 1970, Harold Gleason seemed to feel impelled to issue a statement:

I regret the situation which has arisen with regard to Mr. Roth's investment in land in the Calverton area while he was serving as a member of the Nassau-Suffolk Regional Planning Board. I have worked closely with Mr. Roth for the past 14 years and I know him to be a man of integrity. It would be wrong for me to prejudge this case. The matter will be coming up before the Ethics Committee of Nassau County . . . and the people of Long Island will then have the opportunity to know all of the facts surrounding this matter and the judgment of the Ethics Committee.

This matter is personal in nature. Franklin National Bank is not involved.

It was not a bank matter, but it began to become one when Town Supervisor Jerome Ambro of Huntington threatened to withdraw $1,470,000 of town deposits from Franklin National if I did not resign from the Planning Board. Franklin officials asked him to wait seventy-two hours, and assured him he would be satisfied, according to *Newsday* of February 19.

Now that the bank was being drawn into the publicity, I felt there was no longer any choice. I wrote to Eugene Nickerson and to Leonard Hall, chairman of the Nassau Board of Ethics:

I hereby resign as a member of the Nassau-Suffolk Regional Planning Board because to continue at this time is to risk harm to the Franklin National Bank and its stockholders.

Since my letter to the county executive in which I stated I would not resign and the referral of the matter to the Nassau County Board of Ethics, some public officials have threatened to withdraw substantial funds from the bank. I cannot countenance the risk of possible injury to the bank and its stockholders.

It must be restated here that I have not made any financial gain from my investment of $39,525 in various limited partnerships purchasing real property in Suffolk County, and that at no time have I acted upon or disclosed confidential information. In each instance my participation has been stated in legal notices published in newspapers, and the full agreement has been filed with the County Clerk.

Newsday's headline was, predictably, ROTH RESIGNS . . . UNDER FIRE.

I had heard that at least one director had been accusing me of violating the bank's own code of ethics, which I had prepared. I asked Arthur A. Kaye of the law firm of Bennett, Kaye & Scholly to look into this. He had written on February 18, "The one rule which has relevancy is that under the heading of 'Speculation.' "

"In my opinion your participation in these partnerships . . . was . . . not within the purview of the rule of conduct of the Bank."

On February 19, I sent a brief account of my resignation from the planning board to Franklin's board of directors, together with attachments of my letters to Eugene Nickerson, and requested that these be made part of the minutes of the board meeting of that date. I said, "I regret any concern which this incident may have occasioned."

In July I was in Kaye's office when a call came in for me from Joseph Beisler, Franklin's newest director. He asked me to please come to the board of directors' meeting the following day a half-hour early; he'd like to talk to me. I asked, "What about?" And he said, "Something very important that will come up at the meeting." After I hung up I said, "I think what Beisler wants to see me about is that they will not nominate me as a director tomorrow."

Kaye said, "No, that's unthinkable."

My name had been on the list prepared about ten days before; the meeting would propose the slate to the shareholders at the annual meeting.

I said, "No, it's not unthinkable. I can see by the way they have been acting in recent days that this has been coming. Gleason has avoided me; I tried to get in touch with him and he's always unavailable. He has told people to have nothing to do with me; several officers have helped me, and he reprimanded them."

I knew I had many enemies on the board; not only Gleason, Merkin, and Hein, but Paul Prosswimmer, because I had criticized him for falling down in regard to loans. Now they were ganging up.

The next day, July 18, 1968, when I saw Beisler, he said, "Arthur, I'm very sorry but a majority of the board have decided not to nominate you as a director."

I said, "This is wrong. I know some of the reasons, and they're improper reasons. If you force this thing, it will look very bad."

As chairman I opened the meeting and presided through the various items that came up. And I presented them with the statement from Kaye and my resignation from the Planning Board. I asked that these be made part of the minutes.

There was a little discussion. Hein insisted that he definitely felt there was a violation of the bank's Code of Ethics.

The last item on the agenda was the nomination of directors for the following year. I asked for names to be presented. They were all silent.

Finally, Gleason said, "What are we waiting for? You know the action we agreed to take. Isn't someone going to make a motion?"

William J. Hogan responded by placing names in nomination for the ensuing year. My name was not on the list.

My recollection is that Merkin seconded.

I said, "All in favor say 'Aye.' "

And the majority said "Aye."

"Any opposed?"

There were none, although several had remained silent during the vote.

"Any further business to come before the board?" I asked.

There was none.

I adjourned the meeting at 11:30 A.M. on Thursday, July 18, 1968.

I went home and told my family what had happened. Then I went over to Franklin Square to close out my safety-deposit box and clean out my office. I determined to say nothing in public; not to attend share-holders' meetings, although my family and I were major shareholders; and to do nothing with regard to Franklin for at least two years. I wanted the management and directors to have a free hand; and I wanted it clearly understood that I had no further responsibility for what might happen to the bank. When I left, the Franklin was a dynamic, profitable bank.

A year or so later, the *Newsday* investigative reporter, Arthur Perfall, joined Franklin National Bank as a public-relations executive.

• Postscript

Loew's Inc. chairman Lawrence A. Tisch had quietly acquired a million shares in the Franklin New York Corporation amounting to 21.6 percent of its outstanding stock. Mr. Tisch's investment in 1972 was worth $32 million in stock-market value. His blocks of shares assured him of a seat on the board of both the holding company and the Franklin National Bank.

According to federal banking regulations, anyone owning 25 percent of the shares of a bank or a bank holding company would have to be declared a one-bank holding company. And this would force that shareholder to divest himself of other, nonbank investments.

The Federal Reserve had been investigating Loew's involvement in Franklin, and in 1972 decided that there was a "rebuttable presumption" that Loew's controlled the bank. Had the Fed gone ahead and proved this, Tisch would have been forced to sell Loew's other business interests. He decided to get rid of his Franklin shares. His decision was based in good part on the fact that by March 1972 bank examiners had found Franklin overburdened with bad loans. In fact, in the four years since Arthur Roth had been stripped of his executive responsibilities, Franklin had fallen into such poor financial condition that the comptroller of the currency could have forced a merger or change of management. Instead he chose to accept management's assurances that the bank would clean up its act. In May 1972 Tisch persuaded Paul Luftig, a young and well-regarded executive of Bankers Trust Company, to become president and chief operating officer of Franklin.

Gleason, the bank's chairman and chief executive officer, had proved

253

to be what Arthur Roth anticipated: a smooth-talking public-relations man but a poor administrator as well as an inept banker. Within the first two years as chief executive officer, Gleason had managed to increase the bank's salary outlay by 50 percent, according to *Fortune* magazine. The number of employees, too, had risen sharply as had bonuses and expense accounts. Luftig was supposed to replace Gleason within a few months, but this did not happen.

Kuhn, Loeb & Company, investment bankers, found a prospective buyer for Tisch's Franklin investment: Michele Sindona. A 52-year-old Italian citizen. Mr. Sindona was reputed to a be a successful and very wealthy financier. He represented the Vatican in many large deals; in fact, he was so important there that he could drive into Vatican City without showing any identification at a time of night when the place was barred to others. There were also rumors about this man—that he had close connections with the Sicilian Mafia and was a member of a secret cell of Freemasons to which many of Italy's top politicians, power brokers and Mafia leaders belonged.

Lawrence Tisch took Harold Gleason to meet Sindona in May 1972 at the Drake Hotel (a Loew's property) in New York. Tisch reassured Gleason that if Sindona did buy his (Tisch's) shares, Gleason would be protected by an employment contract. Tisch was asking $45 a share for his holding, some $13 above the market price—a markup of 40 percent. In July, Sindona eventually paid $40, or $40 million, for the block. It is not uncommon for controlling blocks of stock to command premiums, since it might be even more costly to purchase control in the open market; when heavy buying of a stock issue occurs, rumors often raise prices.

Sindona knew of Franklin's difficulties, but was confident the bank was sound because the comptroller of the currency had "approved its balance sheets," according to author Luigi DiFonzo in *St. Peter's Banker: Michele Sindona.*

Sale of a controlling block of stock in an American bank had to be approved by the Federal Reserve and the comptroller of the currency. While authorities were supposed to be investigating Sindona, a radio broadcast over ABC from Italy charged that since 1957 he had been the front man for the Mafia, investing profits from their sale of illegal drugs in legitimate businesses. Nevertheless, the Federal Reserve and the comptroller approved Sindona's purchase of control of Franklin. They never learned—as they could have—that the $40 million Sindona used to purchase the stock was not his own money but came from several foreign corporations that he controlled.

How explain this investigatory laxity? Sindona derived legitimacy in the United States, and also apparently a reputation that made him nearly invulnerable to official probes, from a close association with David Kennedy, a former U.S. secretary of the Treasury. Kennedy's former undersecretary, James Smith, was currently comptroller of the currency. And Sindona burnished his own image further by hiring as his legal representative President Nixon's former law firm, Mudge, Rose, Guthrie & Alexander—one of whose former partners, John Mitchell, was Nixon's attorney general.

The only person to question Sindona's credentials publicly was Arthur Roth. On July 18, 1972, he wrote to Lawrence Tisch, and sent copies to the press, to the Federal Deposit Insurance Corporation, as well as to the comptroller of the currency, the Federal Reserve Board and the New York State Banking Department. He said in part:

> Your sale of [Franklin] stock may have been advisable in so far as Loew's is concerned, but it raises some serious questions for the stockholders and depositors of Franklin National Bank.
> 1. Do you know enough about Michele Sindona to unconditionally recommend him as . . . good for the bank?
> 2. Will there be a full disclosure of his finances, his backers, and detailed biographies?
> 3. Why would he pay $40.00 a share for stock that is currently selling at $32.00, having run up from $28.00 apparently as a result of rumors of this sale?
> 4. What are his intentions regarding additional purchases and what role will he play in the operation of the bank?
> 5. When you sold your holdings at $40.00 a share, did you arrange to see that other stockholders could obtain the same price?
> 6. Don't you think that you could have found many eminent buyers in the United States if you asked a reasonable price for the stock? Would not these prospective buyers also have offered the same deal to other stockholders?
> 7. Franklin has a serious problem in covering its $32,500,000 tax loss carry over. Would not the sale and merger with a United States corporation aid in resolving this problem?
> 8. A bank is built on confidence. Have you considered whether or not this transaction will cause a loss of confidence in the bank?

Roth requested a reply "in an open letter because the stockholders, depositors and the banking fraternity will be interested in your answer.'' Lawrence Tisch never responded, nor did any of the regulatory agencies to which Roth had sent copies.

As a foreign national, Sindona could not sit on the Franklin bank board, but he and an associate, Carlo Bordoni, went on the board of the holding company that controlled 100 percent of the bank without a demurrer from the authorities. About three months after Sindona bought control of Franklin, he began to siphon huge sums of money out of the bank. In October 1972, without authorization by the directors, $15 million was transferred from Franklin to Swiss and Italian banks owned by Sindona.

About this time, Sindona's personal lawyer, Andrew Miller, invited Arthur Roth to meet the new owner. ''Even though he hates you for what you have said about him, I would like him to get to know you.''

The two men met on October 25, 1972, at Sindona's apartment in New York's St. Regis Hotel. Roth brought up the problems of Franklin's bad loans and poor management, and told Sindona that he had to replace Gleason ''even though he's my mistake.'' Sindona, who could assume a variety of personalities, was charming and placating. He didn't know Gleason well enough yet, he said; he was seeing more of the bank's president and CEO Paul Luftig. He said he was planning to cut the bank staff by 250 employees, and that he would personally run the foreign department. He could bring in $1 billion to $2 billion in deposits from overseas, and knew how to make money in foreign exchange. He mentioned a U.S. bank that was reaping huge profits from trading in international currencies—this was the Continental Illinois National Bank (which later had to be saved by the federal government to prevent widespread damage to many other banks).

Asked by Roth why he would pay a large premium for Franklin stock, he replied that in Europe it was common for bank shares to sell for fifty to one hundred times their earnings per share. By his reckoning, he had bought control of Franklin relatively cheaply.

All in all, he won Arthur Roth over with his seeming frankness, candor, and professional competence, as well as his willingness to listen to criticisms and questions and to respond good naturedly.

David Kennedy hired the man who had greatly increased Continental Illinois's foreign deposits and profits, Peter Shaddick, a British national, to run Franklin's international division. Shaddick, given complete autonomy and independence from supervision by Franklin's top executives, quickly ran the bank's trading position in the international money market from a tiny $11 *million* to well above $3 *billion*. Advised by Sindona's associates about which currencies to buy or sell, Shaddick did not know these advisors were taking positions opposite to his in those same currencies. Thus, while Sindona was earning nearly $240 million in the foreign-exchange markets—at one point he nearly destroyed the Italian lira by selling it while buying billions in dollars, Swiss francs, and other currencies—Shaddick was losing some $45 million for Franklin National Bank in the same currencies.

However, he conspired with Sindona's associates to conceal those losses. Working with Sindona banks overseas, he created fictitious rates of exchange and fabricated transactions that did not take place. In fact, he actually claimed profits while losing large sums of money. For example, in March 1973 he stated his international division's profit as $241,000 while actually it had lost $3.6 million that month. The people under him, the traders, pressured to report profits, used a simpler scheme: They simply did not fill out the necessary forms reporting their transactions, but just shoved their papers into drawers. They could report profits because there were no records of losses.

It is not known whether Sindona profited from these illegal currency transactions, or whether the money was pocketed by his associate, Carlo Bordoni. But author Luigi DiFonzo, who devoted several years to untangling many of the complicated financial transactions of Sindona's empire, believes these dealings were part of a plot against Sindona. Bordoni, who Sindona believed to be thoroughly under his control, and Bordoni's wife (who claimed that Sindona had sexually assaulted her) were actually working to ruin Sindona. The goal of their multilayered Byzantine plot was to be the downfall of the Franklin National Bank.

In any case, the foreign transactions and large overnight federal-funds purchases were inflating Franklin's growth far beyond the proper capital ratio. It was now a $5-billion bank, while its capital structure and long-term deposits could support only about $3.5 billion. Arthur Roth decided to confront Sindona with these facts and with Franklin's pressing problems. He dropped in on the Italian unannounced. Sindona received him smoothly and again responded to all of his questions; mainly, his answers consisted of asking for more time. Roth said he would bring up these problems—such as the fact that many of the bank's deposits were short-term, while its loans were long-term and at a rate that was creating losses—at the next stockholders' meeting. Sindona said he would be glad to introduce Roth at the meeting.

Thinking it over, however, Roth decided that if he went public with

Franklin's deficiencies, he might create a panic. Instead of saving the bank, he might destroy it. So he would wait and meanwhile take his facts and figures to the New York deputy controller of the currency, Charles Van Horn, with the hope that government pressure would force Sindona to replace Gleason.

Some months later, in January 1974, the bank hired Norman Schreiber, former chairman of the highly regarded Chicago finance company Walter E. Heller Corporation, to the head of Franklin's Executive Committee. Schreiber was given broad investigatory powers and answered only to the board of directors. He quickly began to assess and revise bank practices.

Nevertheless, in March 1974 a number of banks threatened to refuse to accept Franklin's contracts for foreign currency. And there was another, more serious problem. Sindona had started to create a $200-million company in Italy by selling bonds in that amount in the name of a Mafia-controlled furniture company that had been capitalized at only $1 million. Sindona had guaranteed that any bonds not sold in the public offering would be taken up by Franklin. And since only $103.5 million of the bonds had been bought, Franklin would have had to invest (illegally) $96.5 million in the scheme. Shaddick ordered Franklin's London branch to cover the transaction, thus circumventing U.S. law. But Gleason and others held a meeting and decided that Sindona should make good on the $96.5 million—or the transaction would have to be reported to U.S. banking authorities. Forced into a corner, Sindona had to find the money and this caused him to erupt into a snarling rage.

In March 1974, Arthur Roth visited Van Horn with a devastating analysis of Franklin's *Annual Report*. Van Horn said he had confidence that Schreiber could turn the bank around within the year, and suggested that Roth see James Smith, the comptroller of the currency. First Roth met with Schreiber, and was relieved to learn that they shared the same doubts and believed in the same solutions for the bank, although they differed somewhat over specific numbers. But Roth could see that Schreiber was nervous when they discussed removing Gleason and Sindona; the fact was, Schreiber had been recruited by Sindona and Kennedy. Schreiber was an honorable and independent-minded man; but since he appeared reluctant to seek a change of ownership Roth decided to take his facts to James Smith in Washington.

Meanwhile, Franklin's management fractionated into several groups that did not share information, pushed the bank deeper into trouble. Acting on what he took to be an honest balance sheet, President

Paul Luftig persuaded Manufacturers Hanover Trust to lend $30 million to Franklin and received a promise of another $5 million under certain conditions.

Early in April 1974, Arthur Roth went to Washington to see James Smith, the comptroller. He presented his explosive analysis of Franklin's balance sheet, and Smith looked, listened, and said almost nothing. Getting nowhere, Roth left copies of his worksheets and went to see Brenton Leavitt, the Federal Reserve official in charge of bank regulation. He got a more responsive hearing, but Leavitt, who promised to bring the matter to the Fed's board of governors, did not have the power to change Franklin's management. Only Smith could have done that. Roth sent copies of what he had told Smith and Leavitt to all bank regulatory authorities, and included copies of past letters. There were no responses.

For months Franklin had been awaiting a decision from the Federal Reserve on its petition to take over Talcott International Corporation, a financial institution. Many, including Roth, believed that this merger would help pull Franklin out of its hole. Leavitt was for the merger—he recommended it to the Fed's board of governors. Franklin made it clear that a negative judgment by the Fed, which would of course be made public, could seriously damage Franklin's reputation. In response, the Federal Reserve asked the bank to withdraw its petition rather than suffer the public disgrace (with unpredictable consequences to its stability) of being turned down. But Sindona stubbornly believed that President Nixon could overrule the Fed, and that his Washington attorneys could bring pressure on the president to do this. He neglected to calculate the effect that the Watergate scandal had had on Nixon's power. When on May 1 the board of governors publicly refused to approve the merger, Frankin was suddenly exposed as a poor risk.

Dozens of people called Arthur Roth the next day, saying they had been advised to withdraw their deposits from the bank. Trying to stem the panic, Roth said that Franklin was unquestionably solvent. Then, without an appointment, he went to see Schreiber at his office. Schreiber said that he didn't run the bank; Sindona and Gleason did, and he had no power to replace them. He also told Roth that his visit would certainly be reported to Gleason and that it would be embarrassing to him, Schreiber. He asked Roth not to come to see him again.

Two days later, circumstances took the matter out of their hands: The National Westminster Bank (of London) refused to clear any further Franklin currency transactions. This set off an internal Franklin audit, and it was found that Franklin's New York trader in sterling and French francs had concealed losses of at least $25 million. Paul Luftig recommended to Franklin's Board an immediate merger with Manufacturers Hanover Trust. The motion was carried unanimously.

The comptroller of the currency had taken no action regarding the Franklin. Gleason telephoned Sindona in Italy, telling him of the projected merger with Manufacturers Hanover. Sindona said, "Do nothing until I return." The next day, Tuesday May 2, Paul Luftig informed Van Horn and the Federal Reserve of Franklin's currency-trading losses. He also asked the Federal Reserve for between $100 million and $200 million to tide the bank over for four weeks. The Fed agreed to the loan, but within a day the bank was forced to borrow another $110 million to cover the enormous outflow from savings and business accounts.

On May 9, Roth telephoned Van Horn and told him that the situation was desperate: Leading financial papers had contacted him; they were going to write articles criticizing Franklin. Van Horn said that the comptroller was not worried; that other banks were in trouble. "Franklin is the largest," Roth told him, "and if it goes, it will cause national and international repercussions." But Van Horn was unmoved.

That afternoon, Franklin stock plunged to $8.75 a share. The next day, Friday, May 10, 1974, the Securities and Exchange Commission forced the bank to report publicly on its condition; and Harold Gleason asked the commission to suspend trading in Franklin shares. The bank had a large, but uncalculated, loss in currency trading, he said, and would not pay its quarterly dividend.

Sindona, returning from Europe, placed Carlo Bordoni in charge of Franklin's foreign department—the man who was later disclosed to have stolen more than $25 million from Franklin and two other Sindona corporations. Paul Luftig began negotiating a takeover of Franklin with Manufacturers Hanover on Saturday, May 11. The Manhattan bank was interested in protecting its $30-billion unsecured loan to Franklin, but no deal was struck.

On Sunday, May 12, Sindona designed a projected offering of Franklin stock worth $50 million, designed to save the bank. The offering would be guaranteed by one of his corporations, subject to the approval of Franklin shareholders. Banking authorities helped Sindona and Gleason put out a press release giving the false impression that Franklin was still sound. The release said that losses were only $14 million and covered by insurance; actual losses were more than $40 million, and most were not covered by insurance. Franklin's New York lawyers, Kay Scholer Fierman Hays & Handler, refused to approve the false release and resigned as the bank's attorneys. The employment of Paul Luftig and Peter Shaddick as well as several junior officers was terminated at this time.

Sindona's empire was beginning to collapse in Europe, and this resonated in the United States to the detriment of Franklin. On May 24 the bank had to borrow more than $1 billion from the Federal Reserve to replace its hemorrhaging deposits. On June 20 it was announced that Franklin had lost $65 million in currency and portfolio speculation. Franklin's shareholders refused to approve Sindona's proposed $50-million stock offering. Arthur Roth devised a plan to save the bank that included an investment of $100 million by the board of directors. The plan did not go through.

Sindona and his men continued wheeling and dealing, and the bank remained barely afloat for several months while being repeatedly wounded by more and more bad news. On October 2, 1974 it was forced to borrow nearly $2 billion more from the Federal Reserve. On October 8, Franklin was finally declared insolvent. Takeover bids came in from a number of banks. A banking conglomerate known as European American, owned by several European banks, won the corpse. The next day the signs were changed at all Franklin branches, which opened as the European American Bank. The Franklin National Bank no longer existed.

Michele Sindona was indicted in the United States and in Europe on a variety of counts, including murder, and was convicted of various crimes. He finally died in an Italian prison on March 22, 1986, saying he'd been poisoned.

Carlo Bordoni was sentenced to seven years in prison for his role in the collapse of Franklin. Released to Italian authorities to testify against a number of Sindona associates, he jumped bail in 1982 and disappeared with his wife, Virginia.

Harold Gleason and Paul Luftig were sentenced to three years in prison. Each served one year.

Peter Shaddick testified against Gleason and Sindona, in return for which he received a light sentence of three years in prison.

Depositors and creditors were paid in full.

The F.D.I.C. and Federal Reserve were paid in full together with interest and expenses.

Franklin's common stock was worthless.

W.S.R.

APPENDIX

Statement of the Honorable James E. Smith, Comptroller of the Currency, before the Subcommittee on Financial Institutions, Supervision, Regulation, and Insurance of the House Committee on Banking, Currency, and Housing, Thursday, July 17, 1975

Franklin National Bank

In your letter of June 20th, you requested a "full and complete report" on Franklin.

In anticipation of some of your questions, I have prepared this section of the testimony using the question-and-answer format.

What had been the bank's history over the ten years prior to its failure?

Franklin was chartered by the Comptroller's Office in 1926 and in 1969, the Comptroller approved the corporate reorgnization under which shares of Franklin were acquired by the Franklin New York Corporation. At December 31, 1973, Franklin was the 20th largest bank in the United States with total resources of $5 billion, total deposits of $3.7 billion, and total loans of $2.4 billion. Franklin had a main office in Manhattan and 103 domestic branches, most of which were located on Long Island.

During the five-year period of 1964 to 1969, Franklin had no serious problems or extraordinary deficiencies. The toublesome problems with the bank started about 1969.

Roth was removed as Chief Executive in July 1968

On a balance-sheet basis, Franklin experienced a steady growth in resources from $1.5 billion on 12/31/64 to $5.0 billion on 12/31/73. The growth of Franklin's resources and liabilities was not in itself an indication of unsound condition; however, the continuing inability to manage successfully those resources and liabilities led to the bank's deteriorating condition. Sufficient quality, profits, liquidity, and general confidence in Franklin simply were never developed. As a result, it was in no position to stand and survive the economic conditions which developed and pressed upon all banks in 1973/1974.

Franklin's capital funds grew by only $76 million in the 1964/1973 period while its resources grew by $3.5 billion. Twenty million of that nominal capital growth was from the issuance of stock in 1967 and $56 million from retained earnings.

During its last two years, when the bank's most significant asset and funding growth occurred, its capital funds showed essentially no growth, and its reserve for bad debts declined by $2.6 million.

In spite of rapid growth in the latter years of its existence, Franklin was not successful as an earner. Its old, accumulated assets of poor quality and its management errors left it without the income ability to command confidence. During its last four years, Franklin's net income declined steadily from $21 million in 1970 to $17 million in 1971 to $13 million in 1972 and to a marginal $12 million in 1973. Of that final $12 million, $7.7 million was from foreign exchange trading income which was an additional display of final efforts to override old unsolved problems.

Our bank examiners measure asset quality as a percentage of classified assets to gross capital funds, with 40 percent being a traditional benchmark for asset problems requiring additional attention. In the reports of examination from 1964 to 1969, that classified percentage exceeded 40 percent only two times, 46.2 percent in April, 1965, and 42.3 percent in October, 1966. By September, 1969, it had declined to 16.2 percent. From August 30, 1970 forward, that percentage remained consistently over 40 percent and it was not substantially reduced. It was 58.9 percent in August of 1970, and it was 59.1 percent when the bank was last examined on May 14, 1974.

The final 59 percent was certainly not evidence that the bank was insolvent but the persistence of these high percentages was evidence of management's inability to rid the bank of asset problems which were bearing heavily upon its earning and confidence problems.

While the bank's classified asset percentages were not publicly known, its asset losses were and those losses became extremely heavy for its declining earnings in 1973. The bank had managed to maintain its reserve for loan losses at $31 million during the three years from 1969 through 1971, not through charges to current earnings alone but also through charges to retained earnings. Then in 1972 and in 1973 its net loan losses exceeded its charges to earnings and its reserves declined to $30 million and finally to $27 million.

Franklin's net return on assets declined from 0.63 percent in 1970 to 0.26 percent in 1973. The average return on assets for 47 peer group national banks ($1 to $5 billion) was 0.92 percent in 1970 and 0.74 percent in 1973. By 1973, Franklin was retaining only 3.9 cents of pretax income for each dollar of revenue. The average figure for the 47 peer group national banks in 1973 was 14.8 cents.

While total interest income from loans remained relatively stable, Franklin's total interest expense on deposits increased from $97 million in 1969 to $235 million in 1973.

Franklin's "percentage change in net income from the previous year" was + 30.9 percent, 1968 to 1969. For the 1971 to 1972 comparison, this percentage was –38.9 percent.

In conclusion, Franklin had a history of a marginal existence as a New York City bank with poor earnings and an unimpressive management reputation that ultimately caused a loss of confidence in financial circles.

Most damaging of all, however, was Franklin's incredible expansion by the use of borrowed funds in 1973. At the time we examined the bank in November, 1973, about 50 percent of the bank's liabilities were in the form of volatile, interest-sensitive liabilities. Between our examination in December, 1972 and the one in November, 1973, Franklin had an increase in assets of 29 percent. During the same period its demand and savings deposits declined 5.5 percent. Thus this excessive expansion in assets was almost exclusively supported by short-term money market funds.

Several questions arise as a result of the ten year review of Franklin's activities. Should the Comptroller's Office have taken more affirmative action with Franklin?

In retrospect, the Office did not act aggressively enough to make Franklin put into effect the measures required to correct the situation criticized in the examination report. For example, we might have used our approval of new branch locations more skillfully as leverage to encourage Franklin to raise additional capital and to make other improvements in its performance.

Should the present occupant of the Comptroller's Office have personally involved himself in Franklin's problems at an earlier date?

An objective assessment, benefited by "20-20 hindsight," might indicate that meetings should have been held with the bank's management during the summer or fall of 1973; however, even at that point the explosive danger of the combination of declining earnings and a heavy reliance on short-term interest-sensitive deposits was not sufficiently recognized.

When did the Comptroller become directly involved with Franklin and what steps were taken to deal with the problem?

An examination of Franklin was started on November 14, 1973. This examination revealed the extraordinary growth of the bank, supported by the purchase of short-term volatile funds, and the report reconfirmed the need for additional capital. As of November 14, 1973, total resources had increased by 29 percent since the last examination, and yet the capital of the bank had been increased by less than ½ of 1 percent. The report also showed a substantial depreciation in the securities accounts.

It was apparent that the bank's poor earnings, potential loan losses, and extended foreign exchange position might easily cause a loss of confidence in the bank, which in turn would result in a serious and overwhelming liquidity crisis. In late February, 1974 Regional Administrator Van Horn and Examiner-in-Charge Lake met with me in Washington to discuss the nearly completed examination report. At this time Mr. Van Horn was directed to conduct a meeting with Franklin's Executive Committee and to obtain from the bank a written plan directed at improving the bank's condition, with emphasis on the reduction of all short-term borrowings, the establishment of a clearly defined written loan policy, and a clear definition of the management responsibilities of the senior officers of the bank.

On March 29th this meeting was held and bank officials agreed to prepare and implement the plan. Thereafter, a number of meetings occurred between me and bank officials, especially Mr. Norman Schreiber, who had recently joined Franklin.

Why were their plans not successful?

There was a series of events that prevented Franklin's management from implementing the plans.

On April 18, 1974, Franklin announced net operating income for the first quarter of 1974 of $79,000, or 2¢ per share. The comparable earnings for the first quarter of 1973 were $3,123,000, or 68¢ per share.

On May 1, The Federal Reserve announced its denial of Franklin's bid to acquire Talcott National Corporation.

During the week of May 6, 1974, the Comptroller's Office learned from Franklin that severe losses had occurred in Franklin's foreign exchange operation.

The primary reason, however, that management never had the opportunity to implement their new plans was the money market. Short-term interest rates were spiraling upward at a rapid rate. The sellers of funds began to move to quality, and for the first time a tiered market developed in which the sellers of short-term funds demanded premiums from all but the largest institutions and flatly refused to sell funds to institutions whose performance was seriously below par. As confidence in Franklin declined, the bank was literally frozen out of all sources of short-term funds. To a bank such as Franklin, which depended so heavily on purchased funds, this situation meant certain death.

In a normal money market environment, Franklin might have been saved. But given the highly selective character of this market, there was no hope. We were not dealing with a conventional balance sheet insolvency but with a potentially fatal liquidity crisis.

In a tiered money market, one thing that a bank with excessive reliance on short-term borrowed money cannot afford to lose is that market's complete confidence in the bank, and the events of April resulted in an erosion of confidence.

On Friday, May 10, Franklin announced that it would not declare its regular quarterly dividend. During the same weekend, Franklin announced that extraordinary foreign exchange losses had been discovered, and requested the SEC to suspend trading in the bank's stock. There was general agreement that the announcement would cause a dramatic decline in the ability of Franklin to borrow funds when the bank opened on Monday morning.

What steps did the Comptroller of the Currency take over the May 10 weekend?

A series of meetings and discussions was held over the weekend with representatives of Treasury and the Federal Reserve Board, and senior officials of the New York Federal Reserve Bank.

As a result of the weekend's activities, the Federal Reserve agreed to advance funds to Franklin as needed, within reasonable limits of acceptable collateral.

Contacts were made with representatives of various New York banks to explore the possibility of putting together a quick salvage merger. These inquiries were unsuccessful.

Discussions were held with members of Franklin's management to plan steps to restore confidence in Franklin and to attempt to slow the deposit run-off.

I initiated telephone discussions with Mr. Sindona. He agreed to assign to The Honorable David Kennedy, former Secretary of the Treasury, his power to vote the shares of Franklin Corporation held by the Sindona-owned FASCO Corporation. Mr. Sindona also offered to support additional capital in Franklin through guaranteeing a rights offering of the stock.

The result of all the meetings and discussions held over the weekend of May 10 was a consensus decision to attempt to avert an anticipated run on the bank. It was feared that if Franklin failed, such a failure would have set in motion a panic throughout the domestic and international banking systems.

What happened between the weekend of May 10, 1974, and July 2, 1974, when formal notice was given to the F.D.I.C.?

Our fears of a major liquidity crisis were quickly confirmed on Monday morning, May 13, and the deposit run-off thereafter was immediate and steady. Within 21 business days, Franklin suffered a deposit loss of $1 billion in deposits. Our goal was to protect all depositors and shareholders and, if possible, to save Franklin through a private market solution, without long-term federal assistance. Following the May 10 weekend, we moved ahead on several fronts.

Steps were taken to firm up Mr. Sindona's verbal offer to me to guarantee a rights offering of additional stock up to an amount of $50 million. His offer was presented as a formal written proposal to the Board of Directors of the Franklin National Corporation and was accepted by the Board, subject to later shareholder approval. While such an infusion of additional capital would have fully restored the losses suffered through the unauthorized and unrecorded contracts in foreign exchange, it was never my belief that this action standing alone would be adequate to rebuild market confidence in Franklin to a level that would permit the time for solution of its basic problems of liability structure, asset quality, overhead costs, and earnings.

Clearly the quickest way home to safe harbor was to find a bank of size and high quality willing to acquire either a major ownership position in the Franklin National Corporation or the assets of the bank through a purchase and assumption transaction. In exploring this alternative it was essential that such discussions be conducted by Franklin's officers or a representative designated by management. I suggested that Honorable David Kennedy as an ideal individual to conduct such discussions.

By reason of his acceptance of the sole voting power over the FASCO-held stock of the Franklin National Corporation he was to be an important voice in the future direction of the bank. His vast banking experience, his broad acquaintanceship and excellent reputation in the worldwide banking community offered unique qualifications for this most complex assignment. Likewise, my own high regard for this man, with whom I had served during his term as Secretary of the Treasury, satisfied me that if such a commercial arrangement was realistically achievable, he could put it together.

Secretary Kennedy accepted this assignment and devoted much time and effort to securing a major institutional partner. Based on discussions which I had previously conducted with the major New York banks, Secretary Kennedy and I agreed that the most likely prospects would be among major foreign banks to which Franklin's sizeable territorial base in the New York metropolitan market could be expected to have some real appeal.

At the same time, I requested and obtained agreement from the banks comprising the New York City Clearing House Association to carry out an in-depth analysis of Franklin's operation. This operation was carefully coordinated with the Antitrust Division to guard against any activities that might violate the Federal antitrust laws.

My purpose in seeking this assistance from the New York City banks was two-fold. First, I wanted the knowledgeable judgment of major bank management as to whether or not Franklin was a redeemable entity, assuming the attainment of our private-sector objectives. Second, recognizing that I might ultimately have to decide that the only realistic salvage recourse was with the F.D.I.C., I concluded this evaluation project could contribute importantly to identifying the information which prospective acquirers would need to participate intelligently in an F.D.I.C. receivership sale. In further support of this fail-safe alternative, I instructed our New York Regional Office to begin the task of assembling data, schedules, leases and documentation that might facilitate the F.D.I.C.'s efforts.

By the first of July, based on discussions with Secretary Kennedy indicating no significant interest in Franklin from foreign banking institutions on a commercial basis, and taking account of the somber appraisals I was receiving from the New York Clearing House project, I sadly concluded that the broad requirements of the public interest demanded that I formally request the assistance of the F.D.I.C.

At this point let me acknowledge frankly that there has been criticism of the fact that I did not move immediately in the wake of the events of the May 10 weekend to formally request the F.D.I.C. to initiate discussions aimed at achieving an assisted purchase and assumption transaction such as was used in the case of the U.S. National Bank of San Diego. My decision not to take this step in May, 1974, was a decision on which I believe reasonable persons could fairly disagree.

In summary, the reasoning supporting the decision which I made was as follows:

The immediate problem we faced was not a typical balance sheet insolvency, in which the amount of the liabilities clearly exceeded the value of the assets. Instead, we had an institution suffering a serious liquidity problem directly attributable to a sharp decline in institutional and market confidence in this bank. Thus, I concluded that, if appropriate steps could be taken over a reasonably short time to restore confidence, it might well be possible to cure the liquidity crisis to a point where the time would be available to treat successfully with the bank's more fundamental problems.

What were my reasons for seeking then to avoid a governmentally-supported salvage through the facilities of the F.D.I.C.?

First, Franklin had several thousand shareholders and debenture holders, many of them middle-income residents of Long Island, who deserved by best efforts to preserve some remaining value in their investments. Experience convinced me that the prospects for their salvaging even minimum values after a receivership sale were quite remote.

Second, an F.D.I.C.-assisted transaction for an institution of this size must of necessity take a considerable period of time to consummate. A principal reason for this protracted time period is the fact that public funds are used. The F.D.I.C. must assure that the highest possible bid is obtained to minimize the net utilization of the Corporation's insurance reserves. This requires that every institution for which such an acquisition might be considered a reasonable undertaking be contacted and that a uniform bidding agreement be developed in consultation with the institutions evidencing a serious interest. Additionally, such procedures are necessary to obtain a result free of any questions concerning favoritism towards particular institutions. Recognizing that Franklin's difficulties were creating troublesome conditions in both domestic and foreign financial markets, the public interest appeared best served by the speediest route to solution. I believed that route to be via private, non-governmental arrangements.

Third, I was deeply concerned that a second major bank receivership in the brief span of twelve months would have a most adverse effect on the ability of other banks to obtain capital. All bank regulatory agencies were troubled by the increasing difficulties banks were encountering in raising capital at reasonable cost.

Fourth, I was genuinely convinced at that time that there was a reasonable prospect for success in seeking a private-sector solution. I certainly recognized it was no sure thing and that my decision involved some calculated risk: however, knowing the considerable period of time that would be required by a governmentally-aided solution, I concluded for the reasons stated above that taking some comparatively brief additional time to explore private alternatives was fully justified.

Furthermore, I recognized that even while we were seeking private-sector solutions it would be possible to take some actions helpful to an F.D.I.C. purchase and assumption transaction should our efforts fail. I shall touch on these actions later in this statement.

Those who have not been involved in transactions such as U.S.N.B. might validly inquire why it was not possible to have the F.D.I.C. process moving forward in exact parallel with our private sector explorations. This simply is not possible. To carry out its purposes the F.D.I.C. must contact and meet with banks to discuss the real possibility of a receivership, and the plans for a sale of assets and an assumption of liabilities with the F.D.I.C. acting as a receiver. Once those discussions have ensued, potential acquirers understandably quickly lose interest in a private, commercial transaction which would involve greater attendant risks to their shareholders.

Our efforts to obtain a resolution of Franklin's problem before resorting to an F.D.I.C.-assisted salvage took place on several fronts.

A search was immediately initiated for a new chief executive officer, whose reputation in domestic and international financial circles would begin the process of restoring confidence. This search culminated in the employment of the Honorable Joseph W. Barr.

Mr. Barr, who is well known to many members of this Committee as a former colleague, had a distinguished background in the fields of government and finance, having served as Chairman of the F.D.I.C., Under Secretary and Secretary of the Treasury Department, and as Chairman and Chief Executive Officer of American Security and Trust

Company of Washington, D.C. He was well and favorably known in foreign financial institutions, and a man with whom I was confident we could work effectively under most demanding conditions. My confidence in him was fully justified by his performance. Without him and the qualities of integrity, courage, and decisiveness which he brought to bear on the myriad of problems, I frankly doubt that the successful result in behalf of Franklin's disposition could have been achieved.

The discovery of major problems in the bank's foreign exchange department resulted in the discharge of most of the technically qualified officers in this area. To assist the bank in treating with the continuing serious problems in foreign exchange, we located and secured the employment of Mr. Edwin Reichers, a highly qualified and respected foreign exchange expert.

What happened between the dates of formal notification to the F.D.I.C. on July 2, 1974, and the sale of Franklin to European-American on October 8, 1974?

We continued to move ahead on several fronts in an effort to restore confidence in Franklin and to stabilize its situation. On July 11, 1974, an arrangement was reached whereby the member banks of the New York Clearing House would lend fed funds to Franklin in an amount totaling $200 million.

In an effort to alleviate further liquidity problems, I requested a meeting of representatives of 25 large U.S. banks to discuss selling Franklin's portfolio of Euro-currency loans. It was our hope that at least $100 million of these credits could be sold and Franklin could reduce its reliance on Federal Reserve borrowings. This proved to be an unsuccessful effort because of the interest rates on these credits and because of the liquidity problems of all large banks at that time.

As a result of continuing negative announcements, continuing deposit decline, and management's continued inability to reduce the loan portfolio, on September 30, Franklin's total borrowings from the Federal Reserve Bank of New York exceeded $1.7 billion. By the end of September, total deposits were rapidly approaching the $1 billion mark and total other liabilities were close to $2 billion. The bank was unable to retain any maturing certificates of deposit or other money market liabilities.

In September, Mr. Barr presented the regulatory agencies a plan by which, with substantial assistance from the F.D.I.C., Franklin would shrink, give up most of its national and international business, and become a Long Island bank.

Mr. Barr also suggested that in the event a takeover of Franklin became necessary, it would be beneficial to the interests of the shareholders and to the competitive situation to widen as much as possible the list of potential purchasers. The greatest obstacle to this was the statutory situation which limited the list of potential U.S. buyers to New York State chartered institutions and national banks located in New York. Mr. Barr requested that not only for this case, but also for the future, Congress should act quickly on legislation which would permit the purchase and operation of banks across state lines where necessary to prevent the probable failure of a large institution. Time did not permit the adoption of such legislation before the end came for Franklin, but it is hoped that the Congress will soon provide for such a situation.

I requested the investment banking firm of Blyth Eastman Dillion & Co. to advise us concerning Mr. Barr's proposal. On October 3, the firm advised that the prospects of Franklin's achieving financial viability as an independent banking institution were highly unlikely.

Mr. Chairman, I would be remiss in recalling the events of the Spring and Summer of 1974 if I did not pay special tribute to the dedicated and competent efforts of Mr. Norman B. Schreiber and Mr. Raymond T. Andersen, two gentlemen who joined the senior management of Franklin in early 1974. Each came to Franklin from a long and distinguished career elsewhere in the financial community. Both gave the problems they inherited their best efforts, but time and events simply denied them a fair opportunity to bring about the necessary corrective results.

Based on all the facts available, including Mr. Barr's proposal which conceded that the bank could not survive without substantial massive government assistance, the Blyth Eastman Dillion report, and the negative reports by the New York Clearing House banks, I concluded that Franklin did not appear to be a viable institution.

On October 4, I wrote to the Federal Reserve Bank, briefly reviewing the situation, and asking for the Federal Reserve Bank's views with respect to its continued willingness to lend funds to Franklin. On October 7, the Federal Reserve Bank replied, stating that its emergency credit assistance to Franklin was based on public policy considerations arising from the responsibility of the Federal Reserve System as a lender of last resort and was designed to give Franklin and the Federal banking regulatory agencies concerned a sufficient period to work out a permanent solution to the bank's difficulties. The Federal Reserve Bank also had concluded that the Franklin proposal of September 16, to the F.D.I.C., did not offer a feasible means of achieving the continuation of Franklin as an independent, viable bank. The Federal Reserve Bank advised that it would not be in the public interest for that bank to continue its program of credit assistance to Franklin.

Based upon the continual, daily deterioration of the bank, which resulted in the further erosion of confidence both in Franklin and in the banking system, I became satisfied of the insolvency of Franklin. The Comptroller, as the official charged with the responsibility of determining insolvency and protecting the bank's depositors, is not required to wait until the losses he finds in the bank's assets are actually charged against the bank's book equity capital. The Comptroller's duty is to determine when a bank has reached the point that it will not be able to meet obligations to its depositors in the near future. It was impossible for Franklin to survive without further Federal assistance.

It simply was not in the best interest either of Franklin's depositors and other creditors or of its shareholders to wait for further deterioration in the bank's condition, especially when the alternative of the F.D.I.C.-assisted purchase of the bank at a price including a substantial premium for a going concern value became available. At 3 p.m. on October 8, having become satisfied that Franklin National Bank was insolvent, and acting pursuant to 12 U.S.C. 191, I declared the Bank insolvent and appointed the F.D.I.C. as receiver.

In order to protect all of the depositors of Franklin, the F.D.I.C. moved immediately to accept bids from several major New York banks upon a pre-negotiated contract which provided full protection for all Franklin depositors and other normal banking creditors. The winning bidder was the European-American Bank and Trust Company, a federally insured, New York State chartered institution owned by six large European banks. The following day every banking office of Franklin was opened at the regular banking hour by the European-American Bank. All depositors in Franklin, including holders of certificates of deposit, savings accounts, time accounts, and checking accounts, automatically become depositors of the European-American Bank. The European-American Bank also assumed all existing liabilities to trade creditors of Franklin. The approval of the purchase and assumption transaction avoided any disruption in service for depositors and increased the chances of subordinate creditors for full repayment of their claims.

In summary, our number one goal was to protect the depositors and the banking system of this country, and that goal was achieved. By October 8, Franklin was no longer the 20th largest bank in the country but had become about the 46th largest bank. Of the 65 banks in its size category ($1 to $5 billion in deposits) Franklin had ranked 65th in earning power. This lack of ability to generate earnings, combined with heavy reliance on purchased money, finally created a combination of circumstances which the bank could not bear.

The Franklin crisis was a liquidity crisis; however, we underestimated the rapidity with which a serious liquidity problem can become an insoluble liquidity problem when a marginal bank relies heavily on interest-sensitive, short-term funds, and there is a sudden "move to quality" by the money market participants.

Mr. Chairman, while the Franklin National Bank case is certainly an unhappy event in the annals of American banking history, we should, nevertheless, observe that the highly professional support given to this Office by the Federal Reserve and the F.D.I.C. made possible the full protection of the bank's depositors and also contained matters so as to prevent any ripple effects elsewhere in the banking system. Both of these agencies, including, of course, the Federal Reserve Bank of New York, deserve the highest admiration of the public for outstanding performance in most demanding circumstances.

NOTES

Chapter 2

Page

17 "a truly shameful record . . ." Jesse H. Jones, *Fifty Billion Dollars: My Thirteen Years with the RFC* (New York: Macmillan, 1951), 14.

18 "After midnight . . . ordered them closed." Ibid., 18.
   "a title akin to receiver . . ." Ibid., 21

19 Undercapitalization of banks. Ibid., 13

21 "We weren't too sure . . . one of the worst. . . ." R. Gordon Hoxie, *Facts About Franklin* (unpublished history of the Franklin National Bank, in the papers of Arthur T. Roth), ch. 3, p. 17.

22 "I've been looking for you. . . ." Ibid., ch. 4.

25–26 HOLC information. Arthur M. Schlesinger, Jr., *The Coming of the New Deal* (New York: Houghton Mifflin, 1958), 287–298.

Chapter 3

37 "Before Fannie Mae was a year old . . ." Jones, 151.

43 "especially in the marginal areas . . ." *New York Times*, Nov. 24, 1940, "Long Island Homes Driving Out Farms."

Chapter 4

51 "Many of these borrowers . . . attached to their homes as these." *Long Island Realty*, March 1940.

Chapter 6

Page
75–76 "Other merchandise on display . . . detachable units used in department stores." *Christian Science Monitor,* June 21, 1947.
76 "If I had any money . . . let's just not go into that." *Chickasha* (Oklahoma) *Express,* May 20, 1947.
76–77 "By advertising . . . passes some along to others." "How to Sell Banking," *Newsweek,* June 30, 1947.
78 Grimm recommendation from Grimm & Company financial report of January 5, 1948, in Roth papers.

Chapter 10

121 "Why should these . . . to live and work." Letter from Arthur T. Roth, February 23, 1954, Roth papers.
125 "The consensus . . . in the two counties." *Long Island Daily Press,* October 1, 1956.

Chapter 11

140 Table of relative financial position of mutual and commercial banks from private publication "Resolution to Oust Savings Banks," in Roth papers.

Chapter 12

151 "Only a battle . . . for their healthy growth." *New York World-Telegram & Sun,* August 26, 1958.
153–154 "For a long time now . . . nothing to say at the time." *American Banker,* September 16, 1958.
154 "biggest back-fence brawl . . ." *New York Times,* September 21, 1958.
155 Interview with William Clark. *Chicago Daily Tribune,* September 22, 1958.
156 "impossible to cross the lobby . . ." *American Banker,* September 22, 1958.
"highly unbankerish bang . . ." *New York Herald Tribune,* September 22, 1958.

Page
156–157 Wellman comment and Lyon press conference from *New York Herald Tribune*, September 22, 1958.
159 "Three paramount problems . . . Brigadier of Banking" and "Some are tempted . . . been trying to build." *Savings Bank Journal*, October 1958.
"Commenting on results . . . Miami Beach, Fla." *Chicago American*, September 24, 1958.
160 Reporter's query to "spokesman" from *American Banker*, September 25, 1958. "questioned how much of a victory . . ." *New York World-Telegram & Sun*, October 2, 1958.
161 "They have no intention . . . tax equality." Letter to Arthur T. Roth, in Roth papers.

Chapter 13

163–164 Roth-Rockefeller exchange from record of the Standing Committee on Banks of the Senate and Assembly of the State of New York, Albany, February 18, 1958.
165 "displayed obvious anger. . . ." *New York Times*, September 10, 1959.
169 "Newsmen who observed . . . Wagner wanted $85 million" and "The first clue came . . . three-day cooling-off period." *Independent Banker*, April 1960.
"described the bill as 'the biggest haul since the great bank robbery.' " *New York Post*, March 22, 1960.
170 Letter to stockholders, March 25, 1960, in Roth papers.

Chapter 14

175 Directors' resolution and United Shareholders citation from Report of Annual Meeting, January 27, 1959, and Annual Report of the Franklin National Bank, 1958, in Roth papers.
178 "Although the Treasury had recommended . . ." *Bankers Committee on Tax Equality—Its Objectives, Progress and Achievement*, undated publication in Roth papers.
Forecast of president's policy from *American Banker*, March 20, 1961.
182–183 Roth testimony from hearings on HR8383 before the Committee on Finance, U.S. Senate, 88th Congress, October-November 1963.

Chapter 18

Page

204 "He had really come out swinging . . . scheduled 25 by 1970." *American Banker,* April 29, 1964.

205 "Financing for the small businessman . . . reputable financial institutions." Statement of Joseph M. Landow before New York State Joint Legislative Committee, January 7, 1957.

Chapter 21

235–236 Liptrott-Roth correspondence, in Roth papers.

Postscript

253–254 Comment on Gleason from Sanford Rose, "What Really Went Wrong at the Franklin," *Fortune,* October 1, 1974.

254 Sindona's confidence in Franklin from Luigi di Fonzo, *St. Peter's Banker, Michele Sindona* (New York: Franklin Watts, 1983), 150.

256 "Even though he hates you . . ." Ibid., 152.

INDEX